1986

Sister M.

Speaking the Speech

D1174716

Speaking the Speech

SECOND EDITION

Edwin Cohen

HOLT, RINEHART AND WINSTON

NEW YORK   CHICAGO   SAN FRANCISCO   PHILADELPHIA
MONTREAL   TORONTO   LONDON   SYDNEY   TOKYO
MEXICO CITY   RIO DE JANEIRO   MADRID

Credits

For headlines on p. 48: Copyrighted 1980, *Chicago Tribune*. Used with permission.

For lyrics from "The Big Black Giant" by Richard Rodgers and Oscar Hammerstein: Copyright © 1953 by Williamson Music Co. Copyright renewed, Chappell & Co., Inc., Administrator. International Copyright Secured. All rights reserved. Used by permission.

For quotes on pp. 131 and 133: Reprinted from *How to Lie with Statistics* by Darrell Huff. Pictures by Irving Geis. Copyright 1954 and renewed 1982 by Darrell Huff and Irving Geis. Used by permission of W. W. Norton & Company, Inc.

For lyrics from "Show Me": Copyright © 1956 by Alan Jay Lerner and Frederick Loewe. Chappell & Co., Inc., owner of publication and allied rights throughout the world. International Copyright Secured. All rights reserved. Used by permission.

For "Principles of the Democratic Party: Common Hopes for the Future" by Senator Edward M. Kennedy: Reprinted by permission from *Vital Speeches of the Day*, Vol. 46.

For "Acceptance Address" by Ronald Reagan: Reprinted by permission from *Vital Speeches of the Day*, August 15, 1980 issue.

Art Direction and Cover Design: GLORIA GENTILE
Interior Design: SUZANNE BENNETT
Cover and Interior Illustrations: CHARLES BENTZ

Library of Congress Cataloging in Publication Data
Cohen, Edwin, 1931–
    Speaking the speech.
    Includes index.
    1. Public speaking.   I. Title.
PN4121.C56   1982   808.5′1   82–12055

ISBN 0-03-062006-6

Copyright © 1983 by CBS College Publishing
Copyright © 1980 by Holt, Rinehart and Winston
Address correspondence to:
383 Madison Avenue
New York, N.Y. 10017
All rights reserved
Printed in the United States of America
Published simultaneously in Canada
2 3 4 5   016   9 8 7 6 5 4 3 2 1

CBS COLLEGE PUBLISHING
Holt, Rinehart and Winston
The Dryden Press
Saunders College Publishing

contents

SPEAK THE SPEECH, I pray you, as I pronounced it to you, trippingly on the tongue; but if you mouth it, as many of our players do, I had as lief the town-crier spoke my lines.

Hamlet, Act III, Scene ii
William Shakespeare

Shakespeare's Hamlet offers the above advice to the travelling actors who are about to perform before the King and Queen. The actors, of course, speak an author's words, not their own. As a speaker you will speak your own speeches, as well as researching, organizing, and preparing them.

"Speak the speech," sounds too much like a command, as well as restricting the advice to delivery only. "Speaking the speech," seems less officious and covers the entire speaking process from the first germ of an idea to the post-speech evaluation. I hope you enjoy and learn from SPEAKING THE SPEECH.

Edwin Cohen

to the instructor

We are all aware that the human communication process has not changed much, regardless of the change in analysis, terminology, and pedagogy. Whether we refer to an "orator," a "rhetor," a "speaker," a "source," or a "sender," we are labeling essentially the same object. The same is true of "receiver," "listener," and "audience." Cicero, Daniel Webster, Winston Churchill, and the students in your class face, or faced, essentially the same problems in communicating ideas to their "receivers." All of them had to initiate an idea, organize their thoughts, find a method of presentation, select effective wording, and finally present the idea to an audience. Aristotle identified these five canons of rhetoric as *invention*, *arrangement*, *style*, *memory*, and *delivery*. Today we have names that are more modern and scientific, and we have subdivided some of the concepts for ease of understanding. Still this book, and virtually every public speaking book, follows some variation on the five-canon theme.

I have tried to show how concepts that may be academically divisible defy separation in real life. For instance, some aspects of invention, arrangement, and style go hand-in-hand. The sender encodes the idea into words from inception; organization calls for more sophisticated wording, and style furthers the refinement. In short, communication can be divided into component parts, but at the same time the parts constitute a whole. If a speaker is anxious and tense about delivery, that tension will affect all the other steps, whether we divide the process into five, ten, or one hundred parts.

Nor should we forget that a speech does not exist without a speaker, and the speakers we deal with are inexperienced and unpolished. My philosophy of speech education emphasizes not the speech, but the speaker as a growing human being. Consequently I have devoted an entire chapter to stage fright, anxiety, speech fright, tension, or whatever term happens to be in vogue. I believe that until the student begins to deal with that problem, he or she will not be able to progress, regardless of how efficiently and thoroughly we teach the other aspects of speaking.

I have also included a chapter on listening and evaluating. Evaluation implies a critical stance toward oneself as a speaker, as well as toward others who speak to us. With modern technology bringing dozens of speakers into our homes daily, I believe we had all better learn to listen critically to the political, commercial, and artistic messages that bombard us.

Most of you have found teaching speech-communication a rewarding and fulfilling profession, as have I. This book is designed to help achieve those rewards and fulfillment; but just as a hammer, needle, or baseball bat is only as useful as the person wielding it, so, too, a textbook becomes more useful in the hands of a good teacher.

Second Edition

In this second edition I have tried to incorporate suggestions from instructors who used the first edition, as well as to make changes based on my own experience with it. Many instructors, myself included, felt that the material dealing with stage fright should appear early in the text. The same is true of the chapter about listening and evaluation.

Three new chapters were added, in addition to the reorganization and alteration of previously used material. Chapter 4 describes types of speeches, based on the speaker's intent. Chapter 10 contains material on the body of the speech that appeared in other chapters in the first edition. Chapter 15 deals with groups — material which some critics felt was a serious omission from the first edition.

Most of the other changes are more subtle, although they should add to the general quality and usefulness of the text.

Comments on the first edition were, by and large, gratifying and rewarding. All of the suggestions could not be incorporated since some were contradictory and others did not match the objectives, stated or unstated, of the book, but I have tried to give them all a fair hearing and consideration. I hope you will continue to let me know your thoughts and reactions.

I tried to keep the same style in the second edition because many of you mentioned that as a strength of the book. Also, the style, for better or for worse, is my style and that is what writing a book is all about. I have tried to keep the book readable, while preserving its integrity and adding to its content. I hope that you continue to find it a useful tool in your teaching.

to the student

All teachers like to think that students flock to their classes because the students are fascinated and delighted by the subject matter or by the personality of the teacher. Occasionally those are the reasons why some students enroll in some classes. More often students take a particular class for reasons less flattering but equally valid.

What Are You Doing Here?

If your class in speech-communication is typical, there are a variety of reasons for students being there. The most obvious reason is that some students major or minor in speech. Those students are relatively few and comprise a small proportion of the class.

Sometimes curricula in other departments require a speech-communication course for sound academic reasons—to help students develop speaking skills, think on their feet, or learn organizational and presentational skills.

Sometimes a counselor or advisor recommends a speech-communication course because a student has a specific problem. Unfortunately, sometimes the reasons are not so valid; they seem almost to be traditional initiation rites: "I had to take speech in college, and it scared the hell out of me. These kids have got to be exposed to the same kind of pressure" (almost a direct quote).

Many states or colleges require some form of oral communication course as part of the general requirements for any degree or certificate. Generally they require either oral or written communication, or both. Often the oral requirement is met best by the type of class that you are enrolled in.

Sometimes one student advises another to take a speech-communication class because it is an "easy grade," or whatever the current slang expression is for that type of course. To some people the idea of a speech class being easy may seem to fall somewhere between poor judgment and insanity, but to other people speech classes are easy, just as chemistry or history or calculus is easy to others. A class seems easy when a particular student has an aptitude for that skill. (Of course, it also may be easy because the instructor does not challenge the student.)

Finally, students may enroll simply because they want to take a speech-communication course, or because their schedules have an open spot at a certain hour. The latter is not a good reason; on the other hand, it does help to keep bread and butter (margarine) on the speech teacher's table.

Whatever the reason or reasons that you enrolled, remember you will get out of this class, or any other, just as much as you put into it.

What Will You Learn Here?

What and how much you will learn in your speech-communication class will vary from person to person. Three primary factors influence the amount and kinds of things you learn: your aptitude, your experience and background, and your attitude.

Some of us are able to wiggle our ears; others are not. Some of us excel in athletics, whereas some are complete klutzes; most of us fall somewhere in between. Some have aptitudes for music, mechanics, fine arts, or science. Does it not stand to reason, then, that some people have more aptitude for oral expression than others? Whatever your aptitude in speech-communication, you should be able to learn new skills or sharpen skills you already possess. Unless you have some relevant physical or psychological disorder, you have been communicating orally for a good portion of your life. Almost no one goes through life without some human interaction, certainly no college student.

Whether aptitude shapes experience or experience shapes aptitude is a philosophical argument we will not indulge in here. Probably they are interdependent. The degree of acceptance you received when you first were learning to talk determined many of your later experiences. If those early attempts to communicate were ridiculed or ignored, you probably have not developed skills as fully as someone who received recognition and encouragement. Experiences in elementary and high school, such as being called upon to recite or respond to a teacher's questions, also can have a profound effect. Some students have all sorts of pleasant, rewarding communication experiences in their public school years. Some receive recognition and encouragement in activities such as debate, discussion, or oral interpretation. If your experiences have enabled you to form a positive self-image, you probably will have less difficulty with this class. Your personality and the activities that give you pleasure determine to a great extent the degree and kinds of learning you will experience in this class.

Finally, your attitude toward the class will have a powerful influence upon what you derive from it. If you approach the class with a positive, eager, and open attitude, you will gain more than your classmate who dismisses it as too hard, too easy, too dumb, too intellectual, or too what-have-you. If you do not feel positive, or if you are here against your wishes, try to make the best of the situation. Probably you will learn more than you expect. You even may begin to enjoy the class.

Speaking the Speech

CHAPTER 1

speech communication

1. *How do I communicate with other human beings?*
2. *What are the main components of human communication?*
3. *Why should I try to understand the other person's feelings?*
4. *In what kinds of communication situations do I find myself?*
5. *Why should I learn public-speaking skills?*

As an infant you began to communicate with other humans long before you learned your first word. If your childhood followed normal patterns, your parents learned quickly to distinguish among cries of discomfort, cries of hunger, and cries that were simply exercise. You probably learned also that if you smiled, you got a positive reaction and reinforcement from your family. As your world expanded to include more people, your communication patterns also expanded and became more complex.

The Ways We Communicate

Think of the ways in which we communicate with other people. Oral language is the most obvious and most common method. We write our language also, in many ways: handwriting, printing, typing, and Braille. We have other ways of communicating at a distance: electronic media bring messages around the world; drumbeats communicate over long distances in Africa; whistling carries farther than the human voice; semaphore flags send messages when the roar of the sea and distance prohibit sound communication; and Morse code travels hundreds of miles. At closer range, sometimes a pencil on a desk top taps out answers in a classroom (tsk-tsk!); music and the arts communicate; and so on.

A vital method of communicating is nonverbal communication, the use of the body to send messages. Do children have to explain their feelings when they open

1

birthday presents? Ever walk into a room and immediately sense that something was wrong? How many times a day do we reinforce our verbal messages with gestures that indicate large or small, weak or strong, high or low? Does not the way a person walks convey a message?

Finally, what about the ups and downs, tensions, and changes in vocal patterns? They convey messages in themselves as well as reinforcing verbal messages. It is possible to convey a thought that is the exact opposite of the verbal message; by saying "I love you" sarcastically, you actually indicate dislike.

The Components of Communication

Whether the communication is as simple as pointing to your choice in the cafeteria or as complex as a multilingual debate in the United Nations, human communication involves several basic components. One person *(sender)* wishes to convey an idea *(message)* to another person *(receiver)* and must use some method *(channel)* to do so. The second person, or receiver, will acknowledge or respond to the sender *(feedback)*. Feedback, in turn, implies that the original receiver becomes the sender, and the original sender becomes the receiver. Unfortunately factors in the environment or within the people sometimes impede the process *(noise)*.

In any human communication, at least four of the six components must be present: a sender, a message, a channel, and a receiver. Feedback will probably be present and noise may or may not be.

HUMAN COMMUNICATION MEANS ABSOLUTELY NOTHING.

In the message above, I the author am the sender; the idea expressed is the message; the ink on the paper and the light reflected into your eyes constitute the channel; and you, the reader, are the receiver. If you read the message in a dark room or when someone is talking to you, noise enters the process. If you read the message, decide it is wrong, and phone or write to tell me about it, you have initiated feedback. In oral communication, when people are face to face, feedback is unavoidable, and the possibilities for noise are multiplied greatly.

Any of the six components may occur alone or in multiples. For instance, cheerleaders act as a unit in sending a message. An audience obviously consists of multiple receivers. An emphatic verbal message can have accompanying nonverbal content; you pound your fist on a desk while you shout, "I will not do that!" In that situation there are two messages, although similar, and two channels, aural and visual. When two messages on two channels contradict one another, problems occur. For instance, backing away while saying, "I'm not afraid of you" puts the verbal and nonverbal messages in direct contradiction. Noise too may take many forms simultaneously. Ever sit in a classroom on an exceptionally hot day (1), after a long night with little sleep (2), thinking about the vacation you just took (3), while a construction crew is hammering outside the window (4), and a fly buzzes around the instructor's head (5)? You could add other examples of noise, such as an upset stomach, sunlight in your eyes, tight shoes, sounds from another classroom, people walking by in the hall, a classmate's perfume, and so on. The less the noise and the more in concert the messages, the more effective the communication will be, regardless of how many senders or receivers are involved.

An almost infinite variety of circumstances, experiences, attitudes, and emotions affect the sender's choice of message and channel. Past experiences with the channel and with the receiver may influence the choice. A topic which has offered challenges that the sender has met successfully in the past will lend itself to better communication than one which has caused frustration and failure. Wouldn't you rather talk about something you know and do well than about something of which you are ignorant or at which you have failed? Some people would rather write their important messages; we call them journalists, poets, and authors. Some would rather speak them. Would a sender not communicate better, all other things being equal, with a friend than with someone he or she dislikes or fears? To list all the factors that can affect a sender's choice of message and channel would require a case history of every human interaction. Suffice it to say, communication is a complicated process.

Similar factors apply to the receiver of the message, although the receiver does not always have the choices that a sender has. The sender can decide whether to initiate communication, but if he or she chooses to speak and receivers are within earshot, they must hear. Of course, as soon as the receivers respond they become senders with the same options.

The role of feedback in communication often is overlooked or underplayed. A receiver cannot refuse to receive or, immediately upon receiving, to send feedback. If you receive a message and decide to ignore it, the act of ignoring conveys a message. Pretending to stay calm while your face turns red and your jaw tightens conveys still other messages. The receiver may, of course, give the desired feedback, saying or implying, "I understand and will do what you ask." The point to remember is that whether it is intentional or accidental, there almost always will be feedback. "You cannot not communicate!"

Identification

As you walk across campus any number of people greet you with "Hi" or "How are you?" or some other *social communication*. Usually the person is not really inquiring about your health, but simply acknowledging you as a human being and asking you to do the same. Ever have someone respond with a medical history when you asked how he or she was? You may have regarded that person as a bore, but if you did not mean it, why ask? The answer is, of course, that you were following an accepted pattern for social communication, whereas the other person was not.

In addition to social communication, we engage in other forms of light or uninvolved communication. We ask or give directions to a stranger. We offer advice for safety's sake: "Watch out for the broken sidewalk." We ask for or give a classmate an assignment for a class. We say, "Please pass the salt." All these are examples of purely *informational communication* with little involvement of our personalities and emotions and little risk of failure, embarrassment, or rejection.

When we get into deeper communication, we risk being misunderstood and consequently being embarrassed, ridiculed, or frustrated. Then we begin a process of realizing what the other persons involved are feeling, how they will react, and what we would do in their place. The process is not completely understood, and it has been given many names. In this book we call it *identification*.

The academic principles of identification were eloquently posited by a modern rhetorician and literary critic, Kenneth Burke. The idea, however, is not new; native American folk culture expressed the same concept in the admonition to "Walk a mile in my moccasins." Try to place yourself psychologically in my moccasins or *shoes*, as the more modern expression goes. Then you can understand my problems, motivations, and reasoning.

Suppose a young man and a young woman are contemplating marriage, and that one of them comes from a home with many children but little money, whereas the other is an only child from an affluent home. The one from a large family may fear children as competition and a threat to the family budget. The other may desire many children for companionship and a full family life. If they love one another, each had better attempt to see the other's point of view. If they do not "walk in each other's shoes," they may not get past this vital issue. Temporarily each must *become* the other through empathy and understanding.

During the social upheaval of the 1960s in the United States, middle-class whites were forced to identify with the plight of blacks for the first time, an unpleasant sensation for many. Only by identifying with blacks and attempting to live ghetto life vicariously could the powerful middle class be brought to understand, sympathize, and work for change. Gigantic strides in civil rights were made. To attribute all that progress to the process of identification is vast oversimplification, but without identification most people could never have understood why there was so much discontent.

For normal human communication situations, the more intimate the communication, the more important and higher the degree of identification. A warm, personal conversation between two close friends obviously involves more identification than a superficial conversation between relative strangers; a discussion of philosophy, religion, or other matters "close to the heart" demands more identification than a friendly argument about which baseball team is better. Deep, significant communication cannot take place without an attempt to identify with the other communicants.

Communication Situations

We participate in different kinds of communication situations, sometimes in more than one at the same time. When we analyze these situations, we find some common elements. The number of people involved and the way they identify with one another is one of the more telling aspects. How much of a burden falls to the various participants is another. Finally, the degree and kinds of feedback tell us a great deal.

INTERPERSONAL COMMUNICATION—ONE TO ONE

Interpersonal communication involves a small number of people, usually two, although three or four may be involved. There is no magic number at which interpersonal communication becomes something else. The term *dyadic* is used to describe two-person communication.

The most important factor in an interpersonal encounter is the degree of identification between the participants. The stronger the identification, the better the chances of the communicative act being successful and complete. Both parties share an equal burden in the attempt at understanding. Neither is an expert lecturing the other; rather they are equal partners who constantly send and receive messages. They are like *transceivers*, able to serve both functions simultaneously. Roommates sharing their hopes and aspirations are in an interpersonal situation, as are friends discussing important problems—whether those problems would seem important to you or me is irrelevant. A husband and wife discussing the children, money matters, or relationships with relatives, or two teachers trying to decide how to help a student are other examples of interpersonal communication. In each situation the participants must identify as much as possible, share the burden, and give constant feedback, modifying the conversation by questions and both verbal and nonverbal responses.

SMALL-GROUP COMMUNICATION

Small-group communication is, as the name implies, a communication situation with a relatively small number of persons, but larger than an interpersonal situation. What constitutes a *small* group? Usually from three to eight persons. More than eight usually gets too unwieldy for equal communication.

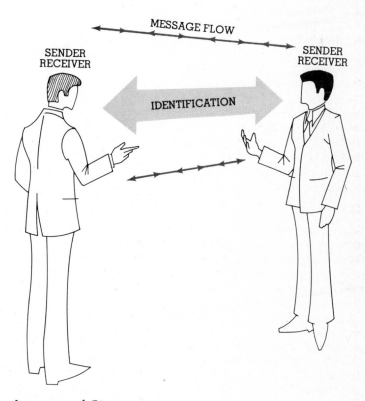

Interpersonal Communication

The small group usually has some specific task to perform, as in a committee. Without a central purpose, the small group becomes a bunch of individuals who happen to be communicating in one place at one time. When there is a specific purpose or task, each member offers individual expertise and, in theory, contributes an equal amount to the task. Absolute equality is virtually impossible, but the tendency toward equal burden and contribution should be pursued. Various members function as leaders from time to time in the ideal small group, while each offers expertise in a different area.

Anyone who analyzes his or her own communication behavior realizes how difficult it is to identify with another. It becomes even more difficult to identify with three, six, or eight others. Identification in the small group is, therefore, not as intense as in interpersonal communication; instead it is directed toward the factors of personality or experience the members share that are germane to the issue or task at hand. In interpersonal communication there is an attempt, or should be, to delve into the other person's inner self; in small-group communication each member should attempt to seek out the pertinent, task-oriented parts of the other. For instance, a committee working on the arrangements for a school dance may include members from widely varied backgrounds. It may not be important to identify with, let us say, the way certain members relate to their families, but it may be most important to understand that a person who comes from a home where money is scarce is sensitive about the cost of the dance. Even if the others are fairly affluent, they should identify with the less affluent members and the constituency they represent. A group attempting to solve an engineering problem does not need to know that one member had a fight with his wife that morning; instead, they must identify with him as an expert in microcircuits. It might ease tensions if they also recognized that this morning the person is more touchy than usual and made the necessary allowances.

In a small group each member is a transceiver, constantly receiving messages and giving feedback through questions, agreement, facial reactions, or other verbal and nonverbal behavior. Feedback may be spontaneous and follow no set pattern. For instance, A may make a point. In response B nods assent, C gets angry, D calls A a liar, E says, "That's what I've been trying to say for ten minutes," and F yawns. Each reacts in a personal and individual manner. The feedback is constant and continually modifies the communication.

PUBLIC COMMUNICATION OR PLATFORM SPEAKING

In public communication the burden of communication lies on one person, the speaker. The politician stands on the platform or appears on the television screen, and the audience listens. There is one sender and any number of receivers. One or two receivers listen to someone spout off from a park bench, or millions listen when a president addresses the nation through mass media. The speaker controls the message, preparing it ahead of time. The receivers are expected to listen, be polite, and applaud or laugh in the right places. The burden of the communication, however, lies with the sender.

If the public speaker has prepared properly, he or she will have analyzed the audience in broad generalities and will attempt to appeal to certain qualities that the audience shares. Political candidates long have been aware that they should discuss farm issues with farmers, industry issues with laborers, and economic issues with management. In the "good old days" politicians would prepare differ-

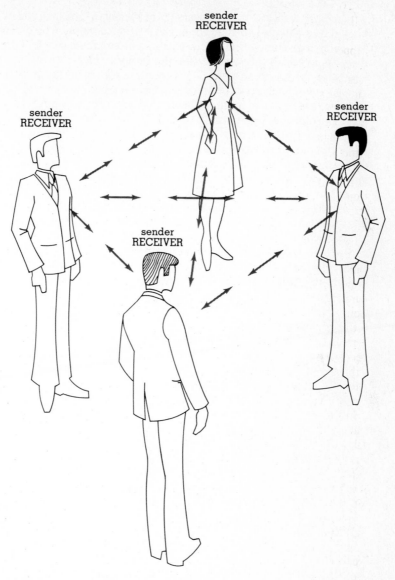

Small-Group Communication. Identification varies with qualities pertinent to the task.

ent, sometimes even contradictory, speeches for various groups. Television has somewhat curtailed that form of dishonesty by bringing the same speech to all groups at the same instant.

Although the sender cannot identify with the mass audience because of its size and passivity, the receivers identify strongly with the public speaker, or at least with certain aspects of the speaker's personality. The politician wants to be known as a parent, war hero, or friend of the common people because most of the voters are family-oriented, patriotic, and common people. Glimpsing these personal aspects of the sender's life, the receivers identify with the sender, or at least with the factors that the clever sender wants them to identify with.

In successful public communication, feedback becomes patterned and plays less of a role than in other forms. When "my candidate" (see how I have identified?) makes a point that I particularly like, I applaud. If the speech contains bad news or makes me angry, I may boo or shake my fist, but the feedback seldom will transcend the space between us. Candidates have been physically abused by audiences, but these candidates usually change their tunes or drop out of politics. Generally speaking, however, Democrats listen to Democratic candidates, Republicans listen to Republican candidates, Methodists listen to Methodist clergy, and nobody listens to teachers. Consequently direct and immediate feedback becomes less important in public communication, although there is no question that the sensitive communicator will note when the audience begins to nod off to sleep, or when the applause comes in the wrong places, or worse yet, not at all. The clever speaker will modify the methods of sending the message, and perhaps the message itself, in order to get the feedback into a more acceptable pattern.

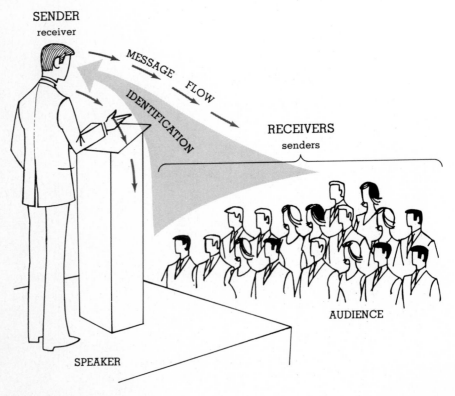

Public Communication

For the live public communicator feedback is always present, but not as intense as in other kinds of communication. To the degree that the receivers identify, the speaker succeeds. Politics, law, education, and religion are the strongest bastions of this kind of communication. It cannot be beaten for conveying messages to many receivers in a short amount of time, but for give and take or for depth, public communication pales beside interpersonal and small-group communication.

SPECIALIZED COMMUNICATION

The final type of communication is specialized communication, which is a combination of interpersonal and public communication. Although the two might seem mutually exclusive, many situations involve specialized communication.

Suppose you go to your counselor or advisor for advice about your schedule, your career, or some personal matter. The counselor, by virtue of the position and information that he or she possesses, will become the dominant communicator. The dominance will not be as pronounced as in the platform situation, and there will be some latitude for feedback and response. The advisor, however, will assume the largest share of the informative process. You, the student, may react and steer the conversation, but you have gone to the advisor because of his or her expertise, and, therefore, the advisor dominates the communication. The same

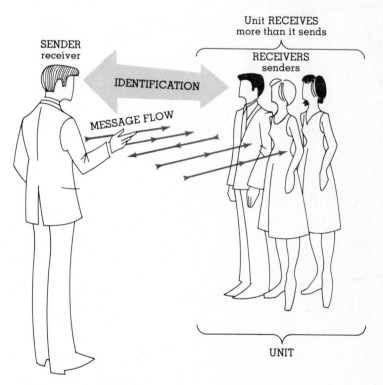

Specialized Communication

situation exists when a family enters a place of business, such as an automobile showroom, to make a purchase. The salesperson will bear the burden of the communication, although the good salesperson will be acutely responsive to the family's feedback. A person listening to a medical doctor or nurse prescribe health procedures also constitutes a specialized situation. The physician should respond to the patient's fears and anxieties but bear the burden of the communication.

In specialized communication one person, by virtue of experience or expertise, is the sender, and most of the communication act focuses on that person. Another person or group acting as a unit receives the communication and offers a degree of feedback. The communication is primarily sender-to-receiver, but there is some feedback and resultant modification. The good salesperson, sensitive physician, or interested advisor utilizes feedback to some extent, but because the person is a specialist, he or she will control the situation and determine the intellectual content of the message.

BEYOND THE CATEGORIES

As you may have observed, communication, like most human endeavors, does not fall into easy, neat classifications. We can say there are four or ten or seventy-six kinds of communication situations, but there actually is an almost infinite number, depending on Who, Where, and Why. Who is communicating with whom? Where are they communicating? Why are they doing it? The type of communication can change in the middle of an event. A candidate for office may speak to an audience (public communication) for twenty minutes and then open the floor for questions (specialized communication). After the speech, there may be a social hour at which the candidate engages in interpersonal communication.

The environment can have a profound effect upon the communication act. A hall with good acoustics, a classroom, or a crowded street each affect the way sensitive communicators do their communicating. Only a naive speaker would attempt to communicate the same way in a hall that seats 2000 as in a living room.

The purpose also directs and influences the whole event. Is it to share ideas, to persuade, or to entertain?

You and Public Speaking

In school and after, you will face many kinds of communication situations. With your family you will use mostly interpersonal communication. At work small-group and specialized situations probably will predominate. At the theater, at the movies, or in front of the television set a different kind of communication, theatrical, comes into play. Only certain vocations, notably religion, education, law, and politics, demand much platform communication, but you will use platform communication when an instructor calls on you to "recite" in front of the class. Although interpersonal, small-group, and specialized situations may predominate, public communication can be the most vital form for you to practice and learn.

If you learn the principles of public communication, you will have mastered the method that places the greatest burden on you as sender. If you conquer your anxieties in the situation where the focus is almost entirely on you, you will find communicating in more egalitarian settings much easier. If you prepare for a communication act that centers on one person, you, it becomes relatively easy to prepare for communication acts that center on several persons. If you function in a situation in which you receive minimal feedback, you should function even better where there is more. If you organize and present ideas when you stand alone "with your soul bared," you should be able to do so much better in a cooperative situation. Through public speaking you learn vital principles of communication, and the skills you develop will help you communicate in all other situations.

Any public speech combines a complex series of skills that we must examine individually, but which are only viable when they work together. The best introduction cannot save a speech containing little or no substance, and poor delivery can damage even a well constructed speech. It is virtually impossible, however, to examine a speech as a unit, so we break it into its component parts for study and scrutiny. When all the parts are put together, contrary to the mathematical law, the whole becomes *greater* than the sum of its parts.

As a speaker you must understand your topic and the types, purposes, and occasions for speeches. You must learn to analyze your audience. Organizing and outlining are vital to the speaking process, as are lively, interesting introductions and memorable conclusions. You must master ways of proving your ideas and of communicating facts, including supplementary proofs, statistics, and visual aids. There are basic, time-proven methods for the presentation of a speech. Another concern for virtually every speaker is stage fright or anxiety. It will not go away if you ignore it. Finally, after your speech is finished, you will want to evaluate it, whether it is for a class grade or an outside-of-school situation.

Each of these elements is examined separately in this book, and you as a speaker must examine them separately also. Not all speeches or speakers need them equally. Some speeches need no statistics; sometimes the selection of a topic is almost automatic; some people experience little fear; and organization comes easier for some speakers than for others. Sometimes you conceive of several individual steps at once: "If I give a persuasive speech about why the parking lot needs to be paved, I can bring in a chunk of the torn-up surface as a visual aid and show it to the audience as an introduction." Regardless of order or emphasis, you should examine each element for every speech, even if only to reject it: "I'll be talking about the abstract concept of courage, so I will not need to include any statistical information."

The skills you are about to learn apply not only to speeches in a speech-communication class. You should be able to apply the skills to speeches long after your class is completed. Even more important, the skills you learn in this class will help you to be more perceptive and more critical in your evaluations of what *other speakers* say. When we listen to political speeches critically, we are better informed citizens; when we listen to advertisers critically, we are wiser consumers.

SUMMARY
AND CONCLUSION

Communication is something we often take for granted. We forget that we have been communicating all our lives, in more sophisticated ways as we grow older. Communication is so much a part of our lives, we sometimes ignore its impact on us. The greatest impact comes from communication with other human beings, but we also communicate with animals and even machines.

The six primary components of the communication process are the following:

1. sender
2. message
3. channel
4. receiver
5. feedback
6. noise

These six components, with the possible exception of noise, are present in virtually every communication event, sometimes in multiples, as when a group of receivers listens to the message of one sender. Whether two people are involved in the most superficial social communication or great numbers are involved in earth-shaking matters, we must communicate. In fact, *we cannot not communicate.*

Will learning the principles and skills of communication guarantee your success as a communicator in the so-called "real world"? An absurd question! Most people will not experience dramatic change, but they will experience some change. No class can guarantee success in any person's future. Successful work in this class, however, can increase the odds in your favor, and as the chef said about the hard-boiled egg, "There's no beating that!"

Delivering and listening to speeches requires working hard and refining skills; this book is like a set of tools designed to help you do it. It is up to you to use the tools to your best ability.

CHAPTER 2

living with stage fright

1. What are the symptoms of stage fright, and what are their physiological bases?
2. What kind of "threat" does giving a speech pose?
3. Am I the only one with stage fright?
4. How can I control and lessen stage fright?
5. What can the person who cannot function because of stage fright do?
6. Do professional speakers experience stage fright?

Who's afraid of the big, bad wolf? snakes and bears?
speeding cars?
    Certainly not I.
Who's afraid of mountain heights? gory sights?
men from Mars?
    Certainly not I.
Who's afraid to stand up before a group and make
a speech?
    IIIIIII AAAAAAMMMMMM!!!!!!

If you find yourself frightened and anxious about getting up and delivering a speech, do not be surprised. If it offers any consolation, virtually everybody in a similar situation has similar feelings. Some call it anxiety; some speech fright, tensiveness, or communication apprehension; others may have even fancier words for it; but we all recognize and experience the ugliest of uglies, "stage fright."

You Are Not Alone

The London *Sunday Times* (October 7, 1973) reported the results of a survey that asked 3000 people in the United States, "What are you the most afraid of?" Guess which fears finished in the top ten? The fear of *Dogs* ranked number ten, with 11 percent of the respondents listing that fear. *Loneliness* ranked ninth with 14 percent, and *Flying* was eighth, with 18 percent grounded. *Sickness* and *Death* were in a tie for sixth place, each feared most by 19 percent of the people surveyed. Then there was a three-way tie for third place among *Insects and Bugs*, *Financial Problems*, and *Deep Water*, each polling 22 percent. The second highest finisher was *Heights*, with 32 percent, almost one-third of the population, avoiding the Grand Canyon or the Empire State Building. Which fear finished the highest, with a total of 41 percent of the respondents listing it? *Speaking Before a Group!* (It would have been pretty silly to include it in this chapter if it were fear of falling off the flat earth.)

Notice that each of the other nine fears, and the same would apply for many of the fears that finished lower than tenth, includes an element of potential injury or disaster. One can fall from heights; insects and bugs bite and spread disease; financial problems can overturn a person's or family's life; one can drown in deep water; sickness and death are hardly ever considered fun; airplanes have been known to crash; loneliness can lead to mental disturbance; and dogs do bite. The fear, however, that two of every five listed as the one they are *most* afraid of poses no real threat to life, limb, or property. It does, however, pose a real threat to our egos, our sense of well-being, and our self-image. Evidently that is enough to place it at the top of the list.

You might argue that three of five people, therefore, do *not* claim fear of speaking in public as their primary phobia. True, but that does not mean that those three are free of that fear. Having spoken to many groups in many situations in over twenty years in education and other aspects of public life, I would have to place my fear of dogs far ahead of my fear of speaking in public, but that fear still exists and sometimes surfaces strongly. (For those who want to put their anxiety about speaking into perspective, you might note that one of the more exotic phobias is *arachibutyrophobia:* fear of peanut butter sticking to the roof of your mouth. See, you are not so unlucky.)

To say that everyone experiences some degree of anxiety in a speaking situation might be an overstatement, but it is safe to say that almost everyone does. Experienced teachers often have nightmares about being late for class, being in the wrong room, teaching a subject they do not know, or other such anxieties on the night before meeting a new class. Performers with years of experience in front of audiences are often petrified before going on stage. Athletes before a meet or musicians before a concert feel similar emotions to those you and I feel before speaking. Many performers feel that anyone who loses stage fright becomes a self-centered performer placing more emphasis on self than on the game, the concert, the play, or the speech. In slang, the person becomes a "ham" or a "hot dog."

There are a few people who claim not to have stage fright, or who appear to be free of it. Usually that means the stage fright takes a different form or that the person is so poised the audience cannot detect it. Two examples from personal experience illustrate these points. A dear friend from college days appeared in several plays with me. She always claimed that she did not have any stage fright or unusual anxiety about performing. She did not connect stage fright with the fact that she regurgitated after almost every show. Evidently her brain kept the usual symptoms hidden, but once the tension was gone and the show over, whoops! The other case was an outstanding speech student who was head and shoulders better than anyone else in the class. She was a model of poise and decorum, always appearing confident and in complete command of the situation, until she did a demonstration speech that gave us a chance to see her hands. They shook so rapidly that they almost hummed. She admitted that she was always that nervous, but she had managed to keep her nerves hidden from the audience.

Physical Reactions

Why is stage fright so universal when it does not pose a physical threat? Our egos and self-esteem are threatened, evidently to a significant degree. No normal person wants to look like a fool. We want to present ourselves in the best possible light to others. Consequently, a speaking situation does involve peril, not physical but psychological. The brain, therefore, instructs the body to react exactly the way it would at times of physical danger. In essence the brain tells the body, "Get ready to fight off the danger or to run away from it."

When the danger signals reach the brain, it instructs the adrenal gland to start secreting adrenal fluid into the bloodstream. The adrenal fluid brings about specific bodily reactions. First and most important, our senses become more keen because we will have to rely on them to help us fight or run. Blood goes away from the muscles of the stomach and intestines. The sudden rush of blood from the digestive system causes the sensation known as "butterflies in the stomach." The large muscles of the arms and legs become most important in the "fight or flight" reaction, as they must do the punching, kicking, running, or swimming. The extra blood and the oxygen it contains get the muscles so tense that they must function strongly. Our hands shake, our knees knock, and we feel tension in the larger muscles of the body. The extra blood in the extremities causes them to warm and perspire. As they perspire, evaporation cools them rapidly, so we get cold feet and hands. Because the digestive system has been given a lower priority, our salivary glands do not secrete as much, and we experience a dry, cottony mouth, sometimes to the point where it hinders good articulation.

All the symptoms we feel have a basis in physiological reactions to the presence of danger:

1. light-headedness
2. dry mouth
3. hollow feeling in the stomach
4. clammy, sweaty palms and feet
5. shaking hands and legs
6. general body tension

Some people experience all six symptoms; some one or two; some different symptoms at different times. The degree to which we experience the symptoms varies from person to person, from symptom to symptom, and from situation to situation. But the chances are that you will feel some or all of them any time you get up to speak. It is only when the symptoms become so severe that they impede your ability to function that you are in trouble. If you get too light-headed, you may faint. Excessive shaking can prevent our using limbs normally. Most people do not experience such drastic symptoms, but *most people do experience symptoms.*

One final personal example shows the universality of stage fright. Many years ago I was in a graduate class called Psychology of Speech. On the first day of the class the instructor had all the students close their eyes, sitting up straight in their seats. Then he announced that he was going to walk through the class and that he would touch one person on the shoulder. That person would have to stand before the class and deliver a speech. As he described the topic for the speech, he was walking around the classroom, and his voice would sound closer or farther away. He walked around the room talking about the assignment for what seemed like a month, but it was closer to three minutes. Then, without touching anyone, he asked us to open our eyes and describe to each other what we felt. We all felt light-headed, were dry-mouthed, had butterflies in the stomach, and so on. In other words, we all experienced stage fright, and by our confessions, we all experienced it fairly strongly. Although the experiment would work in any group of people, the point is that *the class was composed entirely of graduate students who were speech majors.* Most had competed in speech tournaments; many were teachers; some had been in theater also; but all were speech majors at the graduate level, and all had well-defined feelings of stage fright. None of us wished to look foolish in front of our peers; none of us wanted to be in a situation where we would have to "put up or shut up" about our speaking ability; all felt threatened and, therefore, apprehensive despite the years of experience. So, just who do you think you are that you should escape the curse?

Controlling Stage Fright

If stage fright is normal and almost universal, what can be done to eliminate it, or at least control and lessen it? To the first part of the question, eliminating it, the answer is, unfortunately, "not much." An even more honest answer would be, in most cases, "nothing." Eliminating stage fright is almost impossible. You may find it hard to accept, but there is even some question as to the desirability of eliminating it, were it possible. Stage fright causes our brains and bodies to be at a peak of efficiency. It makes us sharper mentally, helps us do some of the things we want to do, and makes us more aware. Those positive factors offer little or no consolation to people who are so frightened that they find it difficult to remember who they are and what they are doing. Even they should work on reducing and controlling the fear, rather than on eliminating it.

Sometimes well-meaning friends and acquaintances offer tricks or gimmicks that are "guaranteed" to cure stage fright overnight or sooner. Be careful; that same person may have the deed to Brooklyn Bridge or a car that was driven by a little old lady once a week to go to church. Gimmicks and tricks just will not do it. Even if they work for someone else, which is unlikely, that does not mean that they will work for you. We are complex animals, we humans, and we have an almost limitless variety of weaknesses and vulnerabilities. Stage fright is closely related to our self-concept and perception of the world, and no two of us see the world or ourselves alike. Consequently, no two of us can relieve a problem that is basically psychological in the same manner.

By now you are probably saying to yourself, or maybe shouting at the book, "Look, I'm scared stiff. I can't eat. I can't sleep or function normally. I have stage fright because of the speech I have to give tomorrow, and now you tell me that I can't get rid of it. Speech-communication — humbug!"

SOME RELIEF

The outlook is not that bleak. Although stage fright is difficult or impossible to overcome, it is possible to lessen and control it by practicing some time-tested methods of dealing with your speaking situation. All these suggestions are much more easily given than taken. However, if you work at them, over a period of time, they may help you with your fear.

First and foremost, you must *concentrate on your speech*, not on yourself. Think about the points you are trying to make, the structure, and your introduction. The more you concentrate on yourself and your feelings, the more you add to your anxiety. If the cause of your stage fright is concern over looking awkward or ridiculous in public, it stands to reason that the more you think about yourself, the more anxiety you will experience.

As you concentrate on the speech, *practice*. The more you practice, the lower the anxiety level. Not only should you practice your speech often, but you also should practice in front of an audience whenever possible. Of course you cannot practice in front of the audience you will eventually face, but husbands, wives, parents, friends, and anyone to whom you can relate under normal circumstances constitute a small but agreeable audience. It does not matter whether the act of practicing reduces fear, or whether you are reassured by the increased quality of your speech. The result is the same: decreased anxiety, more self-confidence. An added advantage of practicing before a live audience is that they may offer you valuable criticism and help. You must evaluate their evaluations, of course, and be certain that their good intentions relate to the real problems. Whether or not you get this extra aid, you will be well served by practice, especially in front of real, live people.

The stronger your motivation to succeed in the class, the lower the anxiety level. If you can convince yourself that you want to do well, not merely get through a requirement, the odds favor reduction of stage fright; in other words, "get psyched up." The reason that such a change in attitude can be useful is simple. If you want to do well, you will do more thorough research on your topic; you will take greater pains with your organization; all of your preparation will benefit from increased attention to details and reworking; and you will undoubtedly practice more. In short, if you care more, you will devote more time and energy to your preparation, and if you are better prepared, you will be more confident.

A simple physical technique — again it sounds easy on paper — is establishing direct eye contact with the audience as much as possible. Doing that is somewhat like diving into ice cold water: you know it is the only way, but it takes courage! Forcing yourself to look directly at audience members will in turn force you to act the way a confident person acts. Even though the act begins as an unreal performance, somehow people actually gain confidence merely by acting confident. Because you have looked right at your audience and assumed an air of confidence, they will respond more positively to you, and the feedback of their response will inspire you to increased confidence. Too often inexperienced speakers stare at the lectern, their notes, the ceiling, the floor, or anything rather than the people at whom they should look. The reluctance in turn heightens the anxiety and hurts their own cause. Admittedly it is difficult, especially the first time, to look at the audience with an attitude of self-confidence and complete control, but once you do it, the rewards are worth the chill of the first plunge.

Finally, do not worry about eliminating stage fright. You are not going to anyway. Most of us are afraid of being afraid. We are afraid of looking cowardly and silly. The more attention you pay to the fear, however, the stronger it becomes. For the next thirty seconds do *not* think about an elephant. The harder you try not to think about it, the larger it looms in your mind. So too with stage fright. Think about other matters connected with your speech, such as content, organization, and mechanics of delivery. If you concentrate on those things, you will stop concentrating on stage fright, consequently lessening it.

SEVERE ANXIETY

If you experience apprehension to the extent that you are virtually paralyzed and cannot function, talk to your instructor about it in private. Most speech teachers are familiar with this kind of problem. Perhaps your school has a desensitization center where systematic conditioning can help your condition. Perhaps the instructor knows of some other form of therapy. Just sharing your anxiety and knowing that someone is sympathetic may help. This advice is not directed at the person who feels mildly nervous, whose hands shake, and who feels slightly queasy before speaking. Most of us feel that. If, however, you actually find it impossible to function normally and are unable to cope with your fear, seek out your teacher privately or talk to a counselor.

The worst mistake you can make is to drop the course in order to avoid the confrontation of private self and public audience. All avoidance accomplishes is to delay the inevitable or force you further into your shell. To most people stage fright is an annoyance, but to some it is a serious problem. As with any other problem, you are better off confronting it and seeking help.

Tips from Professional Speakers

What do people who speak in public as a necessary part of their vocations say about stage fright? In an attempt to get comments from well-known people who must speak in public, I wrote to a group of individuals in public life and asked for their personal views of stage fright. In order to obtain a cross section, I polled a balance of males and females, blacks and whites, Democrats and Republicans, performers, clergy, sports figures, and other occupations. Many did not answer. Of those who did, four answered giving advice, three had their secretaries relay information, seven more had secretaries say that the person could not respond because of the press of business, and two responded personally saying that they were too busy. At the time the requests were sent out, I was a resident of Indiana, and as you might imagine, Indiana politicians responded more quickly and positively than others.

Bill Mauldin, award-winning cartoonist, author, and lecturer, offered the most intriguing response through his secretary:

Mr. Mauldin has been traveling but I read your letter over the phone to him. He asked me to tell you that he used to have stage fright when public speaking, but he ran for Congress and cured himself of it.

Mauldin's tongue-in-cheek "cure" is a rather drastic course of action, so perhaps we had better mention the other responses as well.

Three of the respondents insisted that they had little stage fright. In each case, however, they went on to give advice for those who do experience it more strongly. Former President Gerald R. Ford (all titles are as of Summer 1978) replied as follows:

You asked specifically about anxiety or stage-fright. In this regard I am pleased to submit the following:

Quite frankly, I had a minimal amount of "stage-fright" in speech making primarily because of my many experiences in competitive athletics, especially high school and college football. Public appearances, whether on a football playing field or on a debate platform, are the same. You learn to build yourself up mentally and physically and then perform according to your planned program. It is a process of training and practice plus an assurance you are ready to perform. There is no reason for stage-fright if you develop a confidence based on proper preparation.

U.S. Representative Adam Benjamin, First District of Indiana, also denies having stage fright to any significant degree. I have heard Congressman Benjamin speak on several occasions, always to audiences of approximately twenty to forty people. Benjamin constantly amazes his audience with his command of facts and figures and his relaxed, informal poise. He is, in my opinion, an outstanding speaker. The advice he gives regarding stage fright is excellent, even though he discounts it as a problem for himself.

Quite frankly, while I might undergo some degree of stage fright, I am not consciously aware of it and take no specific steps to abate it.

I have generally settled into a routine which includes a few light comments seeking identification with the audience, the issue at hand and the facts in support thereof and, finally, a conclusion which offers them some direction in which to proceed. I generally bolster myself with facts, probably many more than I will ever use, and these serve to provide either connecting links, transition or support for my argument.

I have never attempted to memorize a speech, nor can I read a speech very well. Consequently, I generally rely on a regurgitation of a couple of opening thoughts as well as closing thoughts leaving it to my mind to convey the in-between on the basis of the presentation I desire to make.

I have never found that practicing, taping or otherwise trying to get mannerisms niched in for amplification or intonation have worked for me. Of course, I may not be an effective speaker.

Generally, I perceive the audience as persons who are going to be receptive to my remarks. In the event that there is repeating noise, excellent speakers before or after me, or the program has generally extended beyond the tolerance of normal human beings to sit, I shorten my remarks and remain as brief as possible. On the other hand, if I am the only speaker and the audience appears to be interested in my remarks, I will keep my remarks to a nominal length and open myself to questions which are much easier to handle than a monologue.

To avoid stage fright, I find that the best approach is to consider your audience as a number of friends who are interested in something that you might have to say. Talk conversationally as you would to friends, and prepare to sit as soon as you have said what you had planned to say.

Finally, the real answer is to be familiar with your subject matter and be absolutely confident in the accuracy of what you plan to say.

I do not know if this is helpful at all. I imagine that everyone of us has our own style and there is no substitute for experience.

The other respondent who disclaimed stage fright personally was Secretary of Housing and Urban Development Patricia R. Harris. She too gives excellent advice in spite of her own lack of problems with anxiety. She responded through her Assistant for Public Affairs:

Secretary Harris has asked me to respond to your recent letter asking whether she experiences stage fright when speaking before groups. She is happy to say she does not, and cannot recall that she has ever suffered from that affliction.

In the Secretary's opinion, stage fright can be avoided by careful preparation of one's speech, thorough grounding in the subject; familiarity with the content of the speech as written; and a subject matter that is of interest to the audience. Flowery language is unnecessary; one's normal vocabulary prevents straining to remember unfamiliar words.

Senator Birch Bayh of Indiana confesses readily, and somewhat poetically, to feeling the ravages of stage fright. Although he admits suffering from it, he offers excellent advice for reducing the degree of anxiety:

There may be some people with steel in their spines and ice water in their veins who are such masters at the art of public speaking that they escape nervousness and stage fright. Unfortunately, I'm not one of them. I have found that the more important or momentous the occasion, the more I am inclined toward nervousness or stage fright.

I have found that some things can be helpful:

1. Although some people say practice makes perfect, practice has not made me a perfect public speaker by any means, but it has decreased the incidences of stage fright. Perhaps this is overly simplistic, but in my judgment, the more one speaks publicly, the more one can speak publicly without suffering from excessive nervousness. Do it, do it, do it! That's the best formula I know to ease nervousness in public speaking.

2. Know the subject. The more familiar you are with the subject matter, the more confident you are. The more confidence, the less likelihood of nervousness.

3. Get into the subject as quickly and enthusiastically as possible. I have found that in those speeches or Senate floor debates where I have been the most nervous, as soon as I become passionately involved in the subject matter, I tend to lose most of my nervousness. I suppose the key is to be able to harness nervous energy and direct it toward an enthusiastic presentation of the subject.

Dr. Billy Graham, world-renowned evangelist, was unable to respond personally, but his executive assistant Dr. Victor B. Nelson, who is also a minister, offered some advice from his own experience on the pulpit:

Before coming with the Billy Graham Association it was my privilege to be a pastor for many years and I understand some of the problems faced by young speakers. The agony of those early years has not been forgotten. In my personal case, the stage-fright became secondary as I became more and more intensely involved in the message which I had to deliver. Eventually, the criticalness of getting the message across replaced the stage-fright.

The final comments are from Dr. Arthur G. Hansen, President of Purdue University. As president of a major university with a reputation for academic excellence, Hansen often finds himself in a public speaking situation. As a faculty member of Purdue who has heard him speak on several occasions, I can vouch for the quality and excellence of his efforts. Referring to the problem as "anxiety" and readily admitting that he falls prey to it, he also offers some excellent advice:

You are certainly right in that most speakers under certain circumstances do experience stage fright.

In my own case, I wouldn't call it stage fright as much as I would call it a sense of anxiety. It is the same type of anxiety that I used to feel before I ran in a track meet in college. However, there are some tricks I have discovered over the years for bringing down that level of anxiety at the podium.

The first is to intentionally take time. This may be done by turning over several pages of your speech as if you were reviewing it. The second thing is to take several deep breaths and begin talking very deliberately to the audience. It is the feeling of control at that point that usually makes the anxiety drop off.

Too often, I think a student rushes up to the podium, tense and distraught, and begins to speak immediately. There must be that calm moment or two when you take charge of yourself rather than have the event control you.

You may have noticed recurring themes in the various letters, which support the advice given earlier in the chapter. *Preparation* is undoubtedly the most important factor in lessening stage fright, simply knowing your topic as well as humanly possible. Several of the respondents also stressed *practice*. Politicians and others who speak often may repeat a message and theme over and over, merely changing audiences. The politician running for office and religious leader going from place to place, therefore, have a distinct advantage over the speaker in class: they can practice and polish their speeches by presenting them to live audiences and observing which parts are met with positive responses and which are met negatively. In any event, practice may not make you perfect, but as Senator Bayh said, it may decrease the incidence of stage fright.

SUMMARY
AND CONCLUSION

One factor about stage fright that you should not lose sight of is that *you are not alone.* Virtually everyone experiences it to some degree, even many experienced and accomplished speakers. Most novice speakers experience stage fright, and you might do better to worry if you do not contract it. If there is consolation in the old adage that "misery loves company," then be consoled. If there are twenty-five people in your speech class, chances are that 24.75 of them have stage fright to some degree.

Stage fright has as its basis the body's reaction to a real psychological threat. Although speaking in public does not pose a threat to life and limb, it does threaten our sense of well-being. It is stimulated by our desire not to look foolish in front of our fellow human beings. Because there is a real or imagined threat, our bodies react physiologically just as they would when faced with a physical threat that would force us to fight or flee from danger.

What can you do to eliminate stage fright? Little! What can you do to control it? Much! Do not try to eliminate stage fright. Do not believe in, or rely on, gimmicks or tricks to get over it; they simply will not work. Instead, try some of these suggestions:

1. Concentrate on the speech, not on yourself.
2. Practice, practice, practice — preferably with a live audience.
3. Try to motivate yourself to succeed, not just endure, in the class. You are in the class anyway, so give it your best shot.
4. Try to establish and maintain direct eye contact with your audience.
5. Hang tough! Ernest Hemingway defined "courage" as "grace under pressure," and a public speaking situation supplies plenty of pressure for you to exhibit your courage.
6. If your anxiety is so overwhelming that you cannot function normally, seek guidance and help from your teacher or counselor.
7. Remember you are not alone. Virtually everyone who speaks publicly experiences what you do, every time they get up to speak.
8. KNOW YOUR SUBJECT AS THOROUGHLY AS POSSIBLE!

EXERCISES

1. Arrange to talk with someone who often speaks before large numbers of people, such as a member of the clergy, a trial attorney, a faculty member, the president of your university or college, or a politician. Ask that person about his or her experiences with stage fright.
2. Examine your own stage fright carefully. *Write* down your symptoms and try to describe the degree to which they affect you. Then try to identify some of the causes. You must be totally honest with yourself for this exercise to be helpful.

CHAPTER 3

listening and evaluating

1. *What skills are involved in listening?*
2. *How can I become a better listener?*
3. *Why is listening important for evaluation?*
4. *What kinds of evaluations take place in speech class? Which is the most important?*
5. *How do I handle a bad speech habit?*
6. *In what three general areas will my speeches be evaluated?*
7. *What is the most important purpose of evaluation?*

It is the province of knowledge to speak and it is the privilege of wisdom to listen.

Oliver Wendell Holmes

We ain't as good as we should be;
And we ain't as good as we're gonna be;
But we're better than we was!

You may wonder why a book about speaking should deal also with *listening*. Without listeners there is no spoken communication. Listening is more than the physical sensation of hearing, although that is a necessary component. Listening involves absorbing ideas in the mind, where they can be stored, interpreted, recalled, and acted upon.

One objective of a public speaking class, some might say the most important objective, is to educate students as receivers of communication. You will receive many more speeches than you ever will send. You will be bombarded with verbal messages for the rest of your life, messages that tell you who to vote for, what products to buy, and even how to live. If our citizenry cannot listen critically to these innumerable messages, then our society is subject to the whims of political demagogues and advertisers whose sole aims are power and wealth. You, as an educated citizen, have a major responsibility to listen and evaluate messages from countless sources with countless objectives.

According to one study, we listen half again as much as we speak; we speak almost twice as much as we read; and we read almost twice as much as we write.* Yet our school curricula emphasize writing skills over reading, reading over speaking, and speaking over listening. As one interested in oral communication, you should also be concerned with your receiving skills.

As a speaker, you must assume a good deal of the burden of getting the audience to listen. Your manner of presentation and the content of your speech should reach out and virtually grab the audience by the ears to insist that they listen. In order to accomplish that you will need to know some principles of listening and to sharpen your own listening skills.

Listening—an Active Process

We cannot avoid hearing sounds generated near us, unless we have impaired hearing. Hearing is a passive process: sound waves vibrate through the air, strike our eardrums, and make the complicated mechanism of the ear vibrate, sending impulses to the brain, which interprets them as music, speech, fingernails on the chalkboard, an engine racing, or whatever. All that is a passive process; we cannot avoid the sounds.

Listening is an active process; like speaking, it takes some effort. In order to listen, we must put the sounds together in ways that make sense, so that we can recall them and accept, reject, or modify them. How then can we become better, more active listeners?

DO NOT JUDGE TOO SOON

"Look at that long hair! What can a kid who looks like that know about international problems?"
"Where does a woman come off talking about electronics?"
"He's black, and what do blacks know about our problems?"
"She's white, and what do whites know about our problems?"
"Look at that fancy three-piece suit and silk tie! What can an old man like that know about our problems?"

All too often we see one or two obvious components of a complex human being, and we decide immediately what the person is worth. Perhaps we hear one or two brief ideas and decide immediately that the person cannot say anything worthwhile. Prejudgment means instant failure for any attempt to listen. Withhold your judgment, listen carefully to what the person has to say, and then accept or reject the person's ideas based on their substance. Listen with your ears, not with your eyes or with preformed attitudes.

---

*Ralph G. Nichols and Leonard Stevens, *Are You Listening?* (New York: McGraw-Hill, 1957).

KEEP AN OPEN MIND

On the wall in my office is a photograph of an orangutan in an apparently thoughtful pose. The message on the poster reads: "Just when I thought I knew all the answers, they changed the questions." People who have all the answers may just be fooling themselves, but even if you have discovered "truth" about a subject, why not listen? Just maybe the other person can extend your knowledge about the subject. Who knows, you even may change your mind a little bit after hearing all sides of an issue. If the speaker does not alter your opinion, you may learn something that will solidify your position. Listen carefully with an open mind; you can always close it again after the speech, but you may be grateful for having kept it open.

BE READY TO LISTEN

Everybody has problems. Sometimes those problems are hard to leave behind us, but we owe it to the speaker to put personal factors out of our minds and listen to the speech. That advice, like most, is more easily given than taken. It is hard for us to turn off our minds to serious disagreements with loved ones, money needs, upcoming exams, or other personal problems, but the more you can put aside the personal distractions, the more you will gain from another's ideas. You will be more able to listen actively.

DO NOT RUSH IDEAS

A speaker may have to take time and offer many supportive arguments before the idea comes through clearly. For the listener to hear only a fraction of the evidence and judge the entire presentation is unfair to the speaker and, perhaps even more important, unfair to the listener. Listen to the whole message; only after giving the speaker a fair hearing should you evaluate.

DO NOT GET CAUGHT UP IN DELIVERY OR WORDS

Certainly delivery is important. Any message poorly sent will be poorly received, but try to understand and go beyond the problems of delivery. If the speaker stumbles over words, that indicates a need for practice, but it does not necessarily mean that the ideas are not worth listening to.

The same principle holds for word choice; some words are semantically loaded and connote all sorts of meanings to one person that they do not to another. Try to empathize with the words and understand them in the speaker's context, not your own. Do "racist," "reactionary," "establishment," "radical," and "socialist," mean the same things to all people? Of course not. If you can put aside, for a moment, your own personal definitions of loaded words, perhaps you will be able to understand the speaker's definitions. In order to do so, however, you will have to hold back your judgment until the whole idea is presented.

If you learn to listen actively and wisely, you will be a better informed citizen, a more effective speaker, and a better educated person.

Evaluating

As you stand in the classroom delivering your masterpiece of oratory, several kinds of evaluation are happening simultaneously. While you speak you evaluate your speech in terms of your own expectations and the feedback that you get from your listening audience, especially the instructor. The class is evaluating you based on their own experiences with other speakers, their relative interest in your topic, and their relative interest in you as a person. The instructor, meanwhile, is evaluating you in terms of an abstract, mysterious, and imaginary "yardstick" that was formed by having heard and seen many other speakers in similar situations; by your previous appearances in front of the class and the improvement you display; and by the needs of the specific assignment.

These various evaluations have three basic results:

1. The other students unconsciously evaluate their own skills and accept or reject for themselves techniques and mannerisms you display.
2. You digest your evaluation of the immediate feedback and of the more formalized feedback you receive later, resulting in your progress and improvement as a speaker.
3. The instructor's evaluation, sometimes incorporated with students' evaluations, forms the basis for your grade.

Although the grade may seem sometimes to be the most important result, in the long run the improvement and growth that you experience overshadow the grade's importance.

SELF-EVALUATION

We learn to speak by imitation and constant evaluation. As small children we experimented with sounds and other communication techniques, evaluated the results, and adopted those techniques which were most successful for satisfying our needs. If a boy says "chocolate cake" and gets a piece, he will evaluate the communication as successful and try it again next time his sweet tooth needs attention. If he gets a quart of vinegar, he will evaluate the communication as unsuccessful and try something else next time.

This recurring process of trial and error brings about the communication habits that we carry through to our adult lives. In essence evaluation by parents, guardians, and older siblings shapes our communication patterns. As we grow older, we evaluate ourselves and communicate in patterns that are acceptable to the social roles we are playing at the time. We constantly judge ourselves, using standards set by those around us.

You take the most important step in the evaluation process, however, when you begin to judge yourself as an individual. The most important goal of formal evaluation should be to enable you to assimilate criticism and learn to evaluate yourself. When you reach the point of self-evaluation, then you are able to progress much more rapidly toward your own potential. Of course, self-evaluation calls for an ability to look at yourself objectively, without being either too harsh or too lenient.

For a simple example of self-evaluation, let us assume that you have a distracting speech habit, such as excessive use of the expression "you know." In all probability you have not noticed yourself using the expression at all, let alone excessively. Then, lucky you, your life is changed by taking a speech-communication class. Your improvement will follow a pattern something like these five steps:

Step 1: *Lack of realization.* "What the heck is he talking about? I do not use 'you know' too much."
Step 2: *Realization.* "Wow! I guess I did use it a lot."

Step 3: *Hearing yourself.* "Oh. &#%*!. I said it again!"
Step 4: *Catching yourself before you say it.* "Ha, ha, almost."
Step 5: *Habit corrected.* "Gee, I haven't said 'you know' in three weeks, you know."

The change may take a long time, and you will probably need help, especially on the first two steps. Naturally the more complex the problem, the longer the solution will take. The real purpose of classroom criticism is to emphasize your strengths while helping to alleviate or eliminate your weaknesses. All the instructor can do is identify the problem and furnish some guidelines for the solution. It is up to you to heed the criticism and begin the process of change. Vital to that process is an ability to evaluate yourself honestly and realistically.

GRADES

You undoubtedly know by now if your instructor uses an evaluation form, whether it is called "critique," "evaluation," "analysis," "rating," "achievement," "habits," "profile," or some other name. In order to avoid imposing my personal choice of forms, I asked colleagues from several schools to show me the forms they use in their beginning speech-communication courses. I assumed that I would find two or three that would be representative and publish them. Ha, ha! I received thirty-eight different forms, ranging from a blank sheet of paper upon which to write impressions to forms that seemed to require a battery of computers just to understand the method. Rather than choosing one, I devised three "consensus" evaluation forms, based on the thirty-eight responses. (See Appendix B.) Although the language varied, common factors appeared on many forms. There seemed to be an implicit understanding that oral criticism would accompany the written.

Almost all the respondents stressed three aspects of the speech process: *organization, content,* and *delivery.* Whether we consider speaking an art, a process, or both, we can agree, for the most part, that unlike mathematics, the whole is greater than the sum of its parts. Consequently I included a fourth aspect, *overall effectiveness.* All teachers have heard speeches in which the individual aspects were merely fair or passable, yet the overall effect was good, or the converse, in which the individual parts were all good, but the result only fair.

How much weight should be attributed to each of the parts is strictly an individual matter. The better question for you to ask is, "Which part is most relevant to my problems?" Your instructor may assign weights to each heading for grading purposes. Remember, however, that an evaluation should be of use after the class is over and grades have been forgotten.

THE REAL PURPOSE OF EVALUATION

After the class is over, it is no longer necessary to fill in forms or follow standardized procedures for evaluation, for each of you will face differing and unique communication situations. You may wonder why one customer bought your product and another did not. You may notice the look of wonder, dismay, or chagrin on the face of the client whom you thought you had convinced. You may wonder why your family rejected the vacation plans you were espousing. Or you may simply wonder why you are so successful while others are only moderately successful doing the same thing, with the same facts, for the same "audience." When such things happen, that is the time to do some honest, critical appraisal of your personal communication techniques.

SUMMARY
AND CONCLUSION

Learning to be a good listener can help you be a better, more responsive citizen. Listening skills are also vital to your progress as a speaker. You will do well to follow these suggestions in any communication situation, but especially in situations where your primary function is listening:

1. Listen actively.
2. Do not judge too soon.
3. Keep an open mind.
4. Be ready to listen.
5. Do not rush ideas.
6. Do not get caught up in delivery or words.
7. Listen actively. (Were you watching actively enough to realize the repetition?)

Perhaps the most essential listening you will do is listening to yourself in order to evaluate your own speaking performance. Listening to yourself can help you progress more than any evaluation form.

You cannot drag out a chart that conveniently lists speech factors on a five-point scale every time you speak—life does not work that way. Nor do you need to have a formalized, structured way of reporting your self-evaluation—life does not work that way, either. But some hard, incisive self-evaluation can do you a great deal of good. When your communication fails, or when it leads you deeper into problems that it should have solved, you need to analyze your skills. The problem may be at work, at home, with the family, with friends, or with any number of different situations. One thing will always be constant, however: communication problems exist *between people*, so examine the situation in terms of the audience and its response to your message.

Try asking these questions:

1. Did I have sufficient control of myself so as not to *appear* nervous? Did I know my material well enough to allay a good portion of my anxiety? Did I appear to be in control, even if I actually was frightened?
2. Did I know what I was talking about, or was I trying to "snow" my audience?
3. With whom am I dealing? What makes them tick? Did I direct my communication to the personality factors that they exhibit, rather than to my own?
4. Did I present my information in an organized pattern easy for the audience to follow?
5. Did I get the audience's attention properly and begin in such a way that they became involved with me and interested in the topic?
6. Did I know when to stop without becoming boring? Did I end with sufficient dramatic punch so they will remember the important details long after the communication event?
7. Did I give the information in a logical manner, remembering that people feel as well as reason? Did I present myself in as good a light as I presented my facts?
8. Did my appeals to statistical information and the words of other people make sense to the audience?
9. Did I give the other people sufficient information for them to visualize, or in some other way sense, what they needed to?
10. Did I use the physical facilities about me to their best advantage? Did I compensate for problems that were beyond my control?

If you have a touch of Sherlock Holmes about you, you may have noticed that the ten questions above refer to the basic substance of Chapters 2, 5–9, and 11–14, in the order in which they appear in the book. The ten questions supply a good, quick check list for your self-evaluation in any communication situation, although they basically refer to public speaking.

Even if you never do much formal public speaking, you will probably be involved with a good deal of informal public, specialized, interpersonal, and group communication. *The principles are the same.* You will continue to communicate with other people for the rest of your life, unless you become a hermit. While these questions and the principles they represent will by no stretch of the imagination insure success with your fellow human beings, coupled with good listening habits and insightful self-evaluation, they might make the future a little less unsuccessful.

CHAPTER 4

types of speeches

1. *What types of speeches are generally used?*
2. *What are the differences between these types?*
3. *What effect does the intent have upon the type?*
4. *How does the occasion help determine the type of speech?*

Speaker:	The State of Virginia had a population of 4,651,448 in 1970. Its area is 40,817 square miles.
Mean Skeptic:	How do you know? Did you count the people? Did you measure it yourself?
Salesperson:	You should definitely buy this Rolls Royce convertible to best suit your needs.
Less-Mean Buyer:	Huh? Why? Tell me some more about it.

Generations of speech students have heard that there are three basic types of speeches: speeches to inform, speeches to persuade, and speeches to entertain. That is a useful way of dividing and categorizing speeches, especially for assignment purposes. In essence it says that the types of speeches are defined by the purpose of the speaker.

The Intent of the Speech

The three-way division of inform, persuade, and entertain is a bit unreliable for two reasons. First, the divisions themselves may have different emphases within them, and second, because every speech should have some aspect of all three in order to be successful.

The simplistic examples given at the beginning of the chapter illustrate the basic problem. A speaker dispensing pure, factual information must also do some persuading within the speech. We in the audience must be convinced, persuaded, that the speaker knows what he or she is talking about. In the example about the statistics regarding Virginia, a speaker might just state the source of the statistics in order to convince us to accept the facts. With an example as simple as numbers of people and square miles there is not a great deal of room for skepticism once the speaker establishes the sources, but what about less concrete information? One politician may tell us about a program that will need only a 7.35% increase in taxes in order to help 76.82% of the population. Another politician may tell us about the same program, informing us that it needs an increase of 37.86% in taxes and only 12.3% of the population will be affected. Both offer us information, but we have to decide by using other persuasive factors which one we will believe. (The cynics in the group probably won't believe either.)

Conversely, a speaking event in which the main purpose is to convince us to change our opinions or to commit ourselves to some act such as a purchase or a vote must also contain informative, factual elements in order to present us with the basis for persuasion. In the silly example at the beginning of the chapter, the buyer would want to know the price and other factual information about the car. Perhaps the name Rolls Royce or the description "convertible" would be enough to inspire some people to act, but most of us would probably want a little better information.

Finally, any speech must be entertaining enough to keep us awake and stimulate our interest, assuming we use "entertaining" in its broadest meaning.

Speeches to Inform

In an informative speech the speaker presents the information to the audience. There may be little or no feedback depending on the size of the audience and the situation. Examples of informative speeches might include such events as the President of the United States appearing on television to explain a new policy or an international crisis; a Student Council officer appearing at an assembly to describe some new program or regulation; a lecturer talking to a garden club about ferns; or a student talking about the State of Virginia.

The basic purpose of any informative speech is to explain, describe, and/or define some basic topic for the audience. Any one speech may include some or all of these purposes. In order for the audience to understand the new parking regulations, the speaker must explain why the regulations were changed, describe the new regulations, and perhaps, define the term "small car," as opposed to "full-sized." The physician may explain the reason for taking a certain medicine; the chemist may describe the chemical reactions that take place; and the chemistry teacher may define terms necessary to understand the chemical reaction.

The more abstract a subject is the more it will need to be defined by the speaker. A speech about capitalism will need definitions of individual words and of concepts such as ownership of property, real property, and investment. The thrust of the speech itself will be definition of the abstract concept.

Description is vital to any speech. The more vivid the description of concrete objects, the more we in the audience will be able to visualize the objects in our imaginations. Both speech and writing will benefit greatly from sharp, clear descriptions of people, objects, and contexts.

In the "how to" speech, the explanation will usually be limited to processes, such as the way a machine or concept works. One could explain, for instance, the process or processes involved in extracting high-grade steel from iron ore, coke, and other raw materials. Again a speaker dealing with capitalism could describe the way that workers spend money made as wages; business then uses the money for investment, salaries, paying bills, etc.; investment institutions lend out the money at increased rates of interest; and so on, explaining the process of cycling and recycling of resources.

Description is vital to virtually any speech, and explanation and definition will appear to a lesser extent in most.

DEMONSTRATION SPEECHES

Another type of informative speech is the demonstration. As the name implies, the speaker will demonstrate a process, showing it in detail. Demonstration speeches often follow a time sequence. If you are demonstrating a process, you begin with step one, proceed to step two, and so on. A photographic demonstration might begin with loading the camera, adjusting it, composing the picture, and finally processing the film. A demonstration speech will *show* what needs to be done, rather than describing or explaining it.

If you are prepared, have practiced all the steps, and have all the necessary equipment, a demonstration may be a fairly easy presentation because the organization is determined by the process itself. Explaining how an interlocking mechanism works may be quite complex and time-consuming. If, however, you can simply show — demonstrate — the process, it should be relatively simple and quick.

Some steps in a demonstration speech may have to be prepared ahead of time. Cooking shows on television are an excellent example of demonstration speeches. If a certain dish needs to cook for three hours, you can be sure that the one prepared before our very eyes will not be the one the chef shows us. The final product will have been produced well ahead of time. An artistic process may take hours to complete, but the individual steps can be demonstrated rather quickly. Have a sample of the finished product ready to show your audience.

EXPOSITORY SPEECHES

The most difficult, and most important, category of informative speaking is the expository speech. In the expository speech, you will need to use description, explanation, and definition as necessary to get your point across to the audience. You may also want to demonstrate certain aspects of the topic. By and large, however, you will be dealing with abstract information. The audience will have to work with you to understand your weighty ideas, but you will, in turn, have to motivate them so that they want to hear and learn about the information you are presenting.

You may have a fascinating (to you) speech about methods of keeping time over the centuries, but unless you motivate your audience with a stimulating introduction, their attention may wander off. (More about introductions in Chapter 8.)

You will, of course, need to compile the information you wish to communicate to your audience. If your hobby has been ancient timepieces, you may have a good deal of the research done already. Chances are, however, you will have to get some historical, statistical, scientific, or testimonial evidence in the library or some other place. If you have really done your research well, your problem will be to limit the amount of information you will present to the audience. That will call for some hard choices of what information to use and what to discard. You will also have to decide just how you want to present the information to the audience. Most abstract subjects can be organized in different ways, making them harder than demonstration speeches that usually follow a strict time sequence.

Informative speaking is the heart of the communicative act. Every speech must have some information in it, although the true informative speech will have the presentation of knowledge as its central focus. Some informative speeches will deal with abstract, difficult to comprehend information; these will require a great deal of audience intellectual activity and work. Some informative speeches will deal with *doing*, demonstrating skills that the audience may be able to duplicate. Some will combine aspects of both. A chemistry professor explaining a newly discovered chemical reaction to a group of fellow-scientists represents an informative speech at the most abstract, intellectual level. A demonstration of macramé, cooking, or other skills is at the "doing" end of the scale. (Sometimes the demonstration speech is considered as a separate category from informative, but it is a form of informative speaking — dispensing information.)

Speeches to Persuade

Persuasive speeches usually state a position and then attempt to persuade the audience to accept a belief or value or to perform a specific action. A member of the clergy attempting to convince an audience of a specific belief is an example of the first type of persuasion. If he or she goes further and asks the audience to behave in a certain way, that speech is of the second type.

The persuasive speech always must give an audience information, so they can make a rational choice. Candidates must give us reasons why they are better choices (information) before we will cast our ballots for them (action); salespersons must tell us the merits of the car, shoes, or aspirin tablets (information) to convince us to buy the product (action); you must tell your friends something about a movie (information) to convince them to spend their money on it (action). If in your speech you advocate that the United States withdraw from the United Nations, you had better have some solid information indicating why we should take such a step. The same would be true if you advocated making a greater commitment to or maintaining the status quo in the United Nations. If you are trying to persuade the audience to sign your petition to have the parking lot resurfaced, you must tell them why there needs to be a change and why your plan will resolve the need. If you advocate that all students should be required to take a speech-communication course (a commendable position), you must state the benefits of such a requirement. (Chapter 11 will deal in more detail with methods for persuading your audience.)

Speeches to Entertain

Speeches designed to entertain do not demand much from the audience except to listen and enjoy. The audience is not expected to assimilate information, take action, or change attitudes. Speakers should realize that the speech that entertains one audience may bore, offend, or go over the heads of another.

Any speech, regardless of its intent, must have elements of entertainment, such as devices of language, vivacity, and energy to keep the audience's attention. Entertainment does not necessarily mean simple jolliness. A speech to entertain can deal with more important issues, but usually when it does it creeps over into the informative or persuasive emphasis.

Speeches for Special Occasions

Occasionally you may be called upon to speak at some special occasion. If you are a member of a student body, church group, or club officer, or involved with any organization, you may be called on to introduce someone, present an award, welcome a dignitary, pay tribute to someone, or accept an award.

Perhaps Hamlet gave the best advice for the special-occasion speaker: "Brevity is the soul of wit." In other words, keep it brief; say what you have to say and let the occasion proceed. The audience wants to hear the person you are introducing, so introduce and let the spotlight pass to him or her.

You will need to convey some information to the audience. You may list the person's achievements, successes, and awards. You will want to convey information that specially connects audience and speaker — for example, that the speaker went to your school. If, however, the guest is a famous explorer speaking about adventures in the jungles of New Guinea, nobody wants to hear your interpretation of those adventures. Do your introduction, and then let the person speak — that is what the audience wants to hear.

It is customary to refrain from mentioning the person's name until the end of the introduction. After giving the pertinent information, you might conclude with something like: "It gives me a great deal of pleasure to present Harry Hill" or "Ladies and gentlemen, this year's winner, Sally Smith." The audience, speaker, and purpose of the speech should determine your brief remarks. If you save the name until the end, the audience will know when to applaud and the recipient can come forward during the applause. If you mention the name too soon, confusion can result. The other person should have the spotlight, unless, of course, you receive an award.

We have all seen award programs, such as the Oscar and Emmy ceremonies, where the recipient goes on and on thanking so many people that the thanks become meaningless. If you receive an award, accept it graciously, thank those people who deserve recognition for that specific honor, and then sit down. You will enhance your dignity.

Any of these speaking situations should be well planned. You will have time to prepare your remarks and weed out the unnecessary elements, unless you win an award you did not expect. In that case, you may find yourself dazed and unsure. That is the time to bring out the many skills you will learn in your speech-communication class. Show poise and confidence, and try to get through the situation without becoming totally unglued. On all special occasions, be brief and let the person who should be the center of attention have the focus.

Stating Your Objectives

The objectives of a speech determine the type of speech it will be. Rarely is a speech purely informative or persuasive; most will have elements of both. It is the basic purpose for the speech that determines whether the thrust is informative or persuasive. You will probably have a purpose in the back of your mind for every speech. You will do better if you write down the purpose as a "statement of objectives."

The public speaker should be able to express an objective for every speech in one sentence similar to this: "When my presentation is finished, I want the audience to _____." The blank may be filled in with an almost infinite variety of responses, such as:

"understand the history and principles of Braille"
"make a simple bird using Origami"
"vote for me for Freshman Class Treasurer"
"sign my petition to have more cultural events on campus"
"accept the divine right of kings as the only political philosophy that can save our society."

Your statement of objectives is part of the preparation of the speech, and, as such, it should not be shared with the audience. It is for your private use, to help you direct all points of the speech to a central focus.

Everything in the speech should relate somehow to the statement of objectives. (Later in your preparation you should develop a topic statement within the context of the speech. The topic statement may evolve from the statement of objectives.)

SUMMARY AND CONCLUSION

The three main categories of speeches overlap. It is impossible to persuade someone without giving information. Conversely, when we inform, we are actually persuading someone to accept our version of truth. Finally, if the audience does not find a speech entertaining, they will lose interest rapidly no matter what you say. Entertainment does not mean empty pleasure, but interesting, provocative involvement. Regardless of the emphasis, you should define your goal for every speech with a statement of objectives.

Your information and purpose will be major factors in your presentation, but the most important aspect of your speech is you. Let your personality, thoughts, and ideas shine through the details. Details are important, but you make the speech unique.

EXERCISES

1. Give two examples of speech topics that could be either informative or persuasive.
2. Using a local law or ordinance, such as a speed limit or zoning law, write a statement of objectives for an informative speech about that law and another statement of objectives for a persuasive speech about the same law.

3. You have been nominated for an Academy Award as outstanding actor or actress (or any other category you choose). Now write a statement of objectives for your acceptance speech. Why bother? Surprise! You won!
4. Draw a continuum or chart which shows how much demand is placed upon the audience in each of the types of speeches.

CHAPTER 5

selecting and researching your topic

1. *How do I go about selecting a topic for my speech?*
2. *Where can I find information about my subject?*
3. *What should I keep in mind as I gather information?*
4. *What are some good choices for my first speech?*

Student: Can I see you for a minute?*
Teacher: Sure!
Student: I am having a problem getting a topic for my first speech, and it's due next week.
Teacher: Have you given it any thought?
Student: Oh, yeah, I really have. But I can't seem to come up with anything.
Teacher: Well, as I said in class, everybody is an expert on something. Do you have a job?
Student: I clean up in a pharmacy, but there is nothing unusual or very interesting about my work.
Teacher: How about travel? Ever go anyplace exotic or unusual?
Student: Not really.
Teacher: Hobbies?
Student: Nope!
Teacher: (Glancing at his watch.) Look, I have another class now. Could you see me in my office later?
Student: What time?
Teacher: Oh, about ten o'clock.
Student: Oh, I can't then, I have to go home to take care of my pet eagle.

*Although I would not vouch for the precise wording of the dialogue above, the sense and content is based on an incident that actually happened to this author while teaching a basic public speaking course. It happened as the class was leaving the room after an 8:00 A.M. session.

His pet *eagle!* And yet he thought he had nothing unusual or interesting to tell people. Perhaps if he had thought of a speech as a way of sharing something pleasant with others, he might have thought about sharing his eagle with us. Eventually this student did speak about the problems and pleasures of raising an eagle. Sadly enough, he did not bring the eagle to class because he thought no one would be interested.

The eagle furnished a magnificent topic for a speech. Those readers who have pet eagles undoubtedly are dancing with joy at having such a wonderful topic. But what about the other 99.9 percent of you? Let's see if we can help you search for a perfect topic. A good topic? Any topic!

Meet the Expert—You

Everybody is an expert on something. If nothing else, you are an expert on your-self. You have lived with you all your life, feeling all your pain and all your joy. No one ever will know you better than you know yourself.

Most of us hold back some of what we know about ourselves. We wonder just how much others want to know or should know about "me," whoever "me" is. If you are shrinking at the thought of telling the world your nightmares, relax! Within the context of knowing yourself, you know about things that relate to you. For instance, I could deliver a speech about playing the folk guitar. I could keep the speech fairly technical, stressing the parts of the guitar or how to hold and play it. From my speech you might infer some things about me: I play the guitar; I enjoy folk music; and I am a reasonably articulate individual. I have not allowed any glimpses into my inner self that might be embarrassing or too self-disclosing. Still you would know more about me, as well as about the guitar, from my presentation.

Each of us has knowledge and ideas to share with others. In the process we share some of ourselves with others, too, but in a controllable, nonthreatening manner. You are all experts or can become experts on three types of knowledge: things you already know; things you would like to know, or know better; and things you should know.

THINGS YOU KNOW

From the moment of birth each of us follows and stumbles along a unique path. Even identical twins have unique experiences and emotions. Throughout our lives we meet different people, go different places, and have different things hap-pen to us, so that no two lives are ever identical or even similar. The boy with the pet eagle may have reasoned that his life, home, family, and experiences were similar to millions of other lives, but he overlooked a facet of his life that was unusual and interesting.

It is impossible to catalog all the experiences that any one of us can have. Think of some inconsequential event that changed the course of your life. Perhaps there is the seed of a speech—or short story or poem. At least one hundred people signed my high school yearbook back in the Middle Ages. One acquaintance signed, "See you at El Camino." At the time I did not even know what El Camino was. I learned that it was a new community college near my home and decided to enroll there. I will not bore you with the profound effect of that simple, seemingly inconsequential reference, but it changed my life drastically and irreversibly. Probably everyone reading this book has had such an experience, perhaps not as drastic, perhaps more. Within that experience lie many speeches. Story writers have used that kind of experience as the basis for umpteen novels: *For some reason I turned left instead of right as I usually do, and there she stood!* (You can finish the story yourself.)

Your hobby or avocation can be of great interest to others and furnish a topic for a speech. An experience playing Little League baseball, travelling with the girls' basketball team, collecting stamps or beer cans, operating a ham radio, designing sets for a theater, and other such topics can fascinate an audience. After all, there must be something interesting about the subject, or it would not have attracted you.

The same is true of a vocation. Many of you have not chosen a vocation yet, but probably you have given it some thought. Share those thoughts! Why are you considering being a truck driver or brain surgeon or jockey or college professor? Perhaps you have already held some interesting job after school or in the summer—share it with the class.

Not all of your experiences furnish good topics for speeches. If 75 percent of your class comes from the same high school, they probably would not be interested in a speech about that high school. What if, however, you went to a school that was unique, or at least different from those attended by most of your classmates? Suppose you are an "Army brat" who went to high school in Tokyo or Madrid. Those circumstances would warrant a speech comparing United States high schools with Japanese or Spanish schools. We all take vacations, and many of the experiences mean nothing except to those who were there. In my family, however, we still discuss the vacation to the national parks in the West where we kept running into the "mailman from Detroit" who invariably sang (miserably) at a campfire talent show. That experience may be amusing enough for a speech. If you live in California and went to Hollywood for your vacation, so what? But if you went to New York and saw plays on Broadway, the United Nations, a variety of museums, and a ball game in Yankee stadium, that trip might furnish a good topic. Of course, the opposite is true for the Easterner.

The point is that ideas and topics for speeches abound in your personal experiences, in the things you already know. As you search for them, be aware of what will interest and inform other people in your classroom audience.

THINGS YOU WOULD LIKE TO KNOW

Things you would like to know but never have taken time to research furnish the opportunity of killing the proverbial two birds with one stone: you get to know about a subject you wanted to learn about, *and* you get a topic and information for a speech.

The variety of topics is limited only by your own curiosity. Elephants, the banjo, the history of puppets, why the sky is blue—the list is endless. Perhaps you always have wondered what it would be like to enter a certain profession but never gave it serious consideration. This speech would be an opportunity to find out something about the profession and perhaps even begin to steer yourself in that direction. Whether you pursue it is unimportant. The important thing is that you are learning something about a topic that has piqued your curiosity. Perhaps you have wondered why a certain law is on the books. Investigate it. You may simply gain information; you may gain insight into the factors that led to the law; or you may decide to pursue it further and attempt to change the law or see that it is enforced. The same could apply to a school regulation. Ever wonder about the origin of your family name, or indeed, the origin of your family? (Hope you don't find too many horse thieves or bootleggers, but if you do, so what?) At one time only the upper classes concerned themselves with family background, but now many people are digging back.

THINGS YOU SHOULD KNOW

An offshoot of things you would like to know more about is things you feel you *should* know more about. Do you feel just a touch of guilt about not knowing anything about a certain subject? If there is such a subject buried in your mind, dig it out. A speech class can be a great opportunity for detective work.

Probably your instructor will give you certain guidelines for your speech, assigning a general topic, a specific area, or a certain type of speech. Usually there is latitude within the guidelines, however, for you to search your experiences and interests for topics that you will enjoy speaking about and your classmates will enjoy hearing about.

What Is a Good Topic?

Plato, the ancient Greek philosopher, condemned the field of speech for not having any substance of its own and for relying on other disciplines for its substance. Most speech-communication educators would disagree with Plato, at least on the first part of the assumption. We think we do have some specific skills and information to impart. In one sense, however, Plato was correct: speech encompasses virtually every other discipline because we can speak on just about any issue in any field of endeavor, academic or otherwise.

Over the years I have heard classroom speeches that drew upon about every facet of human culture and understanding. In my early high-school teaching career a Future Farmer of America gave a speech in which he demonstrated how to cut off a lamb's tail. (The blood and bleating inspired angry phone calls from parents of some of the more squeamish students.) Engineering students have spoken about communication codes in blueprints and other engineering documents, as well as the history and function of the slide rule, advocacy for structural codes, and design problems. Students in computer technology have spoken of ways in which humans and machines communicate, coding of punch cards, and details of latest hardware and techniques. Medical and nursing students have contributed speeches about hospital communication, birth control, and a myriad of health problems and solutions. Students have spoken about facets of crafts, music, other arts, politics, religion, athletics, and just about any subject you can name. Your own interests and resources are the only limiting factors within the framework of your assignments.

Not all speeches are equally good, of course, but the difference, based on my observation, is that quality depends on the student and not on the topic. For instance, good engineering students generally give good speeches; weak engineering students generally give weak speeches *regardless of topic.*

The acceptability of topics may vary from situation to situation and from school to school. In some colleges and universities a speech about birth control may be perfectly acceptable while in others it would be embarrassing and considered in bad taste at best. Taste also is relative. A student once gave a well-planned, interesting speech on devices for smoking marijuana. The topic itself caused a little embarrassment at first, but he quickly got our attention and eased the anxiety. He heightened the tension later, however, when he demonstrated how to use one device, bringing out a plastic pouch with a leafy material which he refused to identify. Later he confessed that the material was tobacco, but because no one was sure, the class became restless, and he lost our attention. Regardless of their personal feelings toward marijuana, everyone knew that it was illegal in our state, and I had warned the class against bringing any illegal substances or objects into the class. The failure to identify the substance moved the speech over the line of good taste.

On the other hand, another young man came to class dressed in a raincoat, obviously naked from the knees down, sat behind a desk that hid his lower torso from the class, and then removed the raincoat to reveal his bare chest. He then delivered a speech about nudity. The speech was light-hearted and never vulgar or demeaning. When he was finished, he put on the raincoat, left class, changed into street clothes in the rest room, and returned to class. He would not tell us whether or not . . . To this day I do not know for sure. In both cases, the attitude of the speaker, more than the subject, determined whether or not the speech was in good taste.

In spite of the folk wisdom of "never discuss politics or religion," either subject can be a source for good speeches — or for bad speeches. A speech that informs the class about your religion's history, culture, practices, and appeal to you can be interesting and informative to a class in a public institution. As soon as it becomes an attempt to gain converts, however, you are in trouble. One mature man in one of my classes insisted on speaking about his religion for every assignment. At first it was interesting, but then he began actively seeking converts. Even after I informed him that he must speak about some other topic, he persisted, accepting the low grade (eventually an "F") rather than change the subject. The class became thoroughly bored with the subject and with him, and he did his cause more harm than good in the long run.

Politics and social issues furnish almost endless topics for speeches. During the late 60's and early 70's every speech teacher heard what seemed like thousands of speeches about the Viet Nam military action, both for and against. The same is true of abortion, the draft, and other issues that challenge our minds and stimulate our emotions.

What is a good topic? Almost any topic that has some intellectual substance can be a good topic in the right speaker's hands. Unfortunately, the converse is also true.

Finding a Topic—June 19, 1980

As I write this particular section of the book it is June 19, 1980. You will be reading it much later than that — probably three or more years later. To indicate one simple and yet quite fruitful source for speech topics, we will examine the first three pages of today's *Chicago Tribune*. These are the headlines:

Page 1:   RUMORS FLY, TENSION MOUNTS, AND AN ERA ENDS
ERA REJECTED AGAIN IN HOUSE SHOWDOWN—FIVE VOTES SHORT, BUT IT'S KEPT ALIVE

TOWN FACES A SUMMER OF DISCONTENT—GEORGIA OFFICIALS WORK TO EASE RACIAL TENSIONS

S. AFRICAN COPS KILL 36 IN RACIAL VIOLENCE

THOMPSON CALLS FOR GAS TAX HIKE TO PAY FOR ROADS
BANKERS STALL THE BAILOUT OF CHRYSLER

Page 2:   2 IN HOUSE INDICTED IN ABSCAM

CARTER WANTS TO SELL 100 TANKS TO JORDAN

KARMAL BACKERS REPORTED SLAIN, MUTILATED

BOLIVIANS PILLAGE U.S. CONSULATE

CHURCH SPONSORING CHILD FOOD SERVICE

LAVA FLOW FEARED AT MT. ST. HELENS

Page 3:   JUDGE'S LANDLORD TAX RULING TO HURT HOMEOWNERS: HYNES

'GUNSMOKE' DOC REMEMBERED

BINGE EATING PLAGUES MANY WOMEN: STUDY

SEARS HIRING BIAS SUIT IS DISMISSED

By the time you read this book, many of the topics above will be of no current interest. Many are, of course, local to the Chicago or Illinois area. The Equal Rights Amendment probably has been ratified or rejected; Mt. St. Helens may be dormant again or it may have blown half of Washington off the map. We can only hope, and not too optimistically, that troubles in the Middle East, Afghanistan, and South Africa will have eased, although cynicism tells us that even if those 1980 hotspots are peaceful, others will have taken their places. The important factor is that every one of those sixteen headlines represents at least one topic for a speech. Most represent several possible topics.

Regardless of the condition of the volcano at Mt. St. Helens, there will be other natural disasters, such as earthquakes, floods, hurricanes, and tornados, all of which can lead you to multiple topics for speeches. The Mt. St. Helens story, which takes only about three column inches, might erupt into speeches with titles similar to these:

The Birth and Death of a Volcano
Pompeii and Mt. Vesuvius
The Active World beneath the Earth's Surface
Predicting Volcanic Eruptions
Mt. St. Helens: A Vulcanologist's Dream
St. Helen: Much Nicer than Her Volcano

These are just samples; the list could go on and on. Of course, you would need to do some research about such a subject, but between March and June 1980 each of the national news magazines devoted dozens of pages to Mt. St. Helens, as did most newspapers. You might want to consult with a geologist or vulcanologist. Perhaps a historian might help. Dozens, if not hundreds, of books have been written about Pompeii and other cities destroyed by volcanic action. Perhaps the topic might lead to research and a speech about Krakatoa or some other natural explosion. The possibilities are virtually endless.

The same is true of stories about the Equal Rights Amendment or racial violence in South Africa. Even if those stories are not current, the human race's newfound awareness and growth in the fields of equal rights and racial prejudice can supply unlimited material for speeches. A speech might inform the audience about some leaders in the struggle for equality or it might deal with historical landmarks. It might be built around the legal principles involved, or it might be an attempt to persuade the audience to support, or oppose, a proposed law or candidate.

Look at your local or campus newspaper and try to brainstorm speech ideas from the headlines. Certainly you will not be interested in every subject and every headline, but you will see that those headlines suggest speech topics, even if they are not for you. You will need to expand your information, of course, but once the germ of an idea emerges, digging out the details becomes somewhat easier.

Sources of Information

If your topic is derived from personal experience, your basic research is already done. If not, you will need to gain more information about it. There are several avenues open for obtaining information.

PERSONAL EXPERIENCE

Suppose you are assigned a five-minute informative speech about some form of communication. What are some possible sources of information?

From your personal experience you may be able to glean several basic topics. You might not have thought of them as communication or as a subject for a speech class assignment, but they may well be. Have you trained show dogs—or horses or cats? What forms of communication aided you in training them? Verbal commands did, to some extent. What about nonverbal commands? What about rewards for good behavior or punishment for bad? In short, how do you communicate with your dog? Ever play organized baseball in Little League or on school teams? How do the players and coaches communicate on the field? Why does the guy standing near third base touch his hat, then his belt, then run his arm down the opposite sleeve, go back to his hat, then clap his hands together? If you have played baseball, you undoubtedly could construct a speech around this peculiar and unique form of communication. Suppose you work with color-coded resistors. Is not the coloring on the bands of the resistor a way for the manufacturer to communicate with the worker who repairs the machine? Such a form of communication could apply to virtually anything that has a code, such as clothing tags or milk cartons. All these topics can be taken from personal experience with little or no further research.

THE LIBRARY

Not all subjects can be gleaned from personal experience. Some require further study. The first place to look is the library. There you can delve into almost any subject as deeply as you wish. Sometimes a well-researched topic in a library will lead from one source to three sources to seven to fifteen to a hundred and six, and so on *ad infinitum*. Library research is exceptionally good for obtaining hard facts such as statistics, quotations from experts, and other people's research.

If you are not familiar with libraries and library procedures, ask the librarians for assistance. Usually they are more than happy to help a student who wants information. They are not there to think up subjects for your speeches, however, and you should not expect them to do that for you. Once you know what you want, you will find them valuable in helping you find it.

INFORMAL OBSERVATION

Many people think that personal experience and library research are the only ways to obtain information, but there are others. The simple act of observing other people can be used for gathering information; indeed, you have been using that method for years. Sitting in the lounge and observing can verify or alter some preconceived ideas you have about human habits and attitudes. Of course, the observation must have some statistical or logical basis. Do you have a preconceived idea about the way males and females carry books? Some say that most female students carry their books with their arms forming a right angle across the body, while most males carry them with the arm extended, primarily using the wrist. Which carry over-the-shoulder tote bags? A simple chart like the one below can give you an answer, if you observe enough subjects.

Position	Males	Females
Arm extended down		
Arm at right angle across body		
Tote bag		

SURVEYS AND INTERVIEWS

Much of our information about the world we live in and many of our attitudes are formed by informal observation. We can gather a great deal of information about a specific subject through more formal observation. A questionnaire may give answers about people's attitudes and desires. Unless you are working on a very elementary level ("Do you smoke? Yes? No?"), you may need some aid in preparing your questions. The more complicated the questionnaire, the more difficult it is to prepare it and to interpret the results. You will be better off to gather simple, polarized information in this manner.

Suppose you want to discuss smoking on your campus. You could gather information by observing informally the number of smokers vs. nonsmokers or the number of female vs. male smokers. To gather deeper information you may wish to ask students in your classes why they do or do not smoke, how many members of their families smoke, or whatever else you want to know for your speech.

Still another valuable way of gathering information is the interview. Public officials, clergy, the police, school teachers and administrators, politicians, business people and indeed most people are willing and even anxious to share information and opinions with students who are respectful and confine questions to the area of the person's expertise. If you want to speak about a law, why not ask an attorney his or her opinion about it? Ask a police officer, a politician, or another concerned official. Do not ask the football coach about business nor the executive about football, although each may have an opinion about the subject. An opinion matters most in the person's area of expertise. A college community affords excellent opportunities for interviewing people on many subjects, since college campuses usually have experts in business, philosophy, law, psychology, and most other fields. Most will be more than willing to discuss their subject with you.

Guidelines for Gathering Information

When conducting a survey or interview, you should keep some guidelines in mind. First, be prepared; know what questions you are going to ask and write them out ahead of time. Avoid loaded questions: "Do you think the administration should raise student body fees in order to get money to fix the parking lot so that the students can park closer to class?" There are really four questions implied in that one: (1) raising fees, (2) getting money, (3) fixing the parking lot, and (4) parking closer to class. A better way to ask would be to break the question into its component parts: (1) Do we need parking closer to classes? (2) Do we need to repair the existing lots? (3) If you answered yes to either question 1 or 2, would you be willing to pay an increased fee for the repair? (4) If you answered question 3 *no*, where do you think the administration should get the money?

You also must ask questions fairly. Do not ask, "Would you like to pay lower fees (or taxes)?" How many people in their right mind would answer no? The results of the fee or tax cut should be part of the question. You also should avoid phrasing the question so it solicits one response: "You're not in favor of building a new gym, are you?" will almost surely get a *no* answer, but "Are you in favor of the plans to build a new gym?" should elicit responses on both sides.

If you are stopping people at random to ask questions, make certain that they are fully aware of your purpose. We have become quite cynical about anyone stopping us, and too often your survey may suffer because the respondents are waiting for you to make your sales pitch. If you are nonthreatening and they can see that you are not trying to sell something, most people will be flattered to have the opportunity to make their opinions heard.

Finally, if individuals prefer not to answer your questions, respect their rights. If you make yourself obnoxious and insist upon getting answers, in all probability the offshoot will twist your results. When someone is coerced into answering, chances are the responses will be affected by hostility toward the interviewer.

Whether you use experience, library research, observation, or interviews, you should keep complete notes. Record all pertinent information. You should be able to cite not only the information, but also where it came from. For example, in a speech on smoking in school you might report the results of a survey:

The members of our discussion group asked 347 students the following question: "Would you favor a smoking ban in the cafeteria?" We conducted the survey during the first week of school in order to recommend a course of action. Sentiment was divided equally, with 138 students responding *yes* and an equal number saying *no*. Seventy-one refused to express an opinion. Our conclusion, therefore, is that the campus is divided on the issue, and that present policy should remain in effect.

Try to obtain information from many sources. The more sources of information, the more complete and worthwhile the information becomes. The ideal topic calls on experience, research, observation, and interviews, although most topics utilize only one or two.

As you gather information on a topic, pay special attention to anything that adds an unusual twist. To be different just to be different does not add anything to your speech and will probably point to itself as a gimmick or artifical device. All of us, however, are interested in that which is genuinely unusual.

Finally, do not be afraid to include personal references. Most of us are curious about other people, and we like to "peak through the keyhole" into their lives. Literature, theatre, motion pictures, and television plays appeal to us in part because they allow us to observe other people's "secrets." You can, however, allow people to peer too deeply into private matters. How much is too much? There is, of course, no answer or formula. A registered nurse once gave an interesting speech about methods of birth control. She made some acceptable personal references, but she went too far when she began to describe her husband's anger and resentment when she forgot to take the proper measures herself while they were on a camping trip. The audience started getting nervous. It was as if they had peeked through the keyhole and seen more than they had bargained for. On the other hand, a student giving an informative speech about mental health moved a class to tears by using a specific example whom she identified as her brother in the conclusion.

SUMMARY
AND CONCLUSION

When wracking your brain to get a topic for a speech, remember that you are an expert. Where your expertise lies, of course, varies from person to person. Once you select a topic the library and other repositories of knowledge can help you research and add to your expertise. We all have countless topics within our memories, limited only by our imaginations and experiences. The acceptability of a topic can be determined by using good taste and judgment in relation to the audience for which the speech is intended.

You can find good information in your personal experience, from informal observation, and from surveys and interviews, as well as from more traditional research methods.

Any speech involves a series of choices—how much information, how much persuasion, how many statistics, which proofs, and so on. The degree of personal involvement is another such choice.

EXERCISES

Here are a few suggestions for your first speech. The actual assignment is in the hands of your teacher, who must make assignments that fit an individual pattern of teaching. Even if these suggestions are not specific assignments, you should think about them. They can put you on the track of good topics.

1. *Describe a person, place, or thing* (sound like a noun?) *that most of your classmates would not know.* The *person* could be someone from your family, someone from a different city, or someone you met on vacation. The *place* could be somewhere that you have travelled or somewhere where you would *like* to travel—either real, such as Rome, or fantasized, such as Oz. You might want to debunk the glamor of Hollywood, the romance of Paris, or the idyllic setting of Hawaii, but if you do, you had better know what you are talking about, and you might want to do it humorously. The *thing* could be virtually anything you know about or would like to know about: your pet eagle (again?), the northern lights, moon rocks, the Mona Lisa, or your customized car. The northern lights, moon rocks, and Mona Lisa will involve more research than the other two, and the approach may be more serious, but any of the topics, and nine zillion like them, can be approached seriously or lightly.
2. *Tell the class about a great vacation spot, a good hobby, or your secret ambition.* Again the information can be from experience, research, or both. It can be based on interests real or imagined, such as your desire to be a long distance truck driver or an international sex symbol.
3. *Trace the origin of your family or your family name.* You yourself may find it interesting to discover the background you came from. If there is no information available, or if the information is embarrassing, you might stick to the name itself. Did the Cruikshanks all have bent or bowed legs (crooked shank)? Did the Churchills live on a hill near the church? Can a Schmidt be a baker and a Baker a smith?
4. *Explain the basic principles of a machine or another device that you use frequently but do not understand.* This topic obviously requires theoretical and perhaps practical research.
5. *Tell what you did on your vacation last year.* Forgive us, Charlie Brown and the other "Peanuts" characters. Perhaps a better speech, since this topic is so overused, would be tell us your idea of an *ideal* vacation.
6. *Utilize a newspaper as was suggested earlier in the chapter.* Make a list of several possible speech topics before you choose the one you will present.
7. *Close your eyes, turn your head, and the first thing you see when you open your eyes will be the subject of your speech.*
8. *Tell why you think this book is the finest you have ever read and why you are giving copies to all your friends for Christmas and birthdays.* (Just wanted to see whether you were paying attention.)

If you sense that some of these topics seem a bit trivial or simple for a polished speaker, you are probably a perceptive, intelligent person. As you become more experienced and secure as a speaker, you and your instructor will want to expand your horizons and deal with more challenging material. A steady diet of personalized, simplistic speeches would become as useless for educational purposes as a semester of the traditional "What I Did on My Vacation" essays. You will need to delve deeper into the types of speeches and decide what is appropriate for each occasion or assignment.

CHAPTER 6

audience analysis

1. What is an audience?

2. What do I look for in an audience?

3. How can I use what I know about the audience?

4. What can I expect from the audience I will face in the classroom?

A big, black giant
Who looks and listens
With thousands of eyes and ears,
A big black mass
Of love and pity
And troubles and hopes and fears . . .

He claps his hands and luck is with you,
He frowns and it disappears.
He'll chill your heart
And warm your heart
For all of your living years.

In the song "The Big, Black Giant" from *Me and Juliet*, Richard Rodgers and Oscar Hammerstein II describe a theatrical audience. Of course the "giant" you face, your classroom audience, will be well lighted and have only forty or fifty eyes and ears, but the chances are you will find it frightening and able to chill or warm your heart just as the "big black giant" does the theatrical performer's heart.

Many students assume that the audience they face in their speech class is the first audience that they have ever dealt with. Not so! You have faced many audiences before, regardless of your inexperience in a formal setting. Strange as it may seem, your classroom audience is probably one of the most supportive you will ever face.

What Is an Audience?

A simple definition of an audience is "any number of people whom another person or persons communicate with or entertain." The speaker, singer, actor, athlete, and musician are obvious examples of persons appearing before audiences. If *communication* is the essence of a performer-audience relationship, have you not been "playing" to a variety of audiences all your life?

Chances are you learned at a tender age that one of your parents could be manipulated more easily in certain circumstances than could the other. When certain needs or desires arose, you probably approached the parent who was the softer touch. You also learned early to sense and react to the moods of both. (If both parents failed to come through, perhaps your grandparents were even a softer touch.)

You probably also discovered that certain kinds of arguments and strategies proved more successful than others: "But, Ma, everybody has one!" "I know it will help my grades!" "I'll never make the team with my old one." "Pat's parents said it's all right with them if it's all right with you."

As your universe expanded, you also found certain strategies more successful with brothers and sisters, peers, teachers, coworkers, and professors. Some people can be persuaded with flattery, some with anger, some with straight talk, some with bribery, some with who-knows-what. You undoubtedly found the methods that worked best for you with each individual.

Trying to decide which strategy will accomplish the most in a particular situation, with a particular audience, is called "audience analysis." Whether you are trying to get the keys to the family car for an evening or selling aspirin tablets to 40 million television viewers, you employ audience analysis.

ANALYSIS FOR SPECIALIZED COMMUNICATION

The ancient Greek philosopher and rhetorician Aristotle listed audience analysis as the first step in making a speech. It may seem obvious that audience analysis would be vital for platform speaking or a mass media event, but what about specialized communication situations, where the audience seeks you out and you control the event?

When I taught elementary folk guitar in continuing education courses, I found students with quite varied backgrounds and reasons for studying the instrument. One student had a masters degree from a noted music school and had played lead viola in a major symphony orchestra. Another had a doctorate in folklore and knew virtually all there was to know about the history and forms of American folk music; he wanted to use the guitar as an adjunct to his field. Another student was a singer who wanted a portable instrument for accompaniment. Many others had no musical background at all. Would not each individual need different emphasis in learning the guitar? Teaching the violist the technicalities of music would be a waste of time; he wanted basic chord positions, how to hold the guitar, and the like. The folklorist did not care about the study of music, although some was necessary. The singer wanted popular music and elementary guitar skills. The others? I had to decide what to emphasize and how much detail to give each student. I had to perform *audience analysis.*

Suppose you are a computer programmer at a large university, and a mathematics professor, a historian, and an experimental psychologist ask you to do some work for them. Might you not deal with each differently? The historian may know nothing of the workings of the computer. He wants the project completed and does not care how. The experimental psychologist, on the other hand, may have done many computerized studies and knows the language of computers. She may want to know which program you will be using and what advantages it has over another program. The math professor may know more about the theory and mechanics of the computer than you do, so you will want to be guarded with your "advice." These three communication events may seem similar, but they imply audience analysis and sensitivity.

Would a pharmacist say the same thing to four customers getting the same prescription if those customers were a chemist, a biologist, a retired librarian, and an immigrant laborer? If the drug were dangerous, you might say to the chemist, "Be careful; it contains amylbarbitol." The chemist will understand the problem. You might warn the biologist by saying, "If you take too much, it will cause narcotism." To the retired librarian you might explain that "It contains barbiturates that cause excessive drowsiness if you take too much." You might simply tell the laborer, "Be sure to take it after meals, with a glass of milk, and no more than three times a day. You will get sicker than you already are if you take too much."

ANALYSIS FOR PUBLIC COMMUNICATION

For the public speaker the audience poses different problems, some easy to deal with, some more difficult. "Experts" in specialized situations must analyze the audience instantly. They usually do not know who their clients will be and must react at the moment of the communication event. The public speaker, however, can prepare for the audience, analyze it in advance, and decide which strategies will be most effective for the purpose. The specialized communicator deals with specific audiences, whereas the public speaker must deal with large, varied audiences. The public speaker, therefore, must analyze an audience in terms of trends and attempt to arrive at a composite picture of the "big, black (or well-lighted) giant" with all those eyes and ears.

What to Look for in an Audience

SITUATION

The speaker always should analyze why the audience is there and what it expects. The audience's expectations and desires can alter how you approach the subject. An audience that expects a light, informative speech may become incensed at a persuasive speech about a serious topic, even if they agree with the speaker's position. Conversely, an audience expecting a serious discussion of a serious topic may be bored, at best, with a light, entertaining presentation. In your classroom, however, the audience will be open to virtually any topic, and the informative or persuasive nature of the speech may be predetermined by the assignment. Sometimes you may want your classroom audience to role-play a more specific audience: "For the purposes of this speech you will be a group of senior electronic engineers, and I will be asking you to accept my new design." Lay people can role-play only so far; after a few minutes of highly technical jargon, a typical college classroom audience may become bored simply because they cannot understand. On the other hand, they could easily role-play being prospective parents for an informative presentation about a modern method of family-centered childbirth. That role of prospective parent is one that some already may have faced and many will face in the foreseeable future.

The mood of an audience also may affect the presentation. For example, it is eleven o'clock on a beautiful Friday in autumn, and the buses leave for the big game at noon. You are going to give a persuasive speech on a topic about which the class has shown little interest. You will need a great deal more preparation, humor, interesting anecdotes, and other devices to gain interest than you would were you speaking on the energy problem on a cold, snowy morning. Even when the audience remains essentially the same, as in the classroom, such a drastically different situation requires analysis and more stringent preparation.

SIZE

Perhaps the easiest factor for the speaker to discover in advance is the audience's size. The auditorium, arena, or room where you speak limits the size of a live audience. The size of the class has been established, and only such factors as flu epidemics or spring fever affect it.

The traditional public-speaking professions—education, law, religion, and politics—generally have predetermined audience sizes also. Some clergy speak to congregations of twenty or thirty people, while others have thousands, but each knows approximately how large the congregation will be at any given time. The classroom teacher's maximum audience usually is determined by a board of education. The politician knows ahead of time whether a speech will be given in someone's family room, a high-school auditorium that seats over 500, or an outdoor arena that holds 3000. The attorney knows that the judge and twelve jurors form the only audience that really counts.

If you speak to your board of education, town or city council, or PTA, you will have some idea of size ahead of time. If you are a paramedic and a local service club calls on you to explain the profession's value to a community, you can ask about how many members will attend. Numbers may vary slightly, but a club with 50 members will not suddenly sprout an audience of 8000.

You can deal with an audience of ten or fewer intimately, perhaps even touching their hands. With larger audiences such intimacy becomes less possible. Imagine yourself as a commencement speaker standing on a platform on a football field, addressing 500 graduates and their 1500 friends and relatives. "Smith, Jan; Smith, Jane; Smith, Jean; and Smith, Joan" all become the same. The politician addressing a mass audience must deal with broad issues and control the flow of the communication. Speaking to twenty people in a concerned citizen's family room, however, the candidate can field direct, complicated questions with answers such as "Good question, Charlie. Nobody every asked that before. Let me give you some background and tell you what my views are on that subject." Suffice it to say that the larger the audience, the less such intimacy is possible.

ELECTRONIC MEDIA

Speaking on the electronic media casts a great burden on the communicator. Television audiences suddenly spring into the thousands, hundreds of thousands, even millions. Most of us cannot conceive of a million anything, certainly not a million people. The speaker's responsibility to the audience is multiplied gigantically when the media are involved. The speaker may see only a handful of people in the studio, each of whom is busy doing something other than paying attention to the speaker. A discussion of the problems and confusion that such an audience creates does not fall within the scope of this book, but if your school has videotape equipment, your instructor may wish to give you some exposure to speaking into a "one-eyed, electronic midget" with a potential for millions of eyes and ears.

Many of the other audience analysis factors that a communicator must take into account fall into what is often called "demographics."

DEMOGRAPHICS

Ever wonder on the evening of an important election how the national television and radio networks predict the results with amazing accuracy almost as soon as the polls are closed? They have closely examined the age, sex, ethnic background, and the educational and socioeconomic level of the voting constituency, programming these facts, called "demographics," into highly sophisticated computers. They select a sample audience that fits the demographic profile, see how that group voted, and then predict from that sampling. They must know many demographic facts about the constituency to make accurate predictions. The public speaker is not faced with such an exacting task; still you should attempt to learn about the people who are listening to you.

Age. One important facet of audience analysis is the general age level. Many audiences will be mixed with a wide age range, but many will have a general tendency that can affect the speech. Suppose you are a citizen in a community that has a vital issue pending for the school curriculum. You address a meeting of concerned parents. If the issue deals with kindergarten children, the parents, as a group, will be considerably younger than if it were a high-school or community college issue. Young and middle-aged adults have different needs and see the world somewhat differently. The clever communicator plans strategies utilizing these differences.

A police officer discussing traffic safety with school children will have to approach the subject with the children's age in mind. The ten-year-old's "world" exists within a few blocks of home, a walk, or maybe a bicycle ride. The high-school student thinks in terms of automobiles or motorcycles and has a much broader scope of traffic problems. Undoubtedly the vocabulary would be somewhat different for the two age groups also.

Suppose you are a building contractor who wishes to construct a senior citizens' retirement village. Would not the senior citizens' interests be different from those of middle-aged taxpayers who support the project? The senior citizens might be more concerned with safety, comfort, and accessibility of churches, hospitals, and stores, whereas the younger taxpayers may also be concerned with added financial burden and the way the project would fit into the general pattern of life in the community.

These differences in no way suggest telling the truth to one group and lies to another, or lies to both. What they should suggest is awareness of peoples' differing needs and motivations.

Sex. Although we are currently questioning and changing many of our stereotyped sex roles, the sex of an audience can still determine some of the ways in which a speaker will approach it. Most audiences today will be mixed sexually, but areas still remain where the sexes are separated, such as social organizations and athletic groups.

Many people still feel that certain language is acceptable for male but not for mixed or female audiences. Attitudes are changing, however, and taboos against words and topics previously thought to be "too much for women's delicate sensibilities" are disappearing. The fact remains that women often have different interests by virtue of being the ones *usually* raising children. In most homes, the wife remains the homemaker even though she and her husband work. Moreover, women who work outside the home often experience different problems than men in the same situation. However, sex differences in audiences have much less effect on a speaker now than they had traditionally.

Ethnic Factors.   The ethnic background of an audience can include race, religion, and national origin. How important the audience's ethnic composition is will vary with the topic. In the past few years we have become very conscious of ethnic factors in the United States. As we have become more sophisticated and less narrow in our thinking, we have eliminated ethnic jokes and slurs from our public discourse, if not from private. Speakers who like to begin with an amusing story are usually in trouble these days if they begin with an ethnic story. Most audiences today are sensitive enough to realize that a speaker who begins with a "Polish joke" to a black audience will probably begin with a "black joke" to a Polish-American audience. Although many people indulge in ethnic humor privately, most become uncomfortable with it in a public setting.

Areas of interest that have more appeal to one ethnic group than another still exist. A historian speaking about the colonization of the Americas would discuss different issues with the Sons of Italy than with a group of Iroquois Indians. A talk on the Middle East would draw a Jewish youth group or students of Arab descent more easily than a talk on recent trends in Nigeria.

If your topic is such that ethnic factors need to be considered, then by all means do so. In most circumstances, however, you should treat audiences as similarly as the other factors of analysis permit.

REGIONAL AND SPECIALIZED INTERESTS

Television has eliminated many regional differences in the United States, but not all. Kansas wheat farmers probably will not get excited about a discussion of wages in the automobile industry, whereas a discussion of farm subsidies may bore steelworkers in Indiana.

Often ethnic and regional factors get confused. Busing children to achieve racial integration in schools and the continuing controversy about abortion are two problems that cause passions to run high. Busing obviously has racial roots, but it is primarily a concern of large urban areas. Abortion, which has close religious ties, becomes more of an issue in regions with large religious groups that have taken strong stands on the subject.

BELIEFS AND VALUES

An audience's beliefs and values also can affect the strategies the speaker will use. Beliefs and values may be tied closely to ethnic factors or age. The speaker advocating capital punishment must speak softly and use carefully prepared rational arguments with an audience whose public stance is against capital punishment. The speaker can use more emotion and project more personality to an audience that is sympathetic to his or her views. If a community has taken a stance against pornographic movies, and you advocate that an area of the city be set aside for this kind of entertainment, you will need to keep your remarks as rational and unemotional as possible to avoid making the audience hostile and unreceptive. Let them know that many of your concerns are the same as theirs, and that you see these movies as a way of achieving common goals. Remember "identification"? When you face an audience whose attitudes are different from yours, you need to stress commonality and help the audience identify with you.

Have the courage to express your convictions. A careful analysis can help you get the audience more receptive.

What to Do with Your Analysis

You can use your analysis of the audience in many ways to plan an effective speech.

TACT
You always must be sensitive to the receivers' strong feelings and interests. Most audiences will tolerate different opinions if they are presented rationally and with respect for the other side's feelings. To antagonize and alienate an audience seems foolish. Careful audience analysis can help you plan a speech that says what needs to be said as firmly but inoffensively as possible.

VOCABULARY
Audience analysis, especially of age, should affect your vocabulary. You do not use the same language to a group of third graders as to a group of mature adults. Educational level also plays a part in language, as *may* ethnic and regional factors.

HUMOR
Humor can be a fine tool for the speaker who can use it well, but it must be tempered by demographics. A story that sends one group into peals of laughter (or at least a few chuckles) may be completely lost with another group. The clever speaker alters anecdotes to fit the situation. I have heard speakers use a story about a man out of work who wrestles a lion so hard that the lion eventually whispers, "Not so hard, do you think you're the only _____ out of work?" The blank has been filled in by "high-school teacher," "speech teacher," "minister," and "steel-worker," depending on the predominant occupation in the audience.

PROOFS
Kinds of proofs and emphasis upon them also should vary with audiences. Accountants and business people may handle statistical information more easily than people in the humanities, who may be more interested in *who* said *what* about the issue. That is not to say that social workers or clergy should not be given statistical information, but the information should be in smaller doses and the methods explained more thoroughly.

TIME
Audience composition also can determine the length of time that you speak. Do not expect a group of third graders to sit quietly through ninety minutes of slides

showing churches and cathedrals in France. Architects, artists, and Francophiles might last through it, but not little kids. A visit to Disneyworld or Disneyland, however, may keep the children enraptured for that length of time.

CHOICE OF TOPIC
Probably the most important effect of audience analysis, however, will be the choice of topic and the way you handle it. In theory *any* topic can be made interesting for *any* audience by a highly skilled and well-prepared speaker, but that implies, among other factors, thorough audience analysis.

The Classroom Audience

One advantage of giving speeches to the same audience over and over is that you do not need to reassess it constantly. The audience in your class remains essentially the same through the term. A good class project may be to do a thorough demographic analysis of the class. Age, sexual balance, ethnic backgrounds, reasons for being in school, and vocational interests could be some of the factors to consider. (The classroom audience remaining the same also has advantages for your nerves, but, on the other hand, it would be better if you had the opportunity to speak in front of different audiences. Unfortunately, the logistics and finances of education prevent that.)

There is another great advantage to appearing before the classroom audience repeatedly. Each person in that audience, except the instructor, faces similar problems. A classroom audience is usually the most sympathetic, sensitive, kindly, and friendly audience you will contact because, individually and as a group, they want you to succeed. They know that they are in the same boat as you. They will be courteous to you, because they want you to be courteous to them (and for other reasons, let us hope). Seldom are any audiences antagonistic to a speaker unless the speaker's reputation predisposes them to be so, but the classroom audience is even less aggressive because, unlike the speaker in a normal situation, each member of the audience must sooner or later face the "multi-eyed giant."

SUMMARY AND CONCLUSION

Which audience analysis factors are most vital? There is no one answer to that question. Any factor may be vital in one speech and irrelevant in another. Always make a mental checklist to see which factors might affect your presentation:

situation
size
age
sex
ethnic factors
regional and specialized interests
beliefs and values

Eliminate the unimportant factors, but consider them all. That is the first step in speaking; now you are ready to prepare the speech itself.

EXERCISES

Think about the way you might treat the following situations. In each case you will be dealing with the same general topic. What changes would the composition of the three audiences require?

1. You are a member of the narcotics squad of the local police department and do public information work. You describe your job to
   a. a group of eighth graders
   b. a group of college freshmen
   c. a group of pharmacists or physicians

2. You are a representative of the Department of Agriculture whose assignment is to inform people why food prices are so high. You explain to
   a. a group of 100 farmers
   b. a group of 100 urban consumers
   c. a group of 100 food store operators

3. The school board in your community decided that each child should be forced to say prayers at the beginning of the public school day. You are a parent of three children and feel strongly about the issue. You will address
   a. the fifty teachers in the district
   b. the school board
   c. a meeting of 500 concerned parents
   d. a meeting of seventy-five to one hundred parents at a church or synagogue whose leaders sponsored the law
   e. a similar meeting at a church or synagogue whose leaders oppose the law

4. You hold a minor office in your labor union, and you feel strongly that women should have equal work and pay with men. They do not currently have those rights. You will speak to
   a. a meeting of rank-and-file, predominately male union members
   b. a chapter of a group that advocates women's rights
   c. a meeting with other union leaders, no more than eight

5. Reverse the situation in exercise 4. Assume that you are *opposed* to equal work and pay for women. Speak with the same groups.

6. You work with the mayor's office in human relations. Discuss the role of minorities in the United States with
   a. a group of fifty blacks, age eighteen to thirty
   b. a group of fifty blacks, age fifty and older
   c. a local service club that is primarily white, Anglo-Saxon, and Protestant
   d. a meeting of the religious leaders of the community

7. You are an automobile salesman. You have many different models. You must sell to
   a. a married couple about thirty with three children
   b. a college student who is serious about continuing on to grad school
   c. a twenty-year-old single male supporting himself
   d. a twenty-five-year-old female supporting herself
   e. a realtor who uses the car to drive potential customers

CHAPTER 7

organizing your thoughts

1. *Why should I organize and outline my speech?*
2. *Do I need organization outside the classroom?*
3. *How do I go about organizing my ideas?*
4. *What do I do with the outline once it is finished?*

Chaos Cake

Sift 2 cups cake flour, 1¼ cups sugar, 2½ tsp. baking powder, and 1 tsp. salt into bowl.
Add ⅛ cup shortening, 1 tsp. vanilla, and ⅔ cup milk.
Beat 2 min. at medium speed; pour into pans.
Frost with your favorite icing.
Bake 25–30 minutes at 350°
Add ⅛ cup milk.
Beat 2 more minutes.
Add 1 large egg.

You do not have to be an expert baker to realize that adding milk and an egg and beating an already baked cake will result in something less than a gourmet's delight. The only problem with the recipe above is that the order of actions is scrambled; it is a dietary version of a three-car accident. The obvious solution to make it a good recipe is to add the milk and egg *before* the second beating, bake the cake, then frost it. In other words, get the recipe into a time sequence.

Why Make an Outline?

Although a speech is hardly a recipe for a cake, organizing and outlining are equally vital to the finished product. They serve several purposes for the speaker, each important in varying degrees in any one speech.

65

Virtually every speech teacher has heard this comment after a student finishes speaking: "Oh, I forgot to mention that . . . !" If a speech is well organized, all the elements that the speaker wishes to cover are included in the proper order. Leaving out an important point in a speech can be disconcerting and can ruin your efforts. The audience is cheated, and the speaker is disappointed. Of course, *you* do not need to write anything down. After all, you can remember it all when you are nervous and on your feet under pressure. Sure you can!

In addition to making sure that you include all the necessary ideas and facts, the outline helps you arrange them to achieve the maximum effect. In the cake recipe, all the elements were included, but the result was less than successful. Unless you are a rare exception, you will see the relationships of ideas much better on paper.

Finally, you can use your outline to organize note cards for the presentation, or as a memory aid, with key words or phrases keeping you on the track.

Outlining can be vitally important to the speaker as well as the writer, but it should not be an end in itself. To practice outlining as "proper" form offers little other than experience in form. On the other hand, outlining to organize your thoughts may be the single most important facet of speech preparation, other than thinking itself.

The audience also profits greatly from clear organization. When we listen to a speaker, we cannot see the words or the connection between ideas. We must rely on the speaker to carry us from one thought to another easily, with as little noise as possible.

Organization in Everyday Life

Whether we realize it or not, we organize our daily lives to make them easier. For instance, you probably wake up at about the same hour every day, or at least every weekday, and eat your meals on a regular basis. If you drive to school or work, chances are you take the same route with a slight variation or two, but covering about the same distance and time. Obviously your class schedule is organized, and even recreation time is planned. Some organizational sequences become so firmly entrenched that they become unconscious routine or habits. Which shoe do you put on first, left or right? Chances are you normally do the same one first.

Some daily events happen more spontaneously and require instant organization in order to fit in the time allotted. Let us take a simple example. Suppose you have to run errands to the following places:

1. the supermarket
2. the library
3. the bank
4. the gas station
5. the post office

Here is a map of the area you must cover in order to run your five errands and return home.

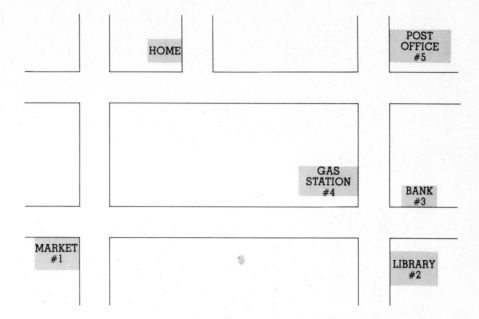

Should you decide to go in random order, there are fifteen possible combinations: any one of *five* for the first place + *four* for the second + *three* for the third + *two* for the fourth + *one* for the fifth = fifteen. A simpler way might be to go in a circle, starting with, for instance, the library if that is the closest to your home. You might, however, rearrange your order if it is an extremely hot day and you need perishables from the market, or if you need gas immediately, or if you need to get money from the bank first. In any event, you will probably decide on an order that represents the easiest and fastest way that allows for the variables of the situation.

The situation just described is much simpler and less intellectually challenging than the organizational problems you face in outlining a speech. The plan for errands includes five main topics and no subtopics. The key to outlining rests in identifying main topics, breaking them down into subtopics, and reducing them to still smaller units.

Methods of Organizing Speeches

Three basic types of organizational patterns apply to speaking situations: patterns based on time, on space, and on topic.

TIME
Most tasks or skills that a speaker demonstrates follow a time pattern. The cake recipe must follow the temporal (a fancy word for time) sequence, or you end up

with a glob of something unappetizing. The same is true for reporting a scientific experiment, telling how to achieve a certain task, or describing the workings of a machine. A time sequence is the easiest of the patterns to recognize and organize.

SPACE

Spatial relationships also provide a built-in organizational pattern. The design of a house is an organizational outline. Would you want a house with the kitchen on the west side of the first floor and the dining room on the east side of the second? The bathroom as the first room you enter from outside the house? The garage in the middle of the basement with no driveway leading to it? The top of a desk also may be spatially organized. I sit with my typewriter in the middle of the desk, the telephone on the left, a radio on the far left, pencils on the right away from the typewriter, and notes farther right. They are arranged this way because I am right-handed, and the radio, which is the farthest away, is least important to what I am doing. The telephone is within easy reach, but at the left side. The pencils and notes, which I constantly use, are on the right side for easy access and marking. The home is organized spatially for privacy and convenience; the desk for convenience.

There is often a close relationship between space and time. You must base travel directions on a sequence in space, but the directions also follow the same sequence in time.

TOPIC

A more difficult type of outline is the topical outline, because you do not have the built-in relationships of time and space. Although the relationships are not so obvious, you can outline your school curriculum by topic, dividing it as follows:

   I. General education requirements
      A. Mathematics
      B. Science
      C. English
  II. Major
      A. Requirements
      B. Electives
 III. Minor
      A. Requirements
      B. Electives

Under each topic you can list subtopics, such as courses that satisfy the mathematics or science requirement.

Topical outlines are usually not as easy to recognize or organize as the curriculum example. The speaker must arrange the topics so that (1) the order makes sense; (2) the most important points get proper emphasis; and (3) the audience can comprehend them. Topical outlines can be constructed along several lines, depending on the purpose and style of the communication.

Cause and Effect.   A *cause and effect* relationship calls for a causal outline. The cause usually is listed first, followed by the effect. If you were to give an informative speech delineating the growth of California in the mid-1800s, you might use the following main topics:

A. The discovery of gold at Sutter's Mill. (Cause)
   (A series of subtopics would follow, such as dates and people.)
B. The impact of the "Gold Rush." (Effect)
   (Subtopics might include population growth, wealth, forming of cities, statehood, communication, and transportation.)

Problem Solution.   You might arrange a persuasive speech with a *problem solution* outline.

A. Puerto Rico faces hardships not known in other areas of the United States. (Problem) (series of subtopics that establish the contention)
B. Granting Puerto Rico statehood would alleviate these problems. (Solution) (series of subtopics demonstrating how the solution would help)

Monroe Motivated Sequence.   For most persuasive speeches the Monroe Motivated Sequence supplies a standard outline, at least as far as the main topics go.

A. Get the attention of the audience.
B. Establish a definite need.
C. Satisfy that need.
D. Give the audience an opportunity to visualize the action.
E. Suggest action for the audience to take.

(See Chapter 11 for a further discussion of persuasion.)

Beyond the Outline—Two Musts

INTRODUCTION — BODY — CONCLUSION
The plans for organizing and outlining are suggestions; there are many more ways of planning the *body* of the speech. Every speech, however, also should have an *introduction* that precedes the body and a *conclusion* that follows. In essence, every speech follows the same pattern:

I. Introduction
II. Body
III. Conclusion

Main topics will fall under each of the major headings, with the most important forming the body.

There is an oversimplified axiom that some speech teachers use to describe the basic pattern: "Tell 'em what you're going to say. Say it. Tell 'em what you said." Let us hope your speeches will not be so obvious in their structure. Basically you will tell the audience what your topic is and get them interested in it; then go into depth with your discussion of the topic; and finally reexamine your ideas in order to plant them firmly in the minds of the audience.

TOPIC SENTENCE

Another device you always should employ is a *topic sentence*—one sentence that describes your basic purpose. Usually the topic sentence will occur at the end of the introduction or at the beginning of the body. If you use the topic sentence too soon, the introduction may not arouse audience interest sufficiently. Too late, and your audience is confused and may not follow your train of thought. Near the beginning of the body of the speech you should say something to the effect of

"The discovery of rich mineral deposits can affect the destiny of a state or country."
"Puerto Rico should be granted statehood immediately."
"Americans eat far too many fried foods, and they are suffering for it."

Although there will be some differences, your topic sentence may be based on your statement of objectives (discussed in Chapter 4). If your statement of objectives says, "When my presentation is finished, I want the audience to *understand the principles of Braille*," for instance, your topic sentence might be (after an introduction), "I would like to share with you some of the history and principles of this remarkable system for the visually handicapped."

The topic sentence serves the same purpose in speech as in writing. For the sender it helps keep the speech on track; it serves as a guidepost to insure that everything within the speech is related to a central idea, much like the statement of objectives.

Outlining: Examples

INFORMATIVE SPEECH

Let us assume that you have an assignment to present an informative speech with the following conditions:

1. four to seven minutes long
2. deals with some form of communication
3. must have visual aids or demonstration
4. must be accompanied by an outline

Let us now further assume that you choose to demonstrate the communication, primarily nonverbal, that takes place on a baseball diamond during a game. Because some of the communication is extremely subtle and not even noticed by the average fan, you want to limit your speech to two or three, possibly four at the most, main headings. Early in the speech you will need to get the audience members' attention and convince them that the topic will have some meaning for them, but for now the selection of the main topics is the first task facing you. After serious consideration (the time you spend will depend in part on your familiarity with the game), you decide to include these three types of communication:

A. coach to batter and runners
B. catcher to pitcher
C. umpire to players and fans

Having selected these three main topics, you go on to subdivide the topics and include the necessary information. You may decide that under each topic you should follow the same pattern, such as

1. information conveyed
2. signal or gesture
3. order

Or you may decide to use a different subpattern for each topic. You settle on a third alternative: for each topic you will give some common and some unique information. If you assume your audience knows little about these signals—a fair assumption in most classes—you will begin each topic with a discussion of its purpose. Once the audience knows the purpose, the details should be easier to comprehend. Therefore your first topic, "Coach to batter and runners," might be subdivided this way:

1. purposes
2. information conveyed
3. basic signals
4. order of signals
5. demonstration, examples

The purposes of the "Coach to batter and runners" signals can be divided into three categories:

a. to inform the batter whether to bunt (may need definition), swing at the ball, or keep from swinging ("take the pitch")
b. to inform the base runner or runners whether they should stay close to their bases, be prepared for a bunt, steal a base, or wait to see what the batter does
c. to convey this information to the batter and runners without permitting the opposition to understand and without delaying the game while the coach runs around telling everyone before every pitch

"Information conveyed" can be divided into the following:

a. bunt
b. steal
c. take the pitch
d. the sign is "off"
e. more sophisticated strategy, such as hit-and-run or run-and-hit

Each topic will be divided and subdivided in similar ways. As you go on you will demonstrate the appropriate signals.

After you have "fleshed out" all three topics and put down the necessary information in the most informative, easy to follow order, most of the outlining is finished. Of course you want an interest-building introduction, which becomes the first part of the outline. After you finish your lecture and demonstration, you want to summarize and draw your conclusions, completing the outline. Your outline in its final form should resemble the outline below. Topics may be in different orders, some details may be added or left out, but basically the *form* of the outline should be similar to what follows.

A Lecture and Demonstration of Signals Used in the Game of Baseball

Statement of Objectives: When I am finished with my speech, the audience should understand some of the nonverbal communication in a baseball game.

I. Introduction (See Chapter 8.)
   A. Attention getter
   B. Motivation for listening and watching
   C. Topic sentence: "The gyrations and movements that may seem absurd to the casual observer actually make sense and are vital means of communication between coaches, players, and umpires."
II. Body:—Communication on the Field (See Chapter 10.)
   A. Coach to batter and runners
      1. purposes
         a. to inform the batter whether to bunt, swing at the ball, or take the pitch
         b. to inform the base runner or runners whether they should stay close to their bases, be prepared for a bunt, steal a base, or wait to see what the batter does
         c. to convey this information to the batter and runners without permitting the opposition to understand and without delaying the game while the coach runs around telling everyone before every pitch
      2. information conveyed
         a. bunt
         b. steal
         c. take the pitch
         d. the sign is "off"
         e. more sophisticated strategy, such as hit-and-run or run-and-hit
      3. basic signals
         a. bill of cap
         b. hand to letters
         c. sleeve
         d. belt
         e. other more sophisticated signs
      4. order of signals
         a. varied
         b. changes
      5. demonstration *(order and form in the hands of the speaker)*

B. Catcher to pitcher
   1. purposes
      a. to allow both to know where and how fast the ball should be thrown
      b. to give the signal so the other team cannot steal it and inform the batter
   2. information conveyed
      a. fast ball
      b. curve ball
      c. change of pace
      d. other more sophisticated pitches
      e. placement of the pitch: high or low, inside or outside
   3. basic signals
      a. one finger
      b. two fingers
      c. fist
      d. second signal given
      e. points to direction of pitch
      f. catcher hides the signal from opposition
      g. pitcher accepts or "shakes off"
   4. demonstration
C. Umpire to players and fans
   1. purposes
      a. to inform the players and coaches of the progress of the game
      b. to keep the fans informed
      c. to keep order on the field and reduce the number of arguments
   2. information conveyed and basic signals *(consult rule book)*
      a. safe = palms down
      b. out = fist, usually with thumb extended in a gesture moving toward the back of the ear
      c. strike = strong gesture with right hand
      d. ball = gesture, usually not as emphatic, with the left hand
      e. others
   3. demonstration and examples
III. Summary and conclusion (See Chapter 9.)

PERSUASIVE SPEECH

Without going into as much detail with the subtopics, let us outline a persuasive speech using the Monroe Motivated Sequence as a model. The speech will advocate the mandatory use of air bags for automobile safety.

Statement of Objectives: When I am finished with my presentation, I want the audience to support the movement to require air bags in every automobile.

I. Introduction (attention getter)
  A. Show large photos of auto accidents
  B. Describe accident(s) in which victim was thrown through windshield
II. Body
  A. Establish need
    1. statistical information about accidents
      a. number yearly
      b. deaths
      c. serious injuries

         2. loss represents
            a. dollars
            b. human terms
         3. problems with seat belts
            a. belt-caused injuries
            b. why people do not use them
            c. easy to bypass
    B. Air bags (satisfy need)
        1. how they work
        2. testimony from experimental users
        3. statistical information from automakers and insurance companies
        4. show short film (visualize the solution)—available insurance companies and automakers
or

        4. vivid description from someone who was "saved" by an air bag
        5. Action
            a. write to legislators (perhaps have forms available)
            b. distribute literature
            c. ask audience to consider air bags with next car purchase
III. Summary and conclusion
    A. Summary
        1. review accident rates
        2. review loss information
        3. review air bags' advantages
        4. review what audience can do
    B. Conclusion—strong ending statement to establish the subject firmly in the minds of the audience

HOW DETAILED SHOULD AN OUTLINE BE?

There is no rule for how detailed an outline should be. Just as the length of a dog's tail depends on the size of the dog, outline length depends on the speech itself. The degree of familiarity that you have with the subject will affect the amount of detail, as will the degree of complexity of the speech. The important point is that the outline is a tool that should help the speaker organize ideas and aid the flow of those ideas. It should also help the audience understand the ideas and be able to make a smooth transition from one idea to another. The outline should be detailed enough to be useful, without bogging you down with unnecessary detail.

After the Outline

Once you have completed your outline, your task is only partially finished. Depending upon how well you know your subject and how confident you are in front of an audience, you may want to use the outline as the "skeleton" for "fleshing out" your speech word for word. Probably only someone who has played baseball or who has been very close to the game would choose a subject such as the one above. That person conceivably could speak from an outline. You may develop note cards using the outline, or even write a manuscript.

    Should you use a one-word outline? A short phrase outline? A sentence outline? There is no simple answer. You will get less confused if you stick to one form or another. Your instructor may insist on a particular form. In any event, the overriding philosophy should be to make the outline useful. Just like whistling or hitting a tennis ball, outlining comes easier to some people, but almost anyone can learn to organize in order to be a better speaker and, indeed, a more efficient and productive human being.

SUMMARY AND CONCLUSION

Organization is vital for the preparation and presentation of a speech, just as it is in everyday life. Basically there are three patterns for organization of speeches: temporal, spatial, and most important, topical. For some informative speeches, you can move from cause to effect. For some persuasive speeches, you will want to go from problem to solution or follow the Monroe Motivated sequence.

No matter how you organize, you must have an introduction, a body, and a conclusion. A topic sentence should be part of your organization.

Although there are many ways to outline, every speech must have some organizational pattern. Which one you choose for a specific speech will depend upon the type of speech and the purpose. The outline should help you develop the completed speech. It is a guide, a map to keep the speaker on the track and insure that all necessary ideas and material are covered during the preparation of the speech. Even if you are so thoroughly familiar with your subject that you feel you do not require an outline—an unusual occurrence, if not blind optimism—simply jot down three or four ideas. From these "shopping list" notes you may find yourself deciding to include other aspects of the subject that had not occurred to you. The outline is to the finished speech what the skeleton is to the body: it is necessary to give support and form. Without it, the body becomes formless and vague. So unless you happen to be a jellyfish, *outline!*

EXERCISES

1. For each of the following subjects select two to five topics and list them in a simple A-B-C or 1-2-3 form. Do not try to do research or make a complete outline. Just list general topics. Example: the value of a college education

   higher lifetime earnings
   easier vocational life
   deeper appreciation of life and culture
   respect and admiration of community

   A. the reasoning behind _____ (a law or regulation)
   B. the basics of playing a specific musical instrument or a specific game
   C. why you like a relative or nonschool-age acquaintance
   D. the advantages of _____ (occupation or vocation)
   E. the _____ crisis
   F. communication in _____ (not baseball)
   G. our greatest president
   H. _____ disease

2. Now take any subject in exercise 1 and subdivide each topic you listed into three to five subtopics, giving you an outline like this one:
Subject from 1 A–H

    1. (topic you listed)
      a. (subtopic)
      b.
      c.
    2.
      a.
      b.
      c.
    3.
      a.
      b.
      c.
      d.
      e.

3. List three to ten steps in a time, space, or time-space sequence (not a recipe or travel directions).

4. In the 1930s Samuel and Bella Spewack wrote a satirical play about Hollywood called *Boy Meets Girl.* The basic idea of the play was that all of Hollywood's movies could be outlined as follows:

    a. boy meets girl
    b. boy loses girl
    c. boy gets girl

The Spewacks oversimplified to make their point and get their laughs. But the process is valid, even if the conclusion is not. Take a television show or movie that you have seen recently and try to break down the plot in a similar, simple manner. For example,

    a. man and woman show up at Rick's place
    b. man must get out of country and needs Rick's help
    c. woman and Rick were lovers years ago
    d. Rick will help the man if she will stay behind
    e. never
    f. Sam plays it again
    g. Rick helps her escape
    h. it looks like a happy ending and that the good guys will win World War II

CHAPTER 8

introducing your speech

1. *Why do I need an introduction for my speech?*
2. *How does the introduction affect the audience?*
3. *When does the introduction begin and end?*
4. *What types of introductions could I try?*

O.K., today I am going to talk to you about not smoking.
  (Hmmmm, I wonder why they are not listening!)

The topic for my speech today is "Why We Shouldn't Smoke."
  (Funny, they look more bored than fascinated.)

Smoking is really bad for you. It causes all sorts of problems.
  (That guy not only looks bored, but he just lit a cigarette!)

Now that you have selected the topic for your speech, analyzed your audience, and organized and outlined the material as thoroughly as possible, you are faced with one of the more difficult aspects of public communication: getting started. You must find that first idea, phrase it, and so introduce yourself and your topic to a group of strangers. It requires imagination and hard thinking to design a successful introduction. Some people are wittier or more clever than others; ideas pop into their heads as soon as they choose the topic. The rest of us too often begin with obvious, uninteresting words that accomplish little except getting us started.

The statements at the beginning of the chapter are three uninteresting, common, and generally unsuccessful introductions. Much of the information they convey is obvious and unnecessary. If you are standing in front of speech class on the day your speech is due, the class would have to be extra dull to assume that you are going to tap dance yesterday or invent the wheel tomorrow. The only worthwhile part of any of these introductions is the statement of the topic. But how dull and unimaginative simply to state the topic and then jump into it.

In this chapter we will explore some common types of introductions, see how and when they serve, and apply some to practical situations.

What Is an Introduction?

There is no such thing as *the* way to introduce a speech, any more than there is only one way to begin a novel or story. An introduction can be one word, several paragraphs, or anything in between. The introduction precedes the body of the speech, but ideally it flows into the body so unobtrusively that the audience is not even aware of the change.

How long should an introduction be? As long or as short as it needs to be within time limits. If you are assigned a five-minute speech, it seems absurd to spend four minutes on the introduction. A good introduction may be one sentence or several paragraphs long. If you find it going on too long, change it, but do not fall back on obvious, uninteresting, and weak introductions like those at the beginning of the chapter.

PURPOSES OF AN INTRODUCTION

Getting Attention.   One function of the introduction is simply to get the audience's attention. The need for getting attention varies according to the situation. At a political rally, for instance, the candidate may have several physical attention-getters. Let us assume that Mary Smith is running for mayor of our community. Mary is on a stage in full view while Harry Jones introduces her. She steps into a spotlight, speaks through a sound amplification system, and the lights on the audience go out. Of course, the audience came there specifically to hear her. She obviously does not need to do a great deal of attention-getting. If Mary were stopping people in a shopping center to make her political pitch, however, she would have to do a great deal more to get their attention.

The classroom speaker is called upon to get up before the group, but the audience probably is unaware of the topic. Candidate Mary's topic we know, at least generally, ahead of time, but we do not know whether student Sammy is going to talk about smoking, pet eagles, or baseball signals. We in the audience need to turn our thoughts from our upcoming date, problems at work, or the fifty dollars we need for the car payment, to the person standing before us.

Focusing on the Topic.   Once the speaker gets the audience's attention, it must be focused on the topic. The introduction must lead smoothly into the subject matter. The degree of difficulty varies. A topic that makes us more appealing to the opposite sex, enables us to make money, or grants some other gratification will need less work to introduce than a topic that makes us think about abstract or difficult concepts.

Helping with Identification.   If we accept the premise in Chapter 1 that when the audience identifies with the speaker, more complete communication takes place, then the introduction serves another function. Speakers may establish their concern with issues that concern us, defining a common ground for identification. Speakers can show concern for their audiences, as well as for issues. If someone is concerned about me, chances are I will identify more with that person. Through word choice, physical mannerisms, and nonverbal cues, speakers also let us know something about themselves. Accomplished speakers, of course, let us know only what they want us to know or what they think we should know, but even these clues help the identification process.

Giving Background. Speakers also utilize introductions to establish their credentials and background, so we trust them. Audiences accept information more readily from someone qualified to give that information. Would you accept lifesaving techniques more readily from a person who has had Red Cross training and who has actually saved someone's life, or from one who does not bother to explain the source of his or her expertise?

The introduction also may furnish some necessary historical information. For instance, a history of tobacco might be a way to begin a speech about smoking.

Setting a Mood. Finally, an introduction helps set the mood, especially for a somber or humorous speech. Although much of the tone was established by the solemnity of the occasion, Abraham Lincoln chose this somber phrasing for his Gettysburg Address: "Four score and seven years ago our fathers brought forth on this continent a new nation, conceived in liberty and dedicated to the proposition that all men are created equal." That language sets a more sober, reflective mood than, "Eighty-seven years ago some men established this country, guaranteeing liberty and equality for everybody."

In summary, the introduction serves the following purposes:

1. to get the audience's attention
2. to lead into the subject matter
3. to help the audience identify with the speaker
4. to establish the speaker's credibility
5. to give necessary background
6. to set the mood

Most introductions do not serve all six functions, but they should get attention and lead into the subject. The importance of each function varies with the speech, speaker, and audience.

APPEALING TO THE AUDIENCE

Any introduction you use must appeal to one or more emotions, drives, or attitudes that prevail in the audience. The drive may be as simple as the innate human desire to know about other people and things. An anti-smoking introduction probably will appeal to the drives for self-preservation, cleanliness, and thrift. An introduction to a baseball signals speech might appeal to general curiosity or to the drive to be accepted by other people, especially of the other sex.

You cannot, of course, get all these appeals into one introduction, but it should at least hint that more elaborate appeals will follow. Most people want to be socially acceptable, desirable to the opposite sex, and have certain possessions or status symbols. We want to stay young and healthy, and know more about the world around us. Without hammering the point so strongly as to alienate your audience, you should appeal to one or more of those drives in order to get your audience interested in you and your topic.

Types of Introductions

Basically there are five types of introductions: the anecdote, startling statement, rhetorical question, quotation, and nonverbal introductions. Often these types overlap and may be combined. Using examples of these types, we will give introductions for two separate topics, an informative speech about the dropping of the atomic bomb on Hiroshima, Japan, and a persuasive speech that is anti-smoking.

As you read the sample introductions, note that in most cases, the introduction closes with a topic sentence that serves as a transition to the body of the speech. Whether the topic sentence is actually part of the introduction or of the body, it serves as a focal point for your ideas.

THE ANECDOTE

The anecdote is a short story that illustrates a specific point. It may be serious or humorous, real or fictional, but it always should make a relevant point and appeal to the audience's emotions as well as their intellect.

The story about the time your uncle got arrested may be amusing or heart-rending, but it probably does not have much relevance to a speech about smoking or atomic bombs. If it does relate to the topic, great—but if it does not, save it for after class or for a speech to entertain.

If the story is true, emphasize the facts of the incident. Mention specific dates and places. They will lend credence to your story, even if they are not totally necessary to it.

Atomic Bomb Introduction: For most Americans the Pacific Theatre of operations in World War II was remote and not connected with their daily lives. Far-off, exotic place names that few had ever heard of became household words: Guadalcanal, Wake Island, Tarawa, Iwo Jima, and the Coral Sea. For most of us who were around then, the war ended September 2, 1945, and the places and romantic names have now drifted into the backs of our memories. For the citizens of Hiroshima, Japan, the war has not yet ended. It still remains vivid and painful in their memories. They live with constant reminders of the day the atomic bomb was dropped on them and the course of history changed forever: August 6, 1945.

Suppose that you have taken an anti-smoking stance in a speech because you recently watched a favorite uncle waste away and die from emphysema or lung cancer. Tell us about it. It will help get the audience's attention and involve them with the subject. It will also aid them in identifying with you as someone with a life outside the classroom. It will give them background about your interest in the subject and set a serious mood. If you handle it well, even audience members who are smokers will listen carefully to your presentation.

Anti-smoking Introduction: Last October 27 I sat in room 526 of the General Hospital watching and listening to my Uncle Fred trying to breathe with lungs that had deteriorated to virtually nothing. I could almost feel the pain that accompanied each breath, and I sensed the exhaustion that the simple act of breathing caused, even when aided by oxygen and modern machines. At 8:07 P.M. I heard some especially difficult breathing followed by silence. Moments later doctors and nurses hovered over his lifeless body. My Uncle Fred was fifty-two years old, and up to a year ago he bragged about smoking two to three packs of cigarettes a day.

Obviously, that example sets a serious, somber mood, and only a foolish speaker would follow it with a humorous look at smoking.

THE STARTLING STATEMENT

The startling statement introduction begins with a statement so unusual that it compels the audience to pay attention. I was privileged to hear a thirty-year-old woman begin an informative speech with "I used to be a hooker." After a pause to let the statement sink in, she went on to tell of her job in the steel mill, a job officially classified as "hooker," someone who works with a crane operator. The woman's speech was about the signals used for communication between the hooker and the crane operator.

The great danger with the startling statement is that it may have shock value but little or no bearing on the speech itself. If the statement or action merely startles without any relationship to the topic at hand, it is a "gimmick." Gimmickry is another quick and easy way to get an audience to tune out the important part of your presentation. In another class a young man began by asking for a dollar bill from someone in the audience. A "volunteer" — set up ahead of time — gave him a dollar, which he proceeded to tear in half. The thought immediately flashed in my mind, "Gimmickry!" As the speech unfolded, however, the torn dollar became an integral part of it. He often gave a similar speech to underprivileged boys in community centers and church groups, telling them the value of a complete education. The torn dollar represented the diminished income the boys could expect if they did not get the proper education. It was not a gimmick, but a solid, startling introduction that became part of the speech itself.

Atomic Bomb Introduction: Look out the window, please, everyone. See those hills about a mile away? Look at the apartment buildings over there in the east. At the stadium to the north. There is the elementary school just to the west with the fine, expensive homes behind the playground. Imagine that all that you can see for the radius of a mile were to vanish, disintegrate, and be burned from the face of the earth. That was the real life situation that faced the citizens of Hiroshima, Japan, on the morning of August 6, 1945, when the first atomic bomb was dropped.

Although the statement itself is not so startling, the sheer horror of the truth is startling enough to get the audience's attention and put some perspective on the immensity of an atomic explosion.

Anti-smoking Introduction: Suppose I asked you to cut five minutes off your life. You'd probably think I was crazy. On the other hand, suppose I offered you a cigarette — you might take it. The net result would be the same, according to statistics furnished by the American Cancer Society. Five minutes per cigarette times two packs, or forty cigarettes, a day equals 200 minutes a day times 365 days a year, which equals 73,000 minutes. In other words, if you smoke two packs of cigarettes a day, this year you will eliminate 50.7 days of your life, almost two months.

The figures are from the author's imagination. The conscientious speaker, how-ever, would have up-to-date information. If indeed those were the facts, they would undoubtedly startle at least some of the audience.

THE RHETORICAL QUESTION

The rhetorical question, unlike an ordinary question, requires no formal answer. When speakers begin with rhetorical questions, they are really saying, "Think about this."

Sometimes a speaker asks a question that requires an answer, such as "How many of you smoke?" Such questions are weak openings because they consume time, and the results may be different than the speaker expects. For instance, suppose you begin an anti-smoking speech with, "How many of you smoke?" and no one raises a hand. Does that mean that the smokers are too shy to admit it? That the audience does not care? Or does it mean that no one smokes?

The rhetorical question, however, simply gets the audience thinking. The rhetorical question, like any other introduction, must be related to the topic. To ask "Would you like to earn a million tax-free, legal dollars next year?" would undoubtedly get everyone's attention. To follow that with a speech describing the impact of the "Peanuts" comic strip would be gimmickry and a sure way to alienate an audience.

The rhetorical question may seem easy, but if it is to have impact and get the audience thinking, it must be well thought out and to the point. "Are computers taking over the world?" will get more thought from an audience than "Have you ever seen a computer?" "Have we already reached the time when computers and other machines control the destiny of human beings?" might be even better. See if you can think of a still better question to introduce a speech about the use and misuse of computers.

If you are introducing a speech about the United States presidency, which would be the best rhetorical question?

1. Who is your favorite president?
2. Do you have to be rich to become President of the United States?
3. Why would anyone want the most difficult, responsible, and criticized job in the world?

Try to come up with a question or two that you might use for such a topic. Remember, it must relate to the topic and attempt to get the audience thinking. Let us look at some questions for our two topics.

Atomic Bomb Introduction: Can the world ever be the same as it was before August 6, 1945? Can the human race inhabit this planet much longer now that we have the wherewithal to obliterate ourselves and virtually all life as we know it? Did the drop-ping of the bomb on Hiroshima, Japan, signal the beginning of the end of the human race, or did it signal the end of the beginning of our struggle to control, utilize, and live with nature?

The thrust that your speech takes will determine just what your rhetorical questions will be and how you want to channel your audience's thinking.

Anti-smoking Introduction: How much would you be willing to pay for the privilege of committing suicide over a forty-year period? Would you be willing to pay $14,600 for the privilege of ruining your heart and lungs, dirtying your clothes and the air around you, and shortening your life by years? *(pause)* If you smoke two packs of cigarettes a day at even fifty cents a pack, that's what you will spend during the next forty years — if you live that long.

The more serious the topic, the more the rhetorical question will have the punch to gain the audience's attention. Anytime you use the rhetorical question, however, you should pause after the question, and let the audience take a second or two to think about it. Let them set their minds so that they will be receptive to the information that follows the question.

THE QUOTATION
Another effective introduction for some speeches is the use of quoted material. Your own literary background places limitations on your ability to use quoted material, but there are good reference works that specialize in quotations. For instance, *The Oxford Dictionary of Quotations*, second edition, published in 1955, lists two entries under "smoking," one by Rudyard Kipling and one by Sir Arthur Helps. Neither would help much for an anti-smoking speech, but for a pro-smoking speech Helps is quoted as saying: "What a blessing this smoking is! perhaps the greatest that we owe to the discovery of America." The index also contains twenty-two entries under "Smoke," two under "Smoked," one under "Smokes," two under "Smoky," and nine under "Tobacco." Your librarian will show you how to use that reference book. The best resource for quotations, of course, is your own reading and search through books, stories, and poems about the subject.

A quotation at the beginning of a speech should have the same qualities that make any piece of literature memorable: strength, beauty, emotion, and appropriateness. It should be long enough to accomplish your purpose, but short enough not to steal the spotlight from the content of your speech. Sometimes when quoting you need to alter the quotation somewhat in order to give information necessary for the quote to make complete sense. With prose cutting is an acceptable practice, but with poetry you almost never alter even a word, although you do not have to quote the entire poem.

Atomic Bomb Introduction: A total of 53,000 of Hiroshima's pre-atomic bomb population of 343,000 is dead. Thirty-three thousand are known to have died almost immediately in that awful flash at 8:18 A.M., (August 6, 1945). . . . On August 20 — 33,000 dead; 30,000 missing and probably dead; 14,000 seriously injured; 43,500 less seriously injured. On September 1, known dead had mounted to 53,000. But no casualty figures could possibly describe the four-and-one-half miles of terrifying desolation — an area where the fear of death will bar permanent residents for years to come. Street cars are running and a few people are walking through the ruins of Hiroshima, but there is nothing standing above the ground except a dozen reinforced concrete buildings — all of which were burned.

Every Japanese-style building in the stricken area has been blasted or burned flat and all that remains in the streets are piles of scattered tiles and black, dead trees. . . . There is no city in the world so terribly destroyed — not Berlin, Hamburg, or any other. . . .

A small Jap(anese) boy, grinning and friendly, approached me in the street. He felt very important at being with foreigners and at having seen the blast from a couple of miles away.

He accepted a chocolate bar with elaborate courtesy. We asked him, through an interpreter, what the blast looked like.

"I thought the moon had fallen down on Hiroshima," the kid answered between bites of candy.

That is the way reporter Clark Lee described his first impressions of the devastation of Hiroshima, Japan, in 1945. Now, almost forty years later, we can look back and take a more objective account of the toll exacted by this one bomb.

The dropping of the bomb on Hiroshima inspired reporters, novelists, short-story writers, and poets to compose hundreds of quote-worthy works. Clark Lee's is just one.

The parentheses added above show that an addition or change was made from the original. The series of periods indicates that some material was left out. These changes do not have to be explained or even mentioned to the audience, but the quote should be as true as possible to the original with only necessary alterations for clarity, smoothness, or good taste, such as changing "Jap," an expression acceptable to most of white America in 1945, to "Japanese," a much more acceptable term today.

Anti-smoking Introduction: "A fire at one end, a fool at the other, and a bit of tobacco in between." That is the way one anonymous writer speaks of smoking. Let's examine the way the "fire" affects the "fool" and drives him to an earlier, poorer grave.

If you prefer verse, this quotation from Frederick William Fairholt's (1814–1866) "Tobacco" might be helpful.

Tobacco, an outlandish weed,
Doth in the land strange wonders breed;
It taints the breath, the blood it dries,
It burns the head, it blinds the eyes;
It dries the lungs, scourgeth the lights,
It numbs the soul, it dulls the spirits;
It brings a man into a maze,
And makes him sit for others' gaze;
It mars a man, it mars a purse,
A lean one fat, a fat one worse.

For a more serious introduction you might ask the American Cancer Society for literature. As with any other introduction, the style of presentation will affect the choice of introductory material. The quotation should always be appropriate to the speech topic, and the more depth to your speech, the more power your quotation should possess.

THE NONVERBAL INTRODUCTION

The nonverbal introduction actually introduces the introduction. Somewhere along the line a speech must become verbal — that is, use words — or it obviously is not a speech. Some topics are ideal for nonverbal introductions, but most are not. A speech, for instance, about the communication on a baseball diamond would lend itself nicely to a nonverbal introduction. The speaker could simply "hang out a set of signs," to use baseball parlance, before beginning to talk about the subject. To attempt a pantomime of an atomic bomb falling would, of course, be ludicrous.

A nonverbal introduction does not have to be a pantomime or dance. A painting or photograph might also introduce a speech wordlessly. Unveiling a cage containing an exotic pet would be a dramatic way to begin a speech about your eagle, alligator, or crabs — all of which I have had in classes over the years. A lighter introduction to an anti-smoking speech might involve lighting a cigarette, coughing, breathing smoke in someone's face, spilling ashes all over, and otherwise illustrating the "evils" of smoking.

The very act of laying out paraphernalia for any speech gets the audience's attention and serves as a form of introduction, as does writing something on the chalkboard in front of the class. You should consider any setup or preparation that takes place in front of your audience as part of a nonverbal introduction, because, like it or not, it will be.

USING HUMOR

Any of the types of introductions will benefit from the judicious use of humor, as will the speech itself. Like any other aspect of an introduction, humor must be related directly to the topic. Humor can be a powerful method for getting an audience's attention *if*

1. the humor is related to the topic
2. the attempted humor is indeed funny
3. the speaker knows how to handle and time humor

Often speakers will begin a speech with an "A funny thing happened to me on the way here tonight" type of anecdote. Frequently the anecdote has absolutely nothing to do with the topic and is simply an amusing way of getting attention. Then the speaker must begin the introduction *after* the anecdote.

As to the second, "if," what is more deadly than a boring story that is supposed to be funny, or a story that sends the speaker into gales of laughter and the audience into fits of yawns?

Finally, if you are going to use humor, know your story and how to tell it. Just try to get an audience interested in your topic after you go through "Oh, no, it was the *man* who said that and the *woman* fainted — wait a minute, it was the woman who said it and her husband fainted — no, it was . . ." Forget it, you've lost them completely!

Of course, no matter how well you can handle humor, how appropriate it is to the topic, and how funny it is, humor should never be used to ridicule individuals or groups. Off-color stories and racial or ethnic slurs are never appropriate. The last thing you as a speaker want to do is offend an audience, making it impossible for them to identify with you when you get into the heart of your topic.

Although anecdotes lend themselves nicely to humor, almost any type of introduction can benefit from it. In skillful hands, it can be a sharp knife, cutting right to the core of the problem. For instance, in an anti-smoking speech, it might be effective to begin by describing the pleasures of smoking while hacking and coughing. A topic of the seriousness of atomic bombs might not be as adaptable to broad humor, but depending on the thrust of the speech, it might benefit from a lighter approach.

SUMMARY
AND CONCLUSION

If the old axiom that "first impressions are lasting" is valid, then the importance of the introduction becomes clear immediately: it establishes the audience's first impression of the speaker and the speech. A good introduction gets you into an audience's good graces and makes them receptive to your ideas. A poor introduction does just the opposite, making it difficult for the speech to succeed.

Although five types of introductions were examined separately, they can be used in combination. Any of them will benefit from humor, but you must always use it judiciously. Like any other aspect of an introduction, humor must be related directly to the topic.

Regardless of topic, type of introduction, and the speaker, the introduction always must appeal to the audience. It must attract attention to the speaker and the subject. Without the audience's attention a speech ceases to be communication and becomes instead an act of no consequence to anyone except the speaker.

EXERCISES

1. A. Write a short introduction for a speech advocating the purchase of compact, economy automobiles.
   B. Do the same for luxury, four-door sedans.
   C. Do the same for sports cars.
2. Think of two effective ways of introducing a speech about the role of computers in our society.
3. Which types of introductions might best serve a speech about the history of musical instruments?
4. Choose two types of introductions for a speech about engineering or your own vocation.

CHAPTER 9

concluding your speech

1. *Why does my speech need a summary and a conclusion?*
2. *What is the difference between the summary and the conclusion?*
3. *How can my summary and conclusion parallel my introduction?*

And so on and so on . . .

Well, (giggle) I guess that's about all I have to say (giggle).

Give me liberty or uh somethin' else.

Any questions?

Golly, folks, I'm done. That is, I have said all that I have to say on the subject. You see, I really don't have any more to say. That is . . . (Sob).

A speech without an ending—a *planned* ending—is like a meal without dessert. No gourmet chef would permit such a thing to happen, because the dessert complements the other taste sensations. The speaker too must leave the audience with a good taste in their mouths, that is, with a well-planned summary of ideas and a conclusion to the speech.

The Summary

After you have completed your speech, you need to refresh the audience's minds by summarizing your main points. Most of us cannot retain vast amounts of detailed information for long. In a ten-minute persuasive speech you may present dozens, even hundreds of bits of information. Some information will be in words or numbers and reinforced by visual aids. Some will be less obvious, such as the nonverbal cues that reinforce the verbal message. Regardless of how you present your ideas, you will inundate your audience with vast amounts of information, not all of which can be retained by even the most attentive receiver. The summary should restate the most important information.

While you are giving the body of your speech, the audience accepts or rejects the ideas you present. If you quote statistics, they accept or reject them based on the sense you make of the statistics, your own credibility, and the source's credibility. The audience need not remember where the statistics came from, so long as they accepted the source as credible when first presented. Nor is it necessary for them to remember that you appeared sincere—an oversimplification—when you presented the information. It is not even necessary for them to remember the details of the statistics, as long as they remember their substance and implication. In your summary, therefore, you do not repeat details, but merely recapture the *meaning* and *importance* of those details. The audience needs to be reminded of the point you were making, not how you made it. If they accepted your information at first, they will accept it again in summary.

The summary deals mainly with intellectual substance. If it deals with emotional appeals, they must be reduced to more logical arguments. In any case, the summary deals only with your main points. Part of the outline's purpose is to identify your most important points. You should reiterate and stress these few points in the summary. You may wish to reintroduce the visual aids that accompanied a specific idea, but the verbal message usually suffices.

A good rule of thumb for summaries is to have one or two sentences for each main point in your outline. Because most speeches have two to five main points, your summary will usually have no more than six or eight sentences.

The Conclusion

If your speech is well organized, the summary should be fairly easy to compose. The conclusion, on the other hand, requires a good deal more thought and creativity. The summary reviews the main points of the speech; the conclusion solidly and permanently implants the ideas in the listeners' memories. The conclusion is not a mere stopping, but a final statement that gives completion, importance, and drama for the audience to respond to and remember. The summary deals primarily with rational appeals, the conclusion appeals to every aspect of the audience members' minds and hearts.

A conclusion may be only a few words in length, possibly only two or three. It may be more lengthy, but the more said in the less time, the better. Effective conclusions are closely allied with the summary, and one flows into the other.

Often we remember the conclusion of a speech, but not the body. Many people can quote, at least approximately, the final sentence from Patrick Henry's speech to the Virginia Convention, March 23, 1775: "I know not what course others may take, but as for me, give me liberty or give me death!" How many people, however, can quote, or even paraphrase, any of the fine, logical arguments Henry presented in the body of his speech? We remember today the conclusion that swayed people in the 18th century.

Winston Churchill was one of the most powerful speakers in history, and one of the first whose speeches were recorded in his own voice, as well as transcribed onto paper. On June 18, 1940, he spoke to Parliament after the fall of Dunkirk and the capitulation of France, concluding with the following, widely quoted sentence: "Let us therefore brace ourselves to our duty, and so bear ourselves that if the British Empire and its Commonwealths last for a thousand years, men will still say, 'This was their finest hour!'" People who remember World War II will be able to tell you who said those famous words, but few will remember when, where, or why they were spoken.

Most of us cannot create conclusions as rich, dramatic, and powerful as Henry's or Churchill's, but each speaker must pay special attention to the conclusion and attempt to make it as memorable as possible. Naturally you will not be dealing with events as momentous as the decision whether to secede from England or as disastrous as the French surrender and defeat at Dunkirk, but within the context of your modest efforts to inform or persuade the audience, you need to stimulate their imaginations and emotions.

No formula can guarantee a powerful, memorable conclusion, but one method that usually bears some success is to parallel the device used in the introduction. If you began with a rhetorical question, you might conclude with a rhetorical question. A better way to refer to the introduction, however, is in terms of content; if the introduction was a narrative about your dying uncle, the conclusion should continue, complete, or otherwise refer to that narrative. The best method is a combination of the two; follow the style and refer to the content of the introduction. This structure aids the audience in their thinking, as well as putting everything into a neat package, giving unity and strength to the speech as a whole.

In Chapter 8 we examined five types of introductions: the anecdote, startling statement, rhetorical question, quotation, and nonverbal introduction. Let us look at some conclusions utilizing these five techniques.

THE ANECDOTE

An anecdote is an especially good conclusion when you introduced the speech with an anecdote, and you can tie the two together. Lighter speeches can make good use of the anecdote, although it can be used also in more serious speeches. To conclude the anti-smoking speech introduced by the story of Uncle Fred's death, you might say something to this effect:

The night they buried Uncle Fred, I took a pack of cigarettes from my shirt pocket and stared at it for what seemed like an eternity. I was going to throw the pack away, but then I decided to keep it. I placed it on the dresser in my bedroom, right next to a picture of Uncle Fred. That was seven months ago, and I haven't touched a cigarette since.

Assume that you have given a speech loaded with statistics and other data supporting a program to preserve our natural resources. After reviewing the facts, you might end with a description of life 100 years from now as you imagine it if we do not become more conservation-oriented:

Imagine yourself in a world with insufficient food for even a portion of the population. Transportation, other than on foot, is reserved for a few rich and powerful people. Perhaps one forty-watt electric light bulb might be permitted in each home, but there will be little or no fuel in winter and no cooling in summer. Our entire way of life will have altered drastically for the worse. That is where we are headed if we do not begin a sound conservation program for our resources. We must begin today; tomorrow may be too late.

The length of your anecdote will depend on the length of the speech itself. One danger of using an anecdote for a conclusion lies in its being too long and becoming boring. If you can avoid that trap, it can be an effective way to conclude a speech.

THE STARTLING STATEMENT

The startling statement is more difficult to use in the conclusion of a speech than in the introduction. By the end the audience already knows your thoughts and feelings. A startling statement usually serves better to lead into something than to tie things up. It can be effective, however, if used judiciously. A student once gave a fine, factual, and informative speech about mental retardation. He never got maudlin or overly sentimental, and he presented the facts objectively. After his summary, however, he paused for a moment, took a breath, and told why he became interested in the topic. Although this wording is not exact, the essence of the statement is this: "I became interested in this subject because it is so close. You see, my younger brother Tommy is severely retarded, and I guess it was just a lucky draw of the cards that it was not me."

Another student did the same thing with a speech about child abuse, withholding until the end the information that she had divorced her husband because he beat their son. In both cases, giving the audience the personal information earlier might have caused embarrassment for both audience and speaker. By waiting, the speakers insured that they could present their facts objectively. The final disclosure made the subject vastly more personal and planted it firmly in the audience's minds.

THE RHETORICAL QUESTION

The rhetorical question also is a good method for bringing a topic home and leaving the audience pondering the subject. The rhetorical question lends itself to more serious topics. Remember, the rhetorical question should not call for a show of hands or a *yes-no* decision. It should direct the audience's thinking along clearly defined lines. A biographical speech might end with a question such as, "What would our lives be like today without the remarkable, inventive genius of Thomas Edison?" A speech about career choices might end with, "What will you be doing in the year 2000?" A speech about President Harry S Truman, the Second World War, nuclear war, or many other topics might end with, "Truman's decision to drop the A-bomb on Hiroshima and on Nagasaki had to be one of the most dramatic and difficult decisions in history. What would you have done?"

One question to avoid for a conclusion is, "Any questions?" Two conditions usually result from that question. If the audience responds to your request, you can lose your train of thought. If they do not respond, you are left with "egg on your face," and an embarrassed silence closes out your presentation. "Any questions?" is weak; it implies that you have not covered everything you should have and leaves the door open for problems. Most important, though, it is not a conclusion; it is at best a stoppage and at worst a detour. Do not use it. Any questions?

THE QUOTATION

The well-selected, dramatically presented quotation of literature can be one of the most powerful ways of concluding a speech. After all, for no cash outlay you are getting writing help from the Bible, Shakespeare, or some other famous author. You get the opportunity to use the words of someone who is recognized as a verbal artist. You should, of course, always give credit to the author whose words you are using, recognizing someone whose talent you think good enough to use for expressing your own thoughts.

A speech about nuclear proliferation, the dangers of a cold war becoming hot, or diminishing resources might end thus: "The question is not dollars. The question is not power or nationalism. Shakespeare's Hamlet said it in one of the most famous speeches in the English language: 'To be or not to be; that is the question.'"

The Bible furnishes a wealth of quotations for speeches, but like any other source it requires prior knowledge. To open the Bible or Shakespeare at random, assuming that you will find an ideal quotation for your speech about a specific topic, is foolish. Another problem with using the Bible in a secular institution results from the various translations used by different religious groups. Most versions are similar, but where there are differences, every group thinks that its version is the correct one. (Noted American novelist John Steinbeck wove an entire novel, *East of Eden*, around the translation of the Hebrew word *timshel* from Genesis 4:7. The verb is variously translated as "must," "will," and "may.")

If you give a speech on semantics or the effects of words on people, what better way to end than with Emily Dickinson's poem, "A Word"?

> A word is dead
> When it is said,
>   Some say.
> I say it just
> Begins to live
>   That day.

Thomas Paine's admonition, "These are the times that try men's souls," has been used to conclude countless speeches, as has his "Tyranny, like hell, is not easily conquered." (Both are from his article "The Crisis.") The sources for your quotations are limited only by your knowledge of literature and your resourcefulness. Remember, there are collections of quotations in most reference libraries. These books index quotations by subject matter, and the better ones cover just about anything.

THE NONVERBAL CONCLUSION

The nonverbal ending occurs infrequently and must be planned meticulously. Nonverbal messages usually accompany and reinforce the verbal message. Used properly, they can furnish dramatic and powerful conclusions. An excellent example of a nonverbal conclusion occurred in a class where a young man limped into the room on crutches, with bandages around his head, his arm in a sling, and his leg in a cast. His speech was a plea for reason. It asked that people not judge things by their appearances. He titled the speech, "Things aren't always what they seem." In the speech he detailed his horror at almost hitting a child with his car, and at the subsequent incident, which deteriorated into a racial confrontation. The situation climaxed when an angry mob attacked him, sending him to the hospital. Throughout the speech he protested his innocence, as he had done unsuccessfully on the street. He closed by again insisting, "Things aren't always what they seem." At that point he tossed aside the crutches, took off the bandages and sling, and removed the cast from his leg. He had gone to great lengths to prove his point; we had swallowed his story completely, primarily because of the apparent injuries. It may sound like gimmickry, but in the context of the class and the assignment, it was most satisfactory. The class and I, however, admitted that we felt a bit angry at having been tricked.

The nonverbal conclusion goes nicely with the demonstration speech. After a series of steps demonstrating a process or procedure, the speaker shows the finished product as a conclusion.

USING HUMOR IN YOUR CONCLUSION

Humor generally will not be as vital to a conclusion as to an introduction. At the beginning of a presentation the speaker must establish rapport with an audience. The speaker who does not establish it by the conclusion is in deep trouble, anyway. If the tone of the speech was light, of course, light humor might be appropriate. Should you wish to use humor in a conclusion, take care that it is inoffensive so your ideas remain paramount in the minds of the audience. The suggestions for humor found in Chapter 8 are also pertinent for humor in conclusions:

1. It must be related to the topic.
2. It must be funny to everyone.
3. The speaker must know how to handle and time it.

SUMMARY AND CONCLUSION

There are many ways to end a speech, and often two or more are used in conjunction to heighten the effect. Every speech needs a strong conclusion following a complete, detailed summary. The needs of the speech, speaker, and audience affect how much emphasis goes to the summary and how much to the conclusion. A basically informative speech usually does not need the depth of emotion in the conclusion that a persuasive speech requires. Depending on the complexity of the topic, speeches need varying amounts of summary. However, you must include both summary and conclusion in order to complete the message and avoid the awkward embarrassment of just stopping. You do not want to leave your audience hanging; they must have a sense of completion in order to digest your thoughts. Avoid the weak, cliché endings such as "Thank you," "Any questions," or "Well, I guess that's about it." Write out your summary and conclusion word for word, giving them as much emphasis as the introduction. Whether you use one or more of the five methods listed or something entirely different, make your summary and conclusion reflect you and your ideas as thoroughly as possible.

Do not spend vast amounts of energy, time, and creativity on the soup, salad, and main course of your spoken "meal," and then expect the dessert simply to happen. The good dessert and the good conclusion of a speech both leave us feeling complete and satisfied. At the same time they follow the old theatrical advice of "Always leave them wanting more." They leave us full, but not stuffed; satisfied, but looking forward to more.

EXERCISES

1. A. Write a short conclusion to a speech supporting the decision to drop the atomic bomb on Hiroshima in World War II.
   B. Do the same for a speech attacking the same decision.
2. A. Write a short summary and conclusion for a speech advocating living in a small community.
   B. Do the same for big city living.
   C. Do the same for suburban living.
3. Think of two effective ways of concluding a demonstration speech about a hobby.
4. What kind or kinds of conclusions might best serve a speech dealing with the history of the alphabet or another communication tool?
5. Write two conclusions for a speech about engineering or any other profession as a vocation.

CHAPTER **10**

preparing the body of your speech

1. *Why is the body of the speech so important?*
2. *What can I do to improve the language of my speech?*
3. *Does the occasion affect the language of the speech?*
4. *Should I use a manuscript or notes?*
5. *What should I put on my note cards?*
6. *Should I memorize the speech?*
7. *How should I practice? How much?*

Your banquet of speech-making will have its appetizing soup and salad, sometimes called "the introduction." At the end your dessert will leave us with a good taste in our mouths—the conclusion. What about the main course, the meat and potatoes of the speech, the body?

Importance of the Body

The introduction sets the mood for the speech, as well as getting the audience in a frame of mind to be receptive to your ideas and thoughts. It should provide a smooth transition to the body which contains those ideas and thoughts. After the body of the speech is completed, the summary and conclusion tie the whole thing together to leave a strong intellectual and emotional response to the ideas you presented. It is in the body, however, where you set forth your ideas in order to inform and/or persuade your audience.

All parts of the speech contain numerous messages, but the central core message, the message articulated in your statement of objectives and verbalized in your topic sentence, appears in the body. It is the body of the speech that furnishes the *raison d'être* ("reason to be" — it sounds more impressive in French) for the whole speech. Without the body the speech has little or no meaning.

In the body of the speech you, the speaker, bring together all the various aspects of speech-making that are discussed throughout the book. You will want to use your best logic in order to inform and convince your audience. The same is true, of course, of other techniques of persuasion. You will need to inform your audience of all vital aspects necessary to understand your ideas. You will have to support your ideas with logical development, valid statistical information, pertinent quotations from experts, and any other means of support you can find. You will also need to reinforce messages through use of sensory aids, primarily visual, graphs, charts, photographs, models, demonstration, and whatever other techniques are appropriate and available.

The Language of the Speech

Throughout the speech you will use many languages, at least one verbal language and several nonverbal languages. The verbal language used for the primary message represents the most important phase of development. Clear, concise, easily understandable language is vital to your speech.

Although there are some differences in style between the written and spoken word, it is no coincidence that people who prepare the best speeches quite often are also good writers. If you can express yourself well one way, you probably will express yourself well the other, although writing does not normally contain the psychological threats that speaking often implies.

USE OF JARGON

Jargon is specialized language that people in a certain field use and understand. Engineers have their jargon, as do lawyers, athletes, and virtually any other group that participates in specialized activities. A speech to a group of engineers about an engineering project can contain a great deal more jargon than the same speech to a general audience. Indeed, for the engineers the jargon will supply a shortcut to understanding and save the speaker a good deal of background explanation. Most of your audiences, however, especially in the classroom, will be general audiences with only a few who are tuned in to the jargon. You will, therefore, have to avoid the use of jargon or you will lose your audience.

In some speeches the use of jargon may help the audience understand the speech better, so that it is worth the time it takes to explain a certain word or phrase and then use it judiciously through the speech. Always avoid the overuse of jargon that may lead you into a closed-circuit or insiders-only speech which will appeal only to those in the know and alienate the rest of the audience.

MOOD AND TONE

Mood and tone are rather vague terms that are hard to define, but they become most obvious when they are not in keeping with the topic of the speech. An extreme example might be a speech about death and dying using slang expressions and "playing for laughs." That is not to say that a serious subject cannot utilize some humor, but it must be done judiciously and carefully. Using people's first names will contribute to the mood and tone of a speech. In a speech about relativity or modern physics referring to "Al" Einstein would jar the mood, as well as being in questionable taste. In a speech about teenage major league ballplayers, however, referring to Al Kaline would be more appropriate than calling him Albert. If you are attempting to deal with a serious subject and trying to establish your credibility, the use of "ain't" or "you was" will defeat your purpose quickly. We in the audience will subconsciously react to such language with thoughts such as, "How does he expect to convince me that he can deal with an intellectual topic when he speaks like an illiterate?"

GRAMMAR
The previous example brings us to grammar and usage of language in general. Bad grammar almost never pays off, unless you are doing a very special, stylized speech. That is not to say that extemporaneous speech must always have perfect grammar; few of us are able to boast honestly of such ability. You should, however, avoid obvious abuses, such as those mentioned before: double negatives; misuses of "you and I"/"you and me;" and subject and verb disagreement.

Obviously this book cannot be a grammar lesson. Your speech or English teacher will be able to provide you with the names of some good style guides if you have a real problem with your grammar.

CONVERSATIONAL STYLE
A speech in which you stand before an audience and attempt to inform and/or persuade them is not a conversational act, so why try to put it in a conversational form? The act of public speaking is quite formal; conversation is not. On the other hand, you do not want to sound phony or unreal when you speak. You must strike a balance between the formal situation in which you find yourself and your own personality. Certainly the audience to which you are addressing yourself will also affect the way in which you utilize conversational style. A conversational style may occasionally be appropriate to a particular speech on a particular occasion, but normally you will want to be a bit more formal making a speech than you are in conversation.

APPROPRIATE TO THE OCCASION
The language of any speech should be appropriate to the occasion, that is, to the reason for giving the speech, to the topic, and to the audience. In ordinary life we select different styles of language for different occasions and different audiences. Chances are your language is somewhat different when you are in a gym or on an athletic field than when you are trying to impress a prospective employer or an important dinner guest. Chances are you will speak differently to your parents if you are asking for money or if you are discussing a political issue as equals. Analyze your audience; think about the topic of the speech; then decide what language and style would be appropriate for that occasion.

CLEAR AND CONCISE VOCABULARY
Many people feel that when they speak they need to use "ten dollar" words to impress their audience. Although some unfamiliar words may be necessary for

explanation, the bulk of the vocabulary should express "you" as well as the topic. There are, of course, many "you's," and your speech-making "you" may be quite serious for a serious topic. Still you do not want to imply through your words that you are someone or something other than yourself. The best word in any given speaking circumstance is that word which conveys the clearest, most precise meaning for the audience and is relatively comfortable for the speaker.

Every word, phrase, and sentence of the speech should be focused on the topic, offering explanation, clarification, or amplification to your central ideas. If you are not sure of whether a sentence is appropriate, try to relate it to your statement of objectives. Does the idea help you to "convince an audience to stop smoking," "inform an audience about the horrors of atomic war," or *(fill in the statement of objectives)?*

VIVID, LIVELY LANGUAGE
Just as in writing, vivid, lively word images will help your speaking convey ideas. It may take you a little extra time to pick and choose the right words, especially in spots in which you want to stimulate the audience's imaginations and senses, but the effort will be well worth it if they understand better and respond more deeply to your speech.

Note Preparation and Memory Aids

Should you use a written-out manuscript for your speech? Notes? Memorization? The answer again is not a simple one. A leader of government must plan speeches word for word because a misplaced "of" or "from" might lead to dire international consequences. Most of us are not in such highly sensitive situations, but we still want to say what we mean and mean what we say.

SPEAKING FROM A MANUSCRIPT
Most beginning speakers are not yet adept enough at thinking on their feet to form the sentences and select just the right words while delivering the speech. Most beginners, and a good percentage of more experienced speakers, choose to write out all or parts of the speech in manuscript form so they can pick and choose words, phrases, and sentences that convey exactly the messages they want. Yet what is more deadly than the speaker who reads from the manuscript and adds no sense of spontaneity? Although the audience will expect you to be thoroughly prepared, they also want the sense that you are talking to them and thinking as you go along. The speaker who works from a manuscript also runs the risk of getting lost and fumbling to get back on the track.

Some instructors require their students to write and speak from manuscripts; others forbid it. When you face a problem that needs precise phrasing, such as an introduction, conclusion, or some difficult passage, write out that part. The most effective speakers are those whose words and ideas seem spontaneous, as if they were popping into the mind during the speech. Using notes rather than a manuscript will help your speech sound and appear extemporaneous. If you must use a manuscript, avoid the studied sound and appearance that too often accompany a manuscript reading. Strive for an extemporaneous quality.

If you work from a manuscript, make sure that it is in good physical condition.

If you carry a bunch of loose papers with dog-eared corners you have at least one strike against you before you open your mouth. Just as you want yourself to look neat and clean, so you should want your manuscript to look the same. Just as it is not expensive to look neat personally, neither is it necessary to spend great amounts of money for a good-looking manuscript. You can purchase an inexpensive folder that will keep your manuscript clean and, at the same time, keep eyes away from your own markings and directions to yourself.

SPEAKING FROM AN OUTLINE

What about speaking from your outline? That is usually not a good idea, because an outline may be so intricate that it will be difficult to read from in a time of tension and stress. The outline's purpose is different from the manuscript's: the outline is a skeleton that needs fleshing out in order to be of value. Chances are that if your outline is simple enough to serve as notes, it is not detailed enough to speak from. If, on the other hand, it is sufficiently detailed to form the basis of your entire speech, it probably is too complex to follow while on your feet.

SPEAKING FROM NOTES

What then is the "best" method for keeping your speech on the track and communicating all the ideas you worked so hard to form? Note cards! Use a series of 3" x 5" or 4" x 6" note cards for jotting down the main points you wish to cover. The number that you use depends on the complexity and length of your speech. If your topic is one with which you are thoroughly familiar, you may just need a word or two on five or six cards to insure getting in all your ideas. If your topic is complex and somewhat new, you probably will want more words and phrases to keep you on the track.

Each card should have no more than three or four key words on it: "Tell the chicken story" or "Demonstrate hand position" or "Current status." The note card can also include information you need to read precisely, quoting a source exactly or making certain your statistics are correct. When you use them as a reminder, however, try to limit yourself to a word or phrase whose complete meaning you can grasp with one quick glance.

Your speech then has three written steps, four if you count research notes:

1. The outline is used to arrange thoughts into a sensible, easily followed order, and serves as a skeletal structure for the manuscript.
2. The manuscript is used to select the best words and phrases while you have the luxury of thinking out each sentence and paragraph.
3. The note cards are used to stimulate your memory and keep you on the track, permitting maximum audience contact.

Memorizing vs. Familiarizing

As bad as most people, especially beginners, sound when they read a speech from a manuscript, they sound even worse when they attempt to memorize a speech. Some people can read a speech and make it sound impromptu and "live," and some people can memorize a manuscript and get the same effect. They are few and usually experienced; most of us are unable to do either.

The problem of losing your place when reading from a manuscript pales beside the problem of forgetting where you are in a memorized speech. Many people actually have to go back to the beginning and start over if they lose their place.

Consciously trying to memorize a speech usually results in disaster. When you practice a speech over and over, however, you cannot help but do some memorizing; "familiarizing" is a better term. You find a word or phrase you like that is right for the situation; you repeat it again and again in practice; and, without even trying, you have memorized it. That is a good situation with highly positive results. The process to avoid is memorizing by repeating words and phrases over and over until they have no meaning. If your instructor requires you to memorize, memorize ideas first and then fill in the words, but never memorize words as an exercise. It is usually futile and self-defeating.

Practicing

Everyone realizes that practice is necessary for presenting a good speech, but how? How much? When? Where? There is no universal answer to any of the questions, certainly not "how." You must find a method that works for you. There are some guidelines that have been successful for most people in most situations over the years.

HOW TO PRACTICE

The closer you can approximate the actual conditions of the speech situation, the more valuable your practice will be. Most of us do not have a room as large as a classroom or twenty-five friends who will drop by to hear our solutions to the world's problems, so we have to settle for home or dormitory conditions. A quiet room is the best place for practice; it will have fewer distractions and enable you to concentrate on what you are doing. Try to assume a physical posture and position that approximate the way you will stand in relation to your real audience.

Speak out loud! You cannot hear the way you will actually sound with your inner ear. Many novice speakers practice silently, and then virtually jump out of their skins when they hear their own voices booming the words they prepared.

Use your notes as you plan to use them in your speech. The best time to discover that a certain note card conveys too little information, or that you cannot handle the cards easily without making some adjustments, is before you face your audience. Adjustments are difficult anytime, but when you are in a public speaking situation, they can become impossible. If you plan to use a lectern for your notes, find something to take the lectern's place in practice sessions. Use a music stand, other suitable furniture, or books piled on a desk to the approximate height.

Time yourself when you speak aloud. Many a five-minute speech has turned out to be ninety seconds long; many seem to be ninety years long and actually do exceed the time limit. Until you are fairly experienced, it is difficult to adjust to the time allotment without doing it out loud.

HOW LONG TO PRACTICE

How long should you practice? As long as necessary. It is highly unlikely that you will achieve perfection even if you practice hundreds of times. If you are satisfied after one or two practices, however, you are probably fooling yourself or settling for a great deal less than you are capable of. Six, eight, or ten times may get you the degree of excellence you are capable of at this stage in your speaking career. Remember, though, it is better to practice five times with two run-throughs each time than once with ten run-throughs. We all have a limit of perfectibility at one session. Several shorter sessions imply preparing long before the assignment is due, but that will also give you more time to think about what you are doing after the groundwork is laid.

The time when it is best for you to practice obviously depends, in part, on factors such as your schedule, outside commitments, availability of space, and whether you are a "night" or "day" person. Again, though, the closer the practice situation is to actual conditions, the better.

Almost all our speech habits are imitative and repetitive. We learn to talk by repeating sounds over and over when we are small. The athlete or dancer will spend hours perfecting the movements of a few small muscles; actors and musicians rehearse hours every day for weeks before performing for an audience. If these people need all that practice, why should we assume that a speaker needs any less? Of course, desire to approach perfection enters the picture also. You may not be as interested in your speeches as the baseball player is in hitting sharp line drives, but you still want to do a respectable job that gives a fair indication of your capabilities. Do not worry about practicing too much and burning yourself out; it can happen, but chances are you and I never will see it happen.

RECORDING YOUR PRACTICE
Should you use a tape recorder to critique yourself? Only if you are able to withstand the shock of hearing your voice radically different from what you are used to. When we hear ourselves speaking, we hear not only the sounds that pass through the air into our ears, but also sounds conducted to the ears by the bones of the head. This extra conduction of sound makes our voices sound different to us from the way others hear us. It happens to everybody, not just you. If you can listen to yourself critically, however, the recorder can offer some hints to better speaking. So can your family and fellow students, but you must remember that their criticism may be based on criteria different from that of your instructor. Their suggestions may be valuable only if you sift them and separate the wheat from the chaff. The best audience, other than a real audience, is you yourself once you have learned to listen to yourself critically and objectively. For some people that takes a long time; for some it never occurs. But the key word is *listen*. Listen to what you are saying and the way you are saying it, not to what you want to say and the way you would like to say it.

SUMMARY
AND CONCLUSION

The body of the speech is probably the most important part of the speech, although all parts must come together to form a "whole." The body carries the primary message, along with the proofs needed to convince and inform the audience.

The language you use will be vital in the degree of acceptance your speech enjoys. Try to avoid jargon unless the entire audience can appreciate it and understand it. If they all understand it, jargon can be a shortcut for you. The audience determines the use of jargon while the topic determines the mood and tone you will want to set. Always use the best grammar you can muster. A conversational style goes over much better with today's audiences than does a flowery, pedantic style. Language must always be appropriate for the topic, the audience, and the occasion, and the language should be as clear and concise and as vivid and lively as possible.

Writing out a speech into manuscript form may be helpful in collecting your ideas and choosing your words. When delivering the speech, however, an extemporaneous style and quality will gain much better audience response. Try not to read from your manuscript or use it for a delivery aid, unless you *must* deliver the speech word-for-word with no variations. The outline of a speech is a useful device for preparation, but it too should not normally be used for performance. The best memory aids are note cards with just a few words each that help keep your place and keep you moving in a logical fashion. Do not memorize; you will probably familiarize yourself with the speech anyway, but a conscious effort to memorize usually leads to a stilted, dull presentation.

When you practice your speech, try, as much as possible, to simulate the conditions under which you will give it. It is better to practice several times for shorter periods than to spend one long, intense practice session.

Finally, no matter how hard you practice, it will never be the same when the time comes to face the audience and do it. A common remark speech instructors hear is, "I was so much better last night in front of the mirror in my bedroom." Undoubtedly! The audience was imaginary, and there was no threat of failure or low grades. But think how much worse the presentation would have been if you had not practiced in front of the mirror in your bedroom. The old adage says "Practice makes perfect." Despite the overstatement, the basic idea is true.

EXERCISES

PRACTICE!!!!

CHAPTER **11**

persuading
your audience

1. *What are the three primary appeals I can use to persuade my audience?*
2. *What is the difference between inductive and deductive logic?*
3. *When is generalization effective? Analogy? Cause and effect?*
4. *What kinds of credibility do I need to establish?*
5. *What is the Monroe Motivated Sequence, and when should I use it?*
6. *What is "argument"?*
7. *What should I do about counter-arguments?*

As you all know, I am a member of seven societies, clubs, and organizations that are known for their patriotic attitudes and works. Each of these organizations is above reproach, and each is regarded as 100 percent American. How can my opponents then accuse me of being un-American? Just because I tried to blow up the White House and sold secret papers to our enemies doesn't prove a thing. Remember, I belong to the . . . .

Cats have four legs.
Socrates is a cat.
Therefore, Socrates drinks milk.
Huh?

Whether you are addressing an audience of millions on radio or selling birdseed to an individual customer, as a speaker you always will be faced with the problem of supporting your contentions, establishing your right to make them, and convincing the audience to accept them. After all, why should we believe people who are paid well to sell a product when they say "Believe me, this product is better than any other on the market?"

Some twenty-four centuries ago Aristotle analyzed the problems facing the rhetorician, or persuader. He contended that a public speaker uses three kinds of appeals, which he called *logos, pathos,* and *ethos. Logos* loosely translates into logic, or the use of logical, rational, and reasoned proofs. He insisted that logical proofs are the most important, because he believed that human beings are basically rational animals. Today we recognize that *pathos,* or emotional appeals, may be even more important than rational appeals. Finally he insisted that the *ethos,* or quality of the speaker, played a significant role; today we call it *credibility* or authority.

Let us examine briefly the kinds of appeals that persuade each of us to make one highly significant investment: buying a car. Some cars can be sold better through rational appeals: "It gets good gas mileage"; "It costs little to run"; "It is the safest car on the road"; "It needs fewer repairs." These are factual, statistically provable points, and only one car can be the "best" in any such category. Other appeals are more emotional or psychological: "It enhances our status"; "It makes us more appealing to friends, especially the opposite sex"; "It is the most stylish"; "It is owned by such-and-such famous person." Finally the dealer, salesperson, and advertiser go to great lengths to sell themselves as well as the car: "Hey, I'm just one of the boys"; "I have your interest at heart"; "I want to be your friend"; "I am really Gary Goodguy in disguise." Logical appeals, emotional appeals, personal appeals — *logos, pathos, ethos!* The ideal speaker or speech appeals to all three.

Logical Appeals

How do we appeal to logic and reason? Aristotle asked that question also. He tried to analyze the ways human beings reason, and he expounded on two basic types of logic: *deductive* and *inductive.* Other thinkers have refined and added to Aristotle's work, but these categories remain the two pillars of reasoning.

DEDUCTIVE REASONING
The *syllogism* that began this chapter was a silly try at deductive reasoning. A proper syllogism states a major premise or, as they say in math, a given: "All cats have four legs." Then it states a minor, more specific premise: "Tabby is a cat." From these two statements we can draw the conclusion: "Tabby has four legs." As for the illustration given at the beginning of the chapter, it may be true that a cat named Socrates likes milk, but we cannot conclude that logically from the evidence stated in the major and minor premises.

What about a situation in which we are presented with only one given: "Tabby is a cat"? From that fact we *infer* that Tabby likes milk. What we have done is fill in the missing major premise that "all cats like milk." It was not stated, but experience tells us that cats like milk. We make a leap of logic and fill in the conclusion ourselves. When part of the syllogism is left unstated but strongly implied, the logical form is called, again in ancient Greek, an *enthymeme.* Notice that the enthymeme is not as exact as the syllogism. The major premise of the syllogism must be universal: "*All cats* like milk." In the enthymeme, however, we hedge the bet by saying,"*All the cats that I have known or heard of* like milk." What we really have is an implied *probability* that most or many cats like milk, and Tabby, being a cat, *probably* likes milk too.

Whenever we deal with the future, we deal in probabilities, whether using the syllogism or the enthymeme. We know, for instance, that throughout recorded history the sun has risen every morning. From science and past experience, we can predict that the sun will rise tomorrow morning at a certain time, but because it is in the future there may be some unpredictable phenomenon that will prevent the sunrise. The probability of sunrise seems so strong, however, that most of us will not give it a great deal of thought.

Deductive reasoning always goes from a broad, general statement to a narrow, specific conclusion, as the example went from all cats to one specific cat. Basically there are three variations on the syllogism or enthymeme, which are determined by key words in the major premise. The major premise, whether stated or not, will imply either (1) *all*, (2) *if*, or (3) *either . . . or*. The premise that deals with *all* will define or categorize something; the *if* premise will deal with time or probability; and the *either . . . or* premise will refine and eliminate choices. Here is an example of each kind:

all   All automobiles have four wheels.
            I own an automobile.
            Therefore, my automobile has four wheels.
if   If automobiles have two wheels, they are hard to steer.
            My automobile has two wheels.
            Therefore, it is hard to steer.
either . . . or
            I can travel either by my automobile or my bicycle.
            My automobile does not work.
            Therefore, I travel by bicycle.

Of course, the last category can have more than two factors, such as "I can travel by automobile, bicycle, bus, train, or rocket." The minor premise then could be, "I have no automobile; the bus does not go where I am going; I do not have enough money for the train; and the rocket exploded on the pad." We have eliminated all the choices except the bicycle, therefore, "I travel by bicycle." In this form deductive reasoning seems childish and obvious, but the good speaker will amplify the parts of the deduction and prove their merit and honesty, resulting in a less formulaic and mathematical form.

The following example might be used as a conclusion to summarize points that were amplified and explained in the body of a speech.

Only four forms of energy are economically feasible for our needs in the immediate future: oil, coal, nuclear energy, and solar energy. The supply of oil is rapidly diminishing and the cost continues to soar as we depend more and more on foreign supplies. The pollution that accompanies the burning of coal has far too great a negative impact on our environment. The dangers of nuclear energy far outweigh its advantages. Consequently, we must turn to the virtually infinite supply of clean, nonpolluting sunlight to meet our ever-expanding energy needs.

When you are using deductive reasoning, however, you might reduce it to the formula of the syllogism in order to test the validity of your conclusions. For example, if you are giving a speech advocating the use of nuclear energy, you might develop the following outline for the body:

A. Energy problems
   1. need for energy growing
      a. developing nations
      b. advancing technology
   2. pollution from present sources
   3. fossil fuel running out
B. Nuclear energy
   1. little or no pollution
   2. readily available
C. Conversion imminent

Your outline would be a good deal more detailed. If you examine the simplified outline closely, however, you can express the three main points as a syllogism:

Major premise: We need energy that is clean and plentiful.
Minor premise: Nuclear energy is clean and plentiful.
Conclusion: Therefore, we need to convert to nuclear energy.

If the first part of the outline dealt only with pollution, and the second part only with availability, reducing to the syllogistic form would show the holes in your logic:

We need clean energy.
Nuclear energy is plentiful.
Therefore, we need nuclear energy.

INDUCTIVE REASONING

Inductive reasoning does exactly the opposite of deductive: it starts with specific facts and develops a general premise. We could observe that Tabby, Cicero, Felix, Morris, and hundreds of other cats drink milk with relish, and from that we generalize that cats like milk; perhaps not all cats, since we have not observed all, but certainly many or most. Of course if we happen to live in an "Alice-in-Wonderland" world and observe that Tabby likes hamburgers, Cicero likes eggplant casserole, Felix likes bacon and eggs, and we know what Morris likes, then we cannot draw any logical conclusions about cats, except that their tastes vary.

Inductive reasoning is perhaps even more open for illogical conclusions than deductive. Almost all of us have fallen into the "Uncle Louie" trap of basing a conclusion on one bit of evidence: "My Uncle Louie never uses his seat belt; he was in an accident and came out without a scratch—therefore, we do not need seat belts." The argument neglects thousands of cases and laboratory tests that indicate that seat belts do reduce the probability of injuries and deaths in auto accidents. We do not have a sufficient body of information from which to draw our conclusion, if we only use Uncle Louie's lucky experience.

Any time you present an argument it must take some form that the reader or listener can understand easily. *Argument* here does not mean shouting and disagreeing, but a way of presenting a persuasive, rational appeal. In order for the argument to make sense to the listener, it must progress from one idea to another smoothly. Of course, no one organizational pattern will work all the time, but the methods presented here have been successful in many presentations of arguments.

Educator and philosopher John Dewey outlined five steps we take to solve a problem.*

1. recognizing the problem or need
2. examining and defining the problem
3. searching for new solutions
4. comparing and testing these solutions
5. selecting the best solution

These steps may occur rapidly in an emergency, or slowly, as in an attempt to solve a political or scientific question. A speaker goes through all these steps, but some may get unwieldy for presentation to an audience. Dewey's process describes the way we think through a problem, rather than the way we present the problem and solution to others.

Monroe Motivated Sequence. In an attempt to incorporate some of Dewey's philosophy into a persuasive pattern for speaking, Alan H. Monroe developed the "motivated sequence."** He articulated a five-step sequence for presenting persuasive appeals:

A. Get the attention of the audience.
B. Establish a definite need.
C. Satisfy that need.
D. Give the audience an opportunity to visualize the solution.
E. Suggest action for the audience to take.

A speech that attempts to persuade an audience to stop eating fried foods might follow this sequence:

A. Show pictures of overweight people. (get attention)
B. Use statistical information; cite medical references. (establish need)
C. Discuss elimination of fried foods from the diet; get specific about calories and health. (satisfy need)
D. Describe life without fried foods; give further statistics and citations. (visualize solution)
E. Present substitute diets; ask them to try for a prescribed period of time. (suggest action)

Argument by Generalization. Inductive reasoning in which the conclusion is derived from a body of evidence is called *generalization.* If we examine the biographies of all one hundred United States senators and discover that eighty-six of them are attorneys and the other fourteen from varied professions, we can assume that law is good academic training for a career in the Senate. That is a generalization, not an absolute, because of the other fourteen senators. If the two

---

*See *How We Think* (Lexington, Mass.: Heath, 1933), pp. 71–78, 91–101.
**See *Principles of Speech Communication* (Glenview, Ill.: Scott, Foresman, 1976).

senators from your state were both speech-communication teachers, you might generalize that teaching speech-communication is the best training for Senators. If you come to that conclusion, beware, because a generalization must have sufficient evidence to be valid — otherwise we are back to "Uncle Louie."

Another misuse of generalization is using evidence that is not representative of the larger picture. A baseball coach would be foolish to train players to use Stan Musial's batting stance. Musial was an enormously successful hitter who made the Hall of Fame, but for most people his stance would fail miserably. One can generalize about cats' eating habits from four cats, for instance, if those cats are typical. If they have been exposed only to filet mignon and banana nut ice cream, however, you cannot draw a valid conclusion from them. Generalization obviously is dangerous ground to tread because the sample of evidence must be sufficiently large and sufficiently typical to be valid. We use generalization often, but when using it in a speech, we should examine our "facts" carefully.

A speech advocating legalization of marijuana might include a list of states and communities where it is permitted in controlled amounts. After listing several places, you might continue:

In state after state, in community after community, pot has been legalized in controlled amounts. These communities have had no significant rise in crime rates. They have had no increase in the incidence of mental disorders. Spaced out "Heads" do not wander the streets in dreamlike trances. These communities have experienced none of the horrors that those opposed to legalization claim. If it works in _____, _____, and _____, why should we doubt that it will work right here in _____?

Argument by Analogy.   Another form of inductive reasoning is reasoning by *analogy*. When we use an analogy, we compare two things that are dissimilar but have sufficient commonality for us to draw conclusions. George Santayana's aphorism that "Those who fail to remember history are condemned to repeat it" implies that we should learn about our mistakes through a process of analogy. Many historians have tried to draw analogies between incidents in ancient history and in the contemporary scene, concluding, for example, that the mistakes made by people in the Roman Empire are paralleled in our society; therefore, we will decay and perish just as did the Romans. Problems arise in using analogy when we draw similar conclusions from situations that are too different or when we simply dismiss the factors that are not similar. Without going into the details of Roman history, we can see that circumstances are vastly different today from what they were two thousand years ago. Modern technology in communication, transportation, and other aspects of life indicates that we are so different from Rome that we cannot use the same measures.

Analogy can be a useful reasoning tool, however, when it is used wisely. If you were to show that a community of similar size and with similar problems to yours tackled one of those problems with a particular solution, and then imply that the solution would also work in your community, you would be on safe grounds of *probability*. To assume that solutions to community problems in an isolated farm community of two thousand people would work in a large, metropolitan area would be foolish. There are too many dissimilarities between, for instance, Chicago and Sunbury, Pennsylvania or between Los Angeles and Lytton, Iowa for the analogy to be valid. The speaker must examine the analogy carefully to insure that it is valid.

A speech advocating a return to a strong central family structure might use the following analogy:

For years people have spoken of their "family trees." When Alex Haley wrote about his family origins, he called his book *Roots*. A family is indeed like a tree, growing in many directions, but always connected to a central point. Just as branches cannot live if they are cut off and scattered, so too, the family cannot survive if its branches are cut away from the central trunk or core. To be strong and healthy, the tree must retain its unity even though there is diversity and individuality within that unity. The family too must retain its unity and draw strength from that unity.

Argument by Cause and Effect.   A final type of inductive reasoning is causal reasoning, or drawing a conclusion from a cause-and-effect relationship: "The heavy snows and fierce winds (cause) make driving extremely hazardous (effect)." We can reverse the process and reason from effect to cause: "The rash of accidents on the streets today (effect) was because of a full moon (cause), or because you did not eat all your vegetables for dinner (cause)."

Is Popeye's great strength derived from spinach (cause and effect) or from some other source? Politicians often assign a cause-and-effect relationship when it is not really valid. For instance, the mayor may take credit for having cured a city's problems when he or she had no control over the real cause. The reverse can be claimed in an election: "My opponent has been in office for four years (cause) and look at the mess we are in (effect)."

A speech against the legalization of marijuana might make these cause-and-effect arguments:

Ready availability and over-the-counter sales of marijuana only will lead to greater numbers of users who have greater dependence upon it. People who might not use an illegal substance will experiment with pot, and while disoriented and unable to use proper judgment, they will drive automobiles, further increasing our already horrible death rate. Marijuana affects reproductive organs, and more innocent children will be born with birth defects. Legalization could very well lead to an entire generation of disoriented zombies ready to do the bidding of whatever demagogue or tyrant takes advantage of them.

Personal Appeals

Although it might seem easy to establish your credibility, you should recognize that different factors are involved for different audiences and situations. During the teenage drug crisis of the 1960s, school authorities tried to convince their students to avoid drugs by bringing in speakers. They found that police, pharmacists, and physicians had little effect on the teens, even though their credentials were excellent. The authorities realized a great deal more success when they brought in speakers with another kind of credibility: personal experience. An ex-addict's testimony, in street language, about the horrors and degradation experienced under the influence of drugs had far more impact than the scientific language and physiological facts that the other experts produced. Establishing personal proofs takes four basic forms: *reputation*, *appearance*, *common experience* or *identification*, and *personal merit.*

REPUTATION

A speaker's *reputation* rests on the audience's respect and friendliness. The speaker probably has established some reputation before the speech begins, and the greeting may be friendly or hostile, respectful or disrespectful. Most audiences are friendly, respectful, and supportive of most speakers, at least at the beginning of a speech, unless the speaker has a strong reputation that goes against the audience's attitudes. (A member of the Communist party probably would not be well received by a meeting of the National Association of Manufacturers, and vice versa.) Generally an audience's attitudes range from eager anticipation to polite acceptance. Rarely does an audience become hostile unless the speaker virtually begs for such reaction. Certainly the classroom audience will be friendly — after all, each person is in the same boat that you are.

If you are a college sophomore advocating that the United Nations should take some specific action, you will have to establish your credibility within the speech itself. If, however, you are president of your student body and are speaking about campus problems to townspeople, they probably will acknowledge your expertise before you even begin. If you are talking about valuable stamps and you indicate that you have been collecting stamps for many years and have a collection worth thousands of dollars, you have established your credibility within the context of the speech. Unless your audience already knows about your expertise, you will have to establish it in your speech, pointing out your research, experiences, or other reasons for knowing the subject.

APPEARANCE

One area that every speaker can use to establish personal worth is *appearance*. The speaker always should dress appropriately for the occasion and audience. You would not raise an issue at a student body meeting while wearing a tuxedo or evening gown, nor would you represent your school or church at a public meeting in cut-offs, a grimy sweatshirt, and bare feet. That appearance might be appropriate with some audiences and in some situations, but it would be offensive to a traditional audience.

Cleanliness and neatness do not have to be expensive. *Appropriate* is the key word for the clothes you wear. On the days when you speak in class, you might want to wear something just a little less informal than your ordinary school clothes — something appropriate for a situation in which you want to convince a group of relative strangers that you have something to say and you are someone worth listening to.

IDENTIFICATION

In Chapter 1 we discussed *identification* as a means of facilitating communication. The speaker helps establish identification with an audience by using the personal appeal of *common experience*. Smart politicians attempting to get votes from farmers emphasize their own background on the farm; the ones trying to appeal to blue-collar workers emphasize their days in the mill or factory; and the ones attempting to win city votes describe their background on the streets of the city. Television has somewhat eliminated this approach because everyone sees it simultaneously, although candidates for office also speak to small, select groups.

A good speaker will attempt to establish as many conditions as possible that allow an audience to identify easily. We in the audience want to know that you, the speaker, are one of "us." The "us" may refer to being college students, Americans, parents, sports fans, or any of a variety of labels that we can attach to ourselves. The identification should be in relation to the topic at hand. Some of these factors for identification can be established nonverbally through appearance, age, and attitude. Other factors will have to be established within the verbal context of the speech itself.

EXPERIENCE

Personal experience and reputation might seem contradictory. How can we appeal to common experience and still maintain that we have uncommon knowledge, that we are experts? The subject matter, the speaker, and the situation dictate to a great degree whether personal experience or reputation should be emphasized.

Most of us want our experts to know more than we do. We want our physicians to know more than we do about medicine, but also to understand our fears and anxieties because they too are human. A senator addressing a commencement class may talk about international affairs with great authority, but how much nicer and more human to appeal to our common experience by recalling his own similar school in a similar community, or the jobs he held while working his way through school. We may go to a counselor for advice with a personal problem and find that, while the counselor maintains an objective distance, she can let us know that she too has similar problems or temptations, without going into detail.

The two personal appeals, experience and reputation, actually appeal to different interests: experience helps establish the person as a human being to whom we can relate, whereas reputation establishes the person's credibility for the specific subject. A police officer may tell a partying group that he too likes a good time and remembers the days when he carried on so (personal experience); but now he has to uphold the law, and throwing water out the fourteenth story of the dorm onto the people below is against the law he must uphold (credibility). The officer's uniform will also help establish credibility.

PERSONAL MERIT

The final type of appeal, *personal merit* or worth as an individual, is much less tangible and less easily reduced to a formula. Throughout your speech you will want to show evidence of human characteristics to which people can respond favorably, such as modesty, sense of humor, sincerity, and regard for other people. Even the most serious subject delivered in a somber atmosphere should involve some of these characteristics and personality traits. The successful speaker usually displays them constantly but subtly.

Emotional or Psychological Appeals

Most people today recognize that although human beings respond to reason, we also have other drives that often override logic. The successful speaker appeals to the psychological, as well as rational, needs of the audience.

Various theorists define our needs differently. One psychologist, Abraham Maslow, developed a hierarchy of needs, insisting that the more basic needs must be satisfied before the next needs on the ladder can be considered.* He lists these needs as follows:

1. physiological needs—nourishment, rest, air, sex, and so on
2. safety needs—protection from external dangers
3. love and belonging needs—acceptance by others, a degree of status, approval of actions, and so on
4. esteem needs—feelings of adequacy, security, competence, and self-esteem
5. self-actualization—fulfillment, realization of potential, creativity

Maslow insists that until our physiological needs are satisfied, we cannot consider safety needs; until safety needs are satisfied, we cannot deal with love and belonging; and so on until we are able to extend ourselves to our full potential. For the speaker this concept implies that it is foolish to offer a person abstractions such as freedom, creativity, or education until the person's physiological needs have been satisfied. Seldom will you encounter a communication situation with people who have not satisfied at least their physiological and safety needs, but when you begin to deal in difficult or abstract ideas, you should at least be aware of such needs.

Perhaps a more practical approach is to remember that we all have needs, desires, and dreams. Reasonably well-adjusted college students have *needs* such as food, shelter, and social acceptance. They also may *desire* success, status, and comfort, placing a good education between need and desire. In private moments they may *dream* of being rich, powerful, or famous. Instead of the perfect lover (dream), most of us settle for a warm, responsive human being who shares life's good and difficult times, thereby satisfying our desires.

The speaker should appeal to motives and aspirations that reflect the better side of our Jekyll/Hyde personalities. Rather than appealing to an audience's racial or ethnic prejudices, the speaker should appeal to pride and self-respect; rather than greed, thrift and personal fulfillment. The speaker who incites an audience to riot might be judged a success if the only criterion were effectiveness and a riot was the goal. That same speaker might also be judged unsuccessful and immoral for using talent and ability to a socially unacceptable end. Adolph Hitler, a gifted speaker in a technical, performance sense, is a good example of a speaker who used fine technique toward ignoble and destructive ends.

Some of the motivations that can become effective appeals in a speech are:

1. wealth
2. power
3. conformity
4. pleasure
5. acceptance
6. comfort
7. reassurance
8. attractiveness
9. self-esteem

*See *Motivation and Personality* (New York: Harper & Row, 1954), pp. 80–92.

Each can be approached positively or negatively, for good or for evil. Speakers should use them for good purposes exclusively.

Forms of Support

However you go about appealing to your audience and refuting counter-arguments, you always will need to support what you say. Even the most informative report must persuade listeners to accept the facts and ideas you present by offering supporting information. Reasoning is one vital form of support; statistics and quotations are two others which are discussed separately in Chapter 12. Here are some other forms of support which deserve mention.

EXAMPLES AND ILLUSTRATIONS
Examples and *illustrations* can be excellent ways of supporting arguments. Any generalization depends on a series of examples or illustrations. "How do I know my plan can work? It worked at Scurvy Tech; it worked at Mesmer University; and it worked at Roly Poly. And these are just three examples of schools that have adopted this plan."

ANECDOTES
Abraham Lincoln, as well as many other speakers, was a master at using an *anecdote*, or a short story, to make his point. Often the anecdote is humorous, but it can be serious. Fables such as "The Fox and the Grapes" are fictional anecdotes that illustrate characteristics of human nature. A speaker getting an audience to act on something that they already agree upon, but which they have been lazy or careless about implementing, might tell the story of the poor golfer whose ball landed on an anthill.

He swung away several times, always missing the little white sphere, but each time killing millions of the little creatures. Eventually there were only two ants left. One turned to the other and said, "I guess it's about time we got on the ball."

COMPARISONS AND CONTRASTS
Ideas that have similarities can be *compared*, and the differences *contrasted*. The careful speaker will compare and contrast whenever it leads to clearer understanding of the situation. Analogy, which implies similarities, needs this form of support in order to make complete sense to all listeners.

DEFINITIONS
Definitions may seem unnecessary in a speech to your peers, but they may be vital. In any speech that deals with technical information you must define the technical terms so that everyone will understand them. If the term is peculiar to a certain group or vocation, it must be defined. Can you assume that everyone in your audience will know what *recidivism* means in a speech about prison reforms? How about *gestalt* in a speech about education? The definition of *resistor* may change from a speech about the Viet Nam war to one about radios. As we saw in Chapter 6, you must analyze your audience to determine what expressions you need to define without boring or offending by assuming less knowledge than

they really possess. Generally you will be safe defining technical terms, jargon peculiar to a specific field, or words that refer to other forms of highly specific data.

One of the greatest problems facing our penal system today is *recidivism*, the tendency of some persons who have spent time in prison to fall back into the criminal act-conviction-imprisonment mode of behavior. If our prisons were doing their jobs, persons who served time would be rehabilitated and would not return to their previous lifestyle.

DESCRIPTIONS

Finally any argument will benefit from *description* in vivid, lively language that enables the audience to establish images in their own minds. Being "trapped by a dog" is not nearly so suggestive or provocative to the audience as being "cornered with no means of escape by a huge German shepherd with his fangs bared, a low gutteral growl in his throat, and muscles tensed to spring at me in an instant."

You may have noticed that some of these methods of support overlap or even depend upon one another. An anecdote will profit from lively description. Illustration may be vital to a comparison or contrast. As mentioned before, illustration is important to generalization, and comparison is vital to analogy. Remember that the *form* of support is not as important as *having* support. The main points of your speech must be bolstered and supported by one or more of these methods, as must the important subpoints. All of the forms work together to help the audience understand your contentions and arguments. Without support, all you have is a series of statements that the audience may or may not accept. With support, they have a basis for following and accepting your ideas and conclusions.

TEST YOUR REASONING

In any type of reasoning, we must be certain of our facts and even more certain of the relationship between the facts and the conclusion. To test your reasoning, try to reduce it to its simplest terms, such as one-sentence statements. Then examine it carefully to see whether it really does what you think it does or what you want it to do. Finally, do not overlook contradictory facts simply because they may hurt your argument. Perhaps your argument is not that good and you should reexamine your entire stance on the issue. If your reasoning passes the test, however, use it to persuade your audience.

Refutation

Regardless of the form of argument the speaker uses, there is always the nagging problem of what to do with counter-arguments. Few problems, if any, have solutions that everyone can agree on. What should you do with the counter-arguments? Ignore them? Slide over them? The answer is, deal with them, not only so that the audience can make up their own minds, but also because the audience generally responds more favorably to an argument that faces the counter-arguments fairly rather than to one that ignores them. If you avoid the counter-arguments, the audience may think you fear that the counter-arguments are more acceptable alternatives.

How do you refute opposing arguments? First, acknowledge their existence. The very fact of acknowledging that there are counter-arguments indicates that you are aware and not afraid of them. Merely acknowledging them, however, will not make them go away or prove their lack of relative merit. So when you say, "I know that opponents of this plan will offer such-and-such as an alternative," you had better be prepared to do some counter-attacking of "such-and-such."

QUANTITATIVE REFUTATION

One method of refutation is to show that in one instance the point may be valid, but taken on a larger scale with a larger quantity of data the counter-argument falls apart. Such quantitative reasoning works especially well against the "Uncle Louie" school of thought: "Occasionally a seat belt may be a hindrance but (valid evidence) and (valid evidence) indicate that in *most* automobile accidents the driver and passengers are far more likely to survive if they are wearing belts," or "Occasionally a Truman, Carter, or Reagan becomes President without legal training, but Ford, Nixon, Johnson, Kennedy, Roosevelt, and so on were trained in the law." Quantitative refutation works well also against *either-or* or *all-or-nothing* types of reasoning.

QUALITATIVE REFUTATION

An even better and surer means of refutation comes from checking the quality of your material. If you quote someone, make sure that person is the best possible source for information on that topic. The same is true for statistics. Who took the survey? How valid were the questions? Is there a direct and absolute relationship between the material you are presenting and the plan you are offering? Also, is your information from a reputable, unbiased source? Did the source have an axe to grind or its own interests to serve? Which is the best source for information about the effects of smoking? The tobacco industry? An anti-smoking society? Or a fact-seeking research team from a university or the government?

How recent is your information? A study showing that most blacks in the United States live in the rural South might have been valid in the 1930s or 1940s, but its validity today would be open to serious questioning. Our world is changing rapidly, and today's "truths" may be tomorrow's myths. President Richard Nixon went to the People's Republic of China and opened the way for friendly negotiations with the "Red" Chinese. If you read Nixon's speeches regarding China in the 1950s, however, you will find his attitude changed considerably. Also, not long ago space travel was a fantasy believed only by science-fiction buffs.

Another way you can test the quality of your argument or a counter-argument is by its *relevancy*. Does it relate to what you are talking about? Is a discussion of *inter*collegiate football as played by large universities relevant to a speech about the value of *intra*mural sports? Probably no more than a description of a supersonic transport plane would be to a speech about hang gliding.

Finally you can and should test your arguments and the counter-arguments by closely examining your *reasoning* and the reasoning of others. Use some of the methods described in this chapter to test reasoning. Strip the argument to its essentials and try to phrase it so it fits the structure of a syllogism or some other form. Make it as much like a mathematical problem as you can, or at least reduce it to its simplest, most direct terms.

SUMMARY
AND CONCLUSION

If your speech has met the standards for thinking, if you have presented your material in such a way that it proceeds from one digestible thought to another, and if you have made it relevant to your audience's situation, tackled the counter-argument, and supported your own ideas well, chances are you will convince at least a segment of your audience. Some listeners will shut out the logic and reasoning and insist on sticking with preconceived ideas. You can, however, reach those who have left their minds open, and even open some that are closed. The stronger your support and appeals, the better your chances for convincing your audience.

EXERCISES

1. Prepare a simple outline for a persuasive speech that urges people to write their representatives asking them to support, or defeat, a bill to appropriate money for further space exploration. Use the Monroe Motivated Sequence.
2. Assume that you are preparing a speech contending that athletes today are faster and stronger than they were forty or fifty years ago. What forms of support might be useful?
3. How might you use inductive logic in a speech about inflation?
4. List some ways that you could use rational appeals in a speech about a new form of preventive medicine. How could you establish your credibility? What kinds of motivational appeals might be useful?
5. Reduce arguments favoring a college education to syllogisms.
6. Find some newspaper, magazine, or television advertisements that illustrate the way the appeals of wealth, power, etc., are used to motivate and persuade consumers.

CHAPTER 12

using statistics and citations

1. *How can statistics help me? How can they fool me?*

2. *What do we mean by "average"?*

3. *How can language affect statistical information?*

4. *Can I use statistics to predict the future?*

5. *Does it matter where I get my statistics?*

6. *What are "unrelated variables"?*

7. *In what ways should I treat citations like statistics?*

A recent survey by De Nehoc and Associates indicates that 36.72 percent of the population can be misled easily by statistical data. — *The Monthly Prevaricator*, February 31, 1942.

Benjamin Disraeli, British statesman of the nineteenth century, is credited with the statement, "There are three kinds of lies; lies, damned lies, and statistics." Disraeli was alluding to the ease with which people intentionally or unintentionally twist the truth by using false or misleading statistics. The speaker informing or persuading an audience often finds that statistical references are vital. Disraeli's admonition does not mean we should never use statistics, but that we must be careful and ethical with them. As speakers or as audience members, we all have an obligation to examine statistics cautiously, to ascertain their real meanings, and not to allow them or their users to imply things that are not there.

Statistics, Their Use and Misuse

In order to describe the proper use of statistics, it is necessary to describe some of their improper uses. Do not be tempted to perform "stagic" (statistical magic) because you feel that your arguments are weak and that a little "twisting" is not the same as a lie. Remember, other people also know how statistics work, and if a speaker uses statistics improperly and gets caught, it is squirm and mumble time.

Whenever you hear or read statistics, ask three questions about them: *What do they mean? What is the source? Are they related to the topic?* If they pass those three tests, chances are they are worth noting.

For a starter let us examine the statement used to open this chapter, which referred to the De Nehoc and Associates survey. What does it mean? Probably nothing. It indicates that one-third or more of the population can be misled easily by statistics. One-third of what population? Kansas farmers? Retired actors? Baptists? Ghetto dwellers? Americans of English descent who have tattoos of snakes on their forearms? The statement *implies* that a cross section of people throughout the United States was polled, but it does not say so.

What about the source, "De Nehoc and Associates"? Some of you already have realized that "De Nehoc" spelled backwards is "Ed Cohen," an unimpeachable source whose integrity is beyond question — except to those who know him well. Assuming that there was a February 31 in 1942, how valid today is information gathered then? After all, people have become vastly more sophisticated and attuned to statistics because of the growing use of numbers in modern technology. And what about the source that quotes the statistic? Do you expect the truth in a "magazine" whose title concerns liars?

Assuming that the citation was honest and not the work of a twisted imagination, it would probably score well on the third question, relationship to the topic. Although .333 in baseball is a good batting average, one out of three affirmatives here casts some pretty dark shadows on the statement. Let us take a deeper look at each of the three questions, and discover how each can save us from being fooled.

WHAT DOES THE STATISTIC MEAN?

The Tricky Average.   One term that is bandied about and abused is "average." We constantly hear about the "average American family," the "average college student," the "average wage earner," and forty thousand other "average" somethings. Just what does "average" mean? How is it used and misused?

Let us assume that at Caliban College there are five speech-communication instructors, named A, B, C, D, and E — not very imaginative names, but they will suffice. Let us further assume that their yearly incomes are as follows:

A — $15,000
B —   15,000
C —   17,000
D —   18,000
E —   56,000

We will not question why E's salary is so much higher; perhaps he is the president's son-in-law, or he may have pictures of the Board of Trustees committing unlawful or immoral acts. Instead, let us continue with some hypothetical examples of the *non-average* average.

Problem 1 concerns the efforts of the staff at Caliban to recruit another speech-communication instructor. They have someone specific in mind. The prospect wants to know about the salaries at Caliban, expecting to get a good, healthy income. We want our salary structure to sound as good as possible, so we say, "The average salary of our speech-communication instructors is $24,200 annually."

Problem 2 finds our Board of Trustees receiving a notice that speech-communication instructors make an average of $16,873.52 nationally. They want to make sure that we at Caliban do not pay too much above the national average. We reply, "The average salary of our speech-communication instructors is $17,000."

In Problem 3 the government decides to levy a new tax, which is computed on the basis of the average salary of the people in particular professions at particular locations. We want ours as low as possible, so we have our accountants inform the authorities, "The average salary of our speech-communication instructors is $15,000."

Which questions got the truthful answer? *All three*, depending on how you define "average."

For Problem 1 we wanted as high a figure as we could get without lying. Consequently we figured the *mean* salary, or the arithmetic average: we added all five together and divided by five, E's salary inflating the figure tremendously. Without E's salary, the mean average is $16,250, a $7950 difference. The $24,200 figure is a valid average, a mean, of the numbers involved.

To answer Problem 2, however, we wanted to show that we are pretty close to the reported national average (whatever that means). Where did we get the $17,000 figure? Simple! We used the *median* or middle figure. That is, half of the people make more than $17,000 and half make less, and E's salary does not inflate the average as much. Indeed, all the figure says is that half of the instructors make between $17,001 and infinity. Since our figure is only $126.48 off the national average as reported by the Board, we look pretty good.

For Problem 3 we wanted the lowest number possible, because the higher the average, the more tax we have to pay. So we used the *mode*, or the number that appears most frequently. Because two of the five make $15,000, that is the modal average.

Which one is correct? All three. All three figures can be defined as the "average," yet there is almost $10,000 difference among them. Which should you as a speaker use? *No, not the one that makes your point best.* You should make clear which kind of average you are using. Usually we assume the *mean* when we say or hear "average," but not always. The numbers were all correct, but the words that accompanied them were deceptive.

Fill in the Empty Spaces.   In the problems above we could have said, "*Only* four people on the staff make less than $56,000." Or we could have said, "Twenty percent of the instructors make $56,000," or "Forty percent make only $15,000." Each of those statements implies a statistical wonder that may not really be representative. Suppose Caliban College really existed, and that it were representative of colleges throughout the United States. Could we say that 20 percent of speech-communication instructors make $56,000 per year? The field would be inundated with applicants trying to make that princely — by college standards — salary. Obviously we have based our conclusion on too small a sample; we have, in other words, reached a conclusion without sufficient evidence.

Insufficient evidence or sampling occurs with statistics other than averages also. Poll-takers frequently report their findings neglecting to note that the sampling is biased or has a special interest. A respondent usually has an interest in a subject when replying to a general or unspecific request for responses. Most of us tend to respond to a survey done in person with what we *think* the person wants to hear.

Survey Taker: Professor Intellect, would you rather read a good book or watch football on television?

Professor I.:   Oh, no question, I'd rather read a good book.

Maybe that is an honest response, but you had better not phone most professors on Super Bowl Sunday. If asked how often we bathe, brush our teeth, or perform some other act that is considered socially desirable, most of us might "fudge" the answer a bit to seem more clean or moral. When the results of the poll are announced, however, we are impressed with what clean, moral, and all-around good people our fellow citizens are. If the survey is sponsored by a company selling toothpaste, you can bet they are depending on you and me to buy more toothpaste because "86.4 percent of Americans brush their teeth twelve times daily," and no one wants to be the smelly offender.

That same toothpaste company might tell us about their toothpaste that results in fewer cavities. "With Shinem cavities are reduced 45.3 percent." The ad generally includes the note that an "independent research organization" conducted the tests. What they may be saying is that 45.3 percent of *one* test group had fewer cavities than the average, but remember that 49.9 percent will have fewer than average, and 49.9 percent will have more. The company may have taken three groups and reported on the one that beat the average. Of course, if you write to the "independent research organization," they will send you the complete test results—ever know anyone who wrote? Why did they not report on the test group that had more than its share of cavities? Obviously that will not sell Shinem. So in addition to too small a sampling, we also have to beware of a *biased sampling* and perhaps the existence of more than one sample.

Another problem with undisclosed information is altering the method used to obtain the result. We read today about alarming leaps in the crime rate, but years ago, in the days of the "cop on the beat," a good portion of neighborhood crime was not reported. Today small crimes may be reported that would have been handled without formal arrest in years gone by. The same is true of diseases. Every year we hear of flu epidemics. Could it be that we now have better methods of diagnosing and reporting such disease? Not too many years ago influenza, or flu, was a frightening, deadly disease. When people had bad colds and were forced to miss work or school, they said that they had "the grippe." Today we call in with "flu." When was the last time you heard of someone having "grippe"? You should not conclude that statistics regarding health are never valid, but you must examine the implied information, the "empty spaces."

"Of the people taking Cureall, 89.6 percent felt better after only four days." Let us imagine that the ad goes on to say that Cureall was given to a large sampling of people and gives us actual numbers of those who claimed they felt better. Where is the catch? Simple, was there a *control group?* Most people will respond on a short-term basis to suggestion. "Take this Cureall; it will make you feel more alive and energetic." So 100,000 people take it and 89,600 report feeling better. If you have a control group that is given the same information and a *placebo,* a sugar-coated pill that has no effect chemically, and still vastly more people respond to Cureall, then it is probably a good medicine. Without a control group, however, forget it. The power of suggestion can be overwhelming, at least on a short-term basis.

If statistics were thrown out of advertising and government reports, newspapers and magazines would shrink by exactly 56.74 percent, and television would program for 3.782 hours per day. (Notice that almost all statistics have a decimal point in them. After all, 50 percent or any round number sounds like an imprecise guess, but 49.987 percent. . . . There is a number with tons of credibility.) After the devastating winter of 1977–1978, a government source announced that there were 116.4 million potholes in the United States. The number (notice the convenient decimal point) was derived from the amount of asphalt that had been ordered by state highway departments. Because 18.2 potholes can be filled with one ton of asphalt and 6.4 million tons of asphalt were ordered, the obvious, exact, unchallengeable number of potholes in the United States *became* 116.4 million. (My pocket calculator came up with 116.48 million, but that would entail rounding off to .5, and that does not sound nearly as precise as .4.) Of course, the study neglected to take into account that some states fill their holes more than others; some have a surplus of highway funds, so they order asphalt for the next year also; some have a deficit, so they are using last year's supply; some were hit harder than others; all roads are not constructed the same way; and one state may have fewer holes per mile or smaller holes. Finally, some representatives let it be known that federal money might be available for pothole-filling, and naturally everybody suddenly needed tons of asphalt. But a federal agency said categorically that there were 116.4 million, and you can be sure that number has become official and irrefutable. (Lest you think that these figures, like some of the others, are products of the author's imagination, this information was gleaned from the Sunday, February 26, 1978 issue of the *Chicago Tribune*, Section 1, page 29. Incidentally, the article also pointed out that the only people in Congress who opposed the bill to allocate money for "pothole relief" were representatives from states where winters were mild and potholes were not a problem.)

Beware of Dangerous Language. When dealing with statistics, we must be careful of the language we use as well as the numbers. Too often there is a tendency to confuse such terms as "average" and "normal." Often "normal" is defined by an average, as with intelligence quotient or IQ. The average IQ is 100 by definition. That is, 100 is average because whatever the average is will arbitrarily be assigned the number 100. If we then call an IQ of 100 normal, does that make someone with an IQ of 97 subnormal? The normal, or average, *range* of IQ is actually 90 to 110. Unfortunately, many people assume that any person who has an IQ measurement below average is subnormal. In doing so, they have put a value judgment on *normal* that may not be valid.

Too often we assume that "normal" equals "desirable." It may be, but not always. For a person with a slower than average pulse rate to try to speed it up to the "normal" seventy-two beats per minute would be absurd and possibly harmful. Some people have slower pulse rates than others, and "normal" is determined only by the usual or average. (In fact a good many long-distance runners have slower than average pulse rates.) Many people consider being called "average" somewhat insulting, but most would agree that "normal" is something to strive for.

The way you phrase your statistical references also can affect the impression you leave with your audience. Assume that you take a survey that indicates that 60 percent — you would probably say "59.8 percent" — of the population brushes their teeth four times a day. When you report these "facts," you may imply that such a practice is healthy, promotes strong teeth, and makes one more appealing. In essence you have defined the 60 percent as the "good guys," which leaves the remaining 40 percent, almost half the population, as "bad guys." The speaker has made a judgment by going from fact to value in one quick step.

As an example of how language can distort facts, let us take a story about two fifteen-year-old boys who are always in competition, Adam and Bob. They decide to have a 100-meter race. At the start Bob slips and loses about 2 meters that he never makes up, and the boys run even the rest of the way with Adam winning by two steps. That night they tell their fathers about the big race, and the fathers ask them to describe it. Their answers are as follows:

Adam: Well, I jumped out to a big lead, easily outdistancing the rest of the field. The only real competition I had came from Bob, but I simply outran the entire group. Bob finished second, yards behind me.

Bob: I should have won. Only one person finished ahead of me, and that was Adam. I would have beaten him too if I hadn't slipped. As it was, I almost nipped him. He just beat me by inches.

Both of the young men tell the truth, but each makes himself seem faster, and each makes the story more dramatic for himself. Two meters can be described as "yards"; after all, 2 meters equal 2 yards 7 inches. Two meters can also be described as "inches," about eighty. Be fair in your language, and do not mislead by connotation.

The Cloudy Crystal Ball.   As our society becomes more complex and our problems more difficult, we tend to rely more on statistics than crystal balls or tea leaves for telling the future. We take current trends and project them into the distant future prophetically describing what that future will be like. The prophecies are usually fraught with doom and gloom, and we can only be happy that cave dwellers did not have computers, or they would have predicted us out of existence by 11,000 B.C. We all have heard predictions such as, "By the year 3257 (again no round numbers) there will be 17.26 people per square foot of land area on the entire earth." Sounds cozy, anyway!

As speakers we must be careful about predicting too far into the future. Colleges and universities erected classrooms, offices, and dormitories like mad during the 1960s and early 1970s, secure in the knowledge that growth would continue, or at the worst level off. Came the middle-to-late 1970s and ouch!: empty dorms, empty classrooms, and empty statistics. Of course there were statisticians who had predicted the decline in college enrollment and who, perhaps rightfully, became smug. Often they went on to paint an even bleaker picture for schools during the final fifth of the century, neglecting the attempts being made to broaden offerings and to appeal to a wider segment of the population. That is where the rub comes in — circumstances change, and often there are factors our statistical crystal balls cannot predict or even suspect.

Just a few years ago people predicted that computers would become the size of houses and even larger. Then along came transistors, and computers shrank drastically. They still had to be large to accommodate the data for massive governmental records or space explorations, but then came microcircuits and the prediction that soon there will be a computer in every home.

It is possible to give statistical information that is valid and up to date, and to do short-range planning and predicting with the use of good statistical information, but when we start predicting decades and centuries into the future, beware. When we review the massive technological leaps that we have taken in the past century, we get some idea of how rapidly the world can change and how unpredictable factors can alter our lives. If someone in my high school graduation class of 1949 had predicted that within twenty years men would walk on the moon, that fortune teller probably would have been laughed at or locked up. If you have valid, reputable statistics that lend themselves to predictions, use them, but you will be wise to confine your predictions to a short-term basis.

In 1954, Darrell Huff and Irving Geis wrote *How to Lie with Statistics*, a delightful and amusing review of some of the statistical errors that we make and perpetuate.* It goes into much more depth than we can in this one chapter, much of which is inspired by that book. In their final chapter, Huff and Geis describe the folly of predicting with statistics.

The number of (television) sets in American homes increased around 10,000 percent from 1947 to 1952. Project this for the next five years and you find that there'll soon be a couple billion of the things. Heaven forbid, or forty sets per family. (p. 140)

They go on to describe some predictions about the population of the United States.

As late as 1938 a presidential commission loaded with experts doubted that the U.S. population would ever reach 140 million; it was 12 million more just twelve years later. There are textbooks published so recently that they are still in college use [1954] that predict a peak population of not more than 150 million and figure it will take until about 1980 to reach it. These fearful underestimates came from assuming that a trend would continue without change. A similar assumption a century ago did as badly in the opposite direction because it assumed continuation of the population-increase rate of 1790 to 1860. In his second message to Congress, Abraham Lincoln predicted the U.S. population would reach 251,689,914 in 1930. (pp. 140–142)

WHAT IS THE SOURCE?
The source of your statistics must be subjected to careful scrutiny in order to establish the data's relative worth. When the Painfree Aspirin Company runs a survey or another kind of study, you can be fairly sure that the results announced to the public will be complimentary and suggest that we all run out and buy carloads of Painfree. Speedee Motors statistics will undoubtedly be favorable to Speedee automobiles. We must always question carefully what axe the company has to grind, or what product they had to sell, although a survey by an interested company is not necessarily invalid.

We can profitably ask the six basic questions that journalists ask: who, what where, when, why, and how.

Who collected the data and *why*? Did that person or organization have some vested interest in the data? Was the information arrived at by a disinterested per-

*Darrell Huff and Irving Geis, *How to Lie with Statistics* (New York: Norton, 1954).

son or group, or by people trying to prove a self-serving point? Not only industry is guilty of conflict of interest in gathering data. Sometimes in the academic world, researchers will skew their data to "prove" the point of view they had before the data were collected. Often we cannot know whether there was self-interest or whether the information was collected objectively. Often government and academic reports have more credibility than others, but examine them carefully.

What was the purpose of the study or information gathering; that is, *why* was it undertaken? Was the information gathered to prove a point, or was it gathered to find out basic knowledge and improve understanding of an issue?

When were the data collected? In an age in which technology moves by quantum leaps, data that are not current become virtually worthless. Figures dealing with finances, population, medicine, and a thousand other subjects become obsolete after a year or so. My first full-time teaching salary in 1957 was $4450 per year, then a fairly good starting salary on a national basis. At that time $10,000 per year was considered a fine income, and $25,000 a year qualified one for the aristocracy. Today $4450 is below the established poverty level, and $25,000 is within the reach of many workers in unskilled or semi-skilled occupations. Even the time of the year can be a factor. What is the most popular sport in the United States? Chances are you will arrive at different figures on that one if you survey the population in mid-October at World Series time or in January at the time of the Super Bowl.

Where were the data gathered? In Minnesota hockey will probably score a lot better than it will in California or Florida, while surfing will not go over so big in Kansas or Nebraska. In order to get a valid answer to a national question, it would have to be asked throughout the country, not in one or two regions. The study must represent the cross section that it purports to.

Most of the statistical information available to you has not one, but two sources. There is the agency or organization that produced the data, such as the Department of Commerce. Probably, however, you will find the data reported in a newspaper, magazine, or other secondary source. In that case, you are wise to question not only the primary source, but also the reporting source. An uninvolved government agency may make a report containing information that can be used profitably by both sides of an issue. A periodical that depends on revenue from, for instance, automobile manufacturers may slant the information to be more favorable to the industry. An environmental group may take the same report and find statistics that condemn the same industry. We therefore must ask the same questions about the reporter that we ask about the originating source: who, what, where, when, why, and how. More importantly, what is the *reputation* of each source? Political considerations, religious affiliations, special interests, and that old devil money can each affect the objectivity with which statistics are reported. Be careful!

IS THE STATISTIC RELATED TO THE TOPIC?

In *How to Lie with Statistics*, Huff and Geis report a study that linked smoking with low grades in college. Although the study is now dated, as an example it is still valid. Let us assume that we can demonstrate a definite correlation between smoking and low grades. The immediate conclusion seems to be "give up smoking and your grades will improve." The implication is that smoking is the *cause* and low grades are the *effect*. Inveterate smokers immediately see that the cause and effect may be reversed here; low grades, and the depression that goes with them, may cause students to smoke. Now smoking is the *effect* and low grades the *cause*. Huff and Geis go on to say:

It seems a good deal more probable, however, that neither of these things has produced the other, but both are a product of some third factor. Can it be that a sociable sort of fellow who takes his books less than seriously is also likely to smoke more? Or is there a clue in the fact that somebody once established a correlation between extroversion and low grades—a closer relationship apparently than the one between grades and intelligence? Maybe extroverts smoke more than introverts. The point is that when there are many reasonable explanations you are hardly entitled to pick one that suits your taste and insist on it. But many people do. (pp. 87–89)

Let us hope that none of the speakers that you come in contact with resort to such foul play, intentionally or unintentionally. We cannot assume a cause-and-effect relationship unless that relationship is demonstrated, not just hinted at and suited to our particular philosophy. Look for the *unrelated variables;* they may be even more important.

During an election campaign in the 1960s, a major political figure was speaking against a proposed job corps project for unemployed young men. Spouting millions and billions of dollars as well as percentages of percentages, he "proved" that it would cost more to put a young man through the job corps program than it would cost to send him to Harvard for a year. "What does sending a man to Harvard have to do with the job corps?" you may ask. The answer is, not much.

Again there were variables in the formula that did not belong there. The government not only would have to feed and clothe the men in the program, but it also would have to purchase land, build housing, supply machinery, supervise and teach new skills, and train the supervisors and teachers. When broken down to a per capita basis for the first year, the numbers legitimately indicated a cost higher than Harvard tuition. Harvard, however, uses centuries-old buildings, and many of their costs were absorbed over a 200-year period, rather than one year. In addition tuition only represents part of the cost to educate a student. The university is heavily endowed by contributions from alumni, industry, and other interested parties. On the surface the politician had a convincing argument, but when examined carefully, it fell apart. Because of the totally different bases for establishing costs, its relationship to the topic was of no consequence whatsoever.

Another example of unrelated variables appears in connecting a college education and earning ability. For years the most vocal argument for attending college was that college graduates make substantially more money than nongraduates. People assumed that going to college was the cause and higher salary was the effect. In recent years, however, the difference between graduates' and nongraduates' incomes has eroded until there is almost none. Why is the difference no longer valid? Perhaps there were other factors that did not appear on the surface. Until the most recent decades, college students came from basically two types of people: the extra-intelligent and the extra-wealthy. Could it be that the extra-intelligent would succeed and make more than average persons, whether or not they attended college? Could it be that the extra-wealthy who had been brought up in a business world and inherited the family businesses would have had a greater income whether or not they attended college? Recent developments in which people of less affluence and less than superior intelligence have attended college seem to bear out the analysis. An average person with a college degree is still an average person, and an above average person with a degree is still above average. Although the degree will present more opportunities to either person, earning power is up to the individual. Fortunately, there are a good many reasons for attending college: unfortunately, we do not hear about them as much.

The point remains, you should examine the facts closely in order to determine three major points about the statistics you send or receive:

1. What does it mean?
2. What is the source?
3. Is it related to the topic?

Graphs, Charts, and Other Statistical Tools

As soon as you present a series of statistics to your audience, expect them to get confused. Most people have a hard time absorbing a battery of numbers, percentages, dollars, and milliliters. As a rule of thumb, whenever you quote more than three statistics, plan to use some sort of visual aid to help your audience understand the numbers and their significance. Graphs, charts, maps, and other tools can make clear a statistic that might be lost without the visual help.

Assume that you are a radical speaker who wishes to illustrate the plight of the worker. Your startling statement might read: "Half of All Workers Earn Below Average Pay!!" That is not really so startling, because if less than half earned below that figure, it would not be the average, or at least not the mean. If you also wish to illustrate dramatically the full implication of this rather undramatic figure, you might decide to use a map. In order to underscore the *half* who are underpaid, you show a map of the forty-eight contiguous states and *half* of them represent the underpaid half of the workers. Naturally you want the chart to show off your point of view, so you block out twenty-four Western states to represent the underpaid, and you use a different color to represent the other half, using the twenty-four Eastern states. Your maps therefore look like this:

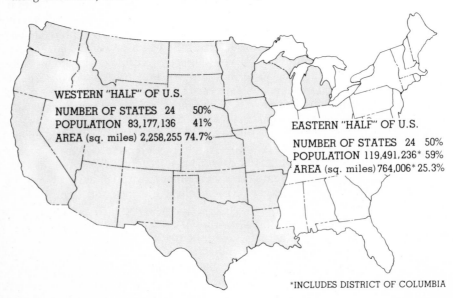

WESTERN "HALF" OF U.S.

NUMBER OF STATES   24   50%
POPULATION   83,177,136   41%
AREA (sq. miles) 2,258,255 74.7%

EASTERN "HALF" OF U.S.

NUMBER OF STATES   24   50%
POPULATION 119,491,236* 59%
AREA (sq. miles) 764,006* 25.3%

*INCLUDES DISTRICT OF COLUMBIA

Of course the Western states represent two to three times the area of the Eastern.

You could show something similar using a map of Europe to dramatically point to the size and strength of the Communist bloc of countries as opposed to the so-called "Western" and independent countries. Because of the size of the U.S.S.R., the "Red" block will appear much larger than the "Free."

Another unplanned abuse can easily occur when you use a graph that gives a false or more dramatic impression just by the way it is composed. Let us assume that E. N. C. Corporation has had the following sales record for the past five years:

year 1 — $8.5 million
year 2 —   8.7 million
year 3 —   8.9 million
year 4 —   9.3 million
year 5 —   9.6 million

An honest bar graph might show the figures thus:

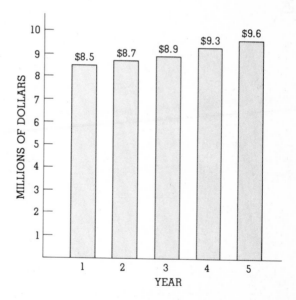

A bar graph showing sales of the E. N. C. Corporation. It appears steady but unspectacular.

That chart shows a steady but unspectacular growth pattern. To impress the board of directors with a dramatic change, however, we can use the same figures and make the graph like the one on the top of page 136, starting with $8,000,000 as the base. The same numbers are represented, but the impression is much more dramatic.

Another abuse of statistics in visual aids can be found in the two-dimensional figure. We want to show how the purchasing power of the dollar has diminished. We discover that just seven years ago ten dollars would buy exactly twice as many

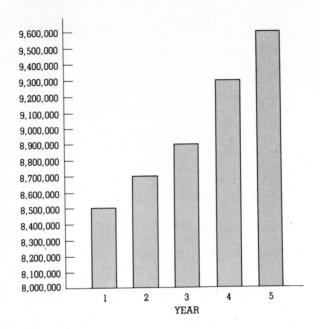

A bar graph showing sales of the E. N. C. Corporation. It appears steady and spectacular.

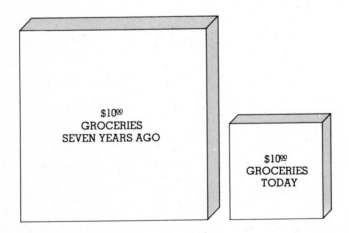

The box at left is actually four times as large as the box on the right. The left box is twice as wide but it is also twice as high. If the third dimension, depth, were in perspective, the box would be eight times as large (2 × 2 × 2 = 8).

groceries as it does today. So we show an illustration of a box of groceries representing what ten dollars buys today. We put that on the right. On the left we show that box of groceries representing what ten dollars would buy seven years ago. (See page 136, bottom.)

Notice that the box on the left represents *twice* the groceries, so we made it twice as big, right? Wrong! True, the left box is twice as high as the box on the right, but it is also twice as wide. Consequently the box on the left actually has *four* times the volume of the one on the right. Again the picture gives a mistaken impression that no honest speaker would want to make.

Although you may not see these abuses of visual aids in your own speeches or in your classmates', you just may find them in advertising campaigns in television, magazines, and newspapers. Look for them, and examine the text carefully. What does the map really mean? Is the graph giving an impression that it should not? Does the figure really represent what it alleges? More important, keep your statistics and visual representations simple. Statistics can be a vital tool for the speaker, but you must treat them as tools: handle them with care and use them for their intended purpose.

Quotations and Citations

Quoting from expert sources can be as powerful a form of evidence as statistics, sometimes even more powerful because of its authoritarian nature. Many of the same problems face the speaker with quotations as with statistics, but because quotations are in the more common language of words, rather than numbers, people are not quite so easily fooled. The speaker must always be on guard not to use them dishonestly and not to impress an audience with source rather than substance. Careful, conscientious speakers examine quotations the same way they examine statistics. The three basic questions comprise a good starting point: *What does it mean? Is it related to the topic? What is the source?* These questions take different forms with verbal citations.

The single most important question both in preparing and in presenting the quotation is "Who said it?" Too often speakers rely on a quotation from a famous person to carry their argument, even when the person is not a good source. There is no denying that the more famous and expert the person is in the field, the more value can be placed on the words. One can gain credibility through experience, study, or a combination of both. An attorney who is an expert on constitutional law is a better source than a trial lawyer if the topic under consideration involves some fine point of constitutional interpretation. If, however, the topic concerns the ability to appeal to an audience of jurors, probably the trial lawyer would be a better source. Quoting from a speech by the Secretary of State may carry a great deal of weight in a speech about foreign policy, but the Secretary's opinion of which team will win the World Series is worth no more than yours or mine. On the other hand a major league ballplayer has little credibility on foreign policy. A person's expertise must be in the sector of life that is under discussion. If there is an unusual circumstance, then you must establish it in the context of the speech, explaining for example that this particular athlete is a Rhodes scholar and an expert on economics.

Although it is vitally important to cite sources, beware of an *appeal to author-*

ity. The fact that some guru favors a course of action may or may not be pertinent. The guru's logic, as exhibited in the quotation, should receive the real emphasis. The words must speak for themselves; they, not the source, form the core and substance of the argument.

You also must examine the quotation to see how pertinent it is. Has the material been outdated? Has the person's point of view changed? Has new evidence been found that negates old ideas? President Richard M. Nixon opened diplomatic relations with the People's Republic of China in the early 1970s, yet during the mid-1950s college debaters quoted then Vice-President Nixon extensively when they argued that "Red China" should not be admitted to the United Nations. Situations change. Conditions change. People change. For some speeches and for some arguments a speaker can legitimately quote sources from centuries past; for some topics a year-old quote is ancient history and obsolete. Examine the quote to see when it was given, where and under what conditions it was given, and whether the situation has changed since.

Speakers must always take full responsibility for quoting in *context.* Taking a statement out of context, thereby altering its meaning, is perhaps the most dishonest step a speaker can take. Suppose someone spends fifteen minutes condemning a murder as vicious, immoral, and unacceptable, but in one spot he adds "I can understand why such a person would act that way." The next day the headline in the *Daily Twister* reads: "So-and-So Sympathizes with Murderer: Says 'I Can Understand Why He Did It.'" If that sounds far-fetched and one more example of the author's capricious imagination, listen to political speakers carefully and read newspaper accounts carefully. You may find it is not that far-fetched after all.

Often we say things ironically, with the tone of voice indicating a meaning exactly the opposite of the words; the adolescent boy says about a girl he hates, "Oh, I love her," or the superconfident boxer says, "I'm scared to death of him." When translated to paper, however, those comments may lose their sense of irony, and the entire context is therefore changed. You owe it to the original source to determine whether your interpretation is indicative of the real sense of the quotation, and whether it is a sincere reflection of the person's ideas. People often have said that one can prove any side of any issue by quoting the Bible or Shakespeare. What they mean is that taking words *out of context,* we can prove what we will.

Just as with statistics, you must be careful of the secondary source of your material. How reliable is the newspaper or magazine that prints the quote? What is its reputation? In what context was the person quoted? A secondary source that has an axe to grind may "accidentally" quote out of context or even misquote. You may not be able to compare several sources in order to establish the reliability of one quotation, but you should make an effort to evaluate the secondary sources and, where possible, go to an original source.

Finally, whenever you quote a person or statistic, you should be sure to give a citation that includes all the necessary and pertinent information and details. Simply to say that "Herman Hogwash says . . ." is not enough. Say *"The Journal of American Bunk* quotes Herman Hogwash in an address to the Association for Retired Preadolescents at Munster, Indiana, in February of 1999 as saying. . . ." If you think enough of old Herman's opinion and his words to want to quote them, give him credit with a complete citation. It is the proper thing to do, and it will increase your credibility and the credibility of your argument.

SUMMARY
AND CONCLUSION

Statistics and quotes from authorities can help you by substantiating the points made in the body of your speech. You must present them fully and honestly. Both can become tools of misdirection when used improperly, and both call for realistic, honest interpretation on your part. You have a moral responsibility to use them fairly and to credit their sources. Whether you use statistical or verbal quotations, ask the following questions:

1. What does it mean?
2. How is it related to the topic?
3. What is the source?

Under the third category you should examine who said it, in what context, when, where, and why. If the answers to these questions show the usefulness of the source, bear out the relationship to the topic, and establish the meaning fully, then by all means use the material, giving full credit where it is due.

EXERCISES

1. Using your library resources, find some statistics relevant to a speech about the price of gold. Prepare a simple visual aid that helps to communicate the information.
2. Get two quotations from conservative politicians about a national program for health insurance. Also get quotes from two liberal politicians, two medical people, and two insurance executives on the same subject. How could you incorporate all these views into an *informative* speech on the subject?
3. Select one common stock and prepare a visual aid showing the monthly fluctuations for one year. (Simply select a date, such as the fifteenth of the month, and use back issues of newspapers for information. Your instructor or a librarian can help you read and interpret the information.)
4. Prepare a visual aid to show how Earned Run Averages or some other sports statistics are computed and what the statistics mean.
5. Choose one topic, such as space exploration, social security, or energy conservation, and find quotations from three United States presidents about the subject. (This exercise is not difficult once you know where to look. Start with *The Reader's Guide to Periodical Literature* in your library.)

CHAPTER 13

using visual and aural aids

1. Why are visual aids important to my speech?
2. Can I appeal to senses other than sight?
3. What types of aids are available to me?
4. What equipment can help me with audiovisual aids?
5. How can I use visual aids most effectively?
6. Where can I find visual aids?

Words, words, words, I am so sick of words.
I get words all day through,
First from him, now from you.
Is that all you blighters can do? . . .

Sing me no songs. Read me no rhymes.
Don't waste my time.
SHOW ME.
Don't talk of June. Don't talk of fall.
Don't talk at all.
SHOW ME.

> Alan Jay Lerner — *My Fair Lady*

Appealing to the Senses

We constantly receive information about the world about us through our senses. Our brains interpret the sensory information they receive, expressing the responses through verbal referents such as *hurt, smooth, sweet, large, small, blue* or an almost infinite variety of other words and phrases.

Unless we have severe visual problems, we receive most of our information through our sense of sight. Although human eyesight is not as keen as that of some animals, especially birds, we center much of our activity around our ability to see. Close in importance is our sense of hearing, *aural* impressions. Our hearing cannot compare to a dog's, for instance, but still we gain much information this way. Our sense of smell stinks (pardon the pun) beside a dog's, and a fish is many times more sensitive to motion and touch than are we. We receive information visually from stars and planets millions and even billions of miles away and from objects only inches from our eyes. Depending on the intensity, we can hear sounds generated hundreds of miles away, but we are usually restricted to our immediate environment for sound. We have tactile responses only to things that actually touch us. Odors and tastes also must invade our immediate territory.

The stimuli that cause the most profound responses, however, are composed of two or more sensations linked together. A chef tries to make food visually attractive, as well as tasty. A breeze bearing natural, woodsy smells may feel better than a breeze carrying polluted, industrial odors. We see a beautiful piece of carved wood or woven fabric, and we want to feel the texture. Automobile dealers want us not only to see the visual beauty of their products, but also to hear the solid, comfortable "thunk" the door makes when it closes.

VISUAL AIDS

Speakers are limited in the way they can appeal to an audience's senses. The audience hears a verbal message. There is some nonverbal visual stimulation from facial expression and gestures and some aural stimulation through vocal inflection and variety. These nonverbal stimuli reinforce rather than offer new information. To reinforce the message further, add selected information, and appeal more widely to the senses, speakers often use devices. Although these aids may appeal to any of the senses, most often they are sight-oriented *visual aids.*

You may not realize how many visual aids surround you. Chances are the classroom in which you deliver speeches has chalkboards. There may be pictures on the walls depicting a foreign country if foreign language and culture classes meet in the room. The colors of classroom walls often are chosen for their tranquil, unobtrusive effect. Maps, charts, graphs, photographs, drawings, and models all aid in the communication of information.

NONVISUAL AIDS

Occasionally aids appeal to senses other than sight. For instance, a speech about metals might be enhanced by allowing the audience, assuming that it is small enough, to feel the comparative weights of equal volumes of lead and aluminum. We all enjoy feeling the texture of smooth objects, and you could easily demonstrate wood before and after sanding to get a smooth finish on a piece of furniture. Softness and temperature also might warrant an appeal to our sense of touch.

Several times I have had students demonstrate baking or other cooking techniques in class. To stimulate the sense of taste, like touch, the object must be within reach of the taster. However, there can be danger in tasting unknown objects or concoctions. Although taste and smell are utilized less than touch, the wise speaker will appeal to these senses also when it is appropriate and valuable.

What Visual Aids Do

A most important rule of thumb for visual aids is: "If they help the audience understand the speech, they are good; if they hinder understanding, they are bad." In any case they will (1) reinforce the verbal message; (2) stimulate or renew interest; and (3) illustrate factors that are difficult to visualize or imagine, or that are beyond the experience of the audience.

Visual aids reinforce the verbal message. Facial expression, hand gestures, and body position are visual aids in that sense, and they should work hand in hand with the verbal message. A visual aid that calls attention to itself and takes attention away from the speaker and speech is not good, or the speaker has used it improperly. Suppose you are giving a speech about your city, and you have a large aerial photograph to augment the speech. If the photograph is on display through the entire speech, audience members may look for familiar landmarks, such as their own homes, or cars in the parking lot. While you are discussing your city government, the audience may be engrossed in the photo; you lose their interest and thereby fail to convey all or part of your message. The clever speaker anticipates such distraction and keeps the visual aid covered until the proper time, then points out the features that are appropriate for the speech and covers it again. That way the aid is used to reinforce, not compete with the message. Charts and graphs in particular can help reinforce the message, but virtually any visual aid should serve that function.

Properly used aids stimulate interest in a positive, sound manner. Pictures of ruins or art might stimulate interest in an historical topic. A picture of the "Winged Victory of Samothrace" sculpture might stimulate interest in a speech about ancient Greece, Greek art, sculpture, the Louvre (where it is housed), or mythology. Maps also stimulate interest and reinforce the message in the history or geography classroom. An old sepia photograph of your grandparents might arouse interest in a speech about your family, life fifty years ago, immigrants, or other topics dealing with your family or the bygone age.

A good visual aid can also stimulate interest in what will be. When the Boeing 747 jetliners were about to appear, a student brought in silhouettes of the then popular 707, a well-known airplane, and the soon-to-be-seen 747, an unknown. The classroom audience was impressed by seeing the size differences, as well as hearing the numbers involved in the specifications. Advertisements that show you "what you can look like" stimulate interest in what will be. You could begin a speech about the craft of macramé either by showing the raw rope or hemp used by the artist, or by showing a completed work and then going over the steps involved in reaching that point. The second introduction is an example of showing what will be.

If you have never worked on an automobile, can you imagine what a carburetor or needle valve looks like? If you have never worked in a theatrical production, would you be likely to know where "up right" is? The speaker who wants to talk about a carburetor should let the audience see one, or a model or diagram, in order to understand what a needle valve is and where it goes. A speaker talking about theater could show a model of a stage, draw a diagram on the chalkboard, or use the room to draw an analogy with the stage.

Often one visual aid accomplishes two or even three purposes. The silhouettes of the airplanes could reinforce the verbal message, stimulate audience interest, and help the audience visualize something beyond their experience. Usually, however, the visual aid has one primary purpose, and the other effects are simply added value.

Virtually any speech will profit from good use of visual aids. There may be exceptions, but the wise speaker examines every speech closely to see where aids might be used. A demonstration speech almost demands a visual aid, whether it is concerned with explaining carburetors, baking cookies, or giving baseball signals. The machine itself, a sample of the finished product, or someone actually demonstrating a procedure constitutes a visual aid. If the object is too large or unavailable, a photograph, scale model, or drawing will suffice. It would be difficult to get a 747 into most classrooms, but a scale model or a silhouette presents no problem.

Any speech that involves statistics or lists of facts is helped immeasurably by visual aids. The human mind can grasp only so many facts, percentages, or other bits of information aurally; eventually it needs visual help. Graphs, charts, or simply listings that the audience can see help them understand and retain facts. Which is easier to understand, someone reading off the following statistics — 26 percent in 1950; 42 percent in 1955; 39 percent in 1960; 47 percent in 1965; 44.3 percent in 1970; and 53.4 percent in 1975 — or the following bar graph.

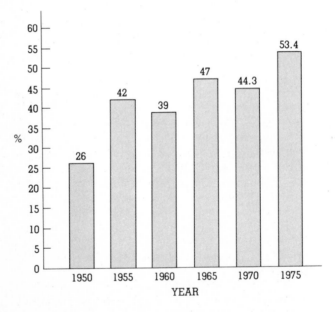

A bar graph showing the percentage of left-handed shortstops suffering tennis elbow in selected years.

Of course, for either the reading of statistics or the graph to make sense they must be explained thoroughly and sensibly within the context of the speech.

If a speech is about people or places, photographs, slides, or even motion pictures can help. The proper photograph or portrait also can set the mood for a speech, as well as simply showing who or what you are talking about. Think how much a photo would add to a speech about your favorite athlete, poet, or general, or about an exotic or unusual place, such as Hawaii or Yellowstone.

Speeches that deal with abstract issues such as politics, law, philosophy, or religion require much more imagination in seeking valuable visual aids. How many people who have heard thousands of words about the fall of Richard Nixon's administration would recognize a picture of the Watergate complex in Washington? Political speeches often deal with dollars, percentages, or raw statistics; you can use charts and graphs again. A speech about the Aztec religion in my class was aided greatly by a large picture of the Aztec calendar stone. In a speech dealing with abstractions, you must exercise imagination and seek out visual aids that reinforce the verbal message, stimulate interest, and visualize difficult concepts.

Types of Visual Aids

Keeping in mind that your own creativity and imagination are the best sources for visual aids and that no one source can cover all kinds, let us examine some common aids that might be used in a typical classroom. Graphs and charts are perhaps the most common types and the most useful for conveying statistical information.

Graphs

The *bar graph* is useful for visualizing comparative statistics. It uses bars of different heights to compare amounts. In the example below, the vertical range represented the percentage and the horizontal the time in five-year increments. In the example on page 146, the vertical lines represent the average yearly salary in dollars and the horizontal lines various professions.

The *pie graph* is useful for conveying information about several factors that are closely connected. A fictitious example on page 147 (top) represents the expenditures of a family on an income of $15,000.

Another type of graph is the *line graph*, which illustrates progression or regression of one factor over a period of time. Similar factors can be compared on such a graph. Newspaper cartoons abound with examples of businesses using line graphs to chart their profits or losses. (See page 147, bottom.)

LIVE EXAMPLES
Any time it is feasible to use a live example, the audience will gain a great deal from seeing it. Over the years I have seen all sorts of pets used as visual aids in the classroom: dogs, birds, and even crabs. Some students have brought younger brothers or sisters or their own children to class for examples. Animals and children, however, pose problems that inanimate objects do not: they are notorious scene-stealers and easily, without trying, take the attention away from the speaker. It is also unfair to subject the speakers who precede or follow you to the whims and outbursts of your younger brother or the unpredictable behavior of your loveable pooch. If you use children or animals, check first with your instruc-

A bar graph of the average income for selected, very selected, professions for 1937.

tor and try to be the first or last scheduled speaker, so you can keep the little darlings out of the hair of others.

MODELS

When it is not feasible to bring in the actual object because of size, complexity, or unavailability, you can often substitute a model. Whereas an internal combustion engine would be impractical, even dangerous, in a classroom, a scale model could give the audience needed information and an opportunity to visualize parts and their relationship to one another. Model airplanes, ships, or automobiles can be used in a variety of speeches. The history of transportation, or of one branch of transportation, would benefit from models, as would a description of the function of certain types of ships. If the models are in scale, they can vividly illustrate size differences and characteristics. Cut-away models are excellent for illustrating functions of the various parts of any machine. A demonstration of lifesaving techniques, such as artificial respiration, can be greatly enhanced by using a life-size dummy. The Red Cross, military, and civil defense agencies can provide such models, as can a nursing department or school.

A most dramatic anti-smoking demonstration was highlighted by a student operating a homemade "smoking machine." His machine had a small bellows,

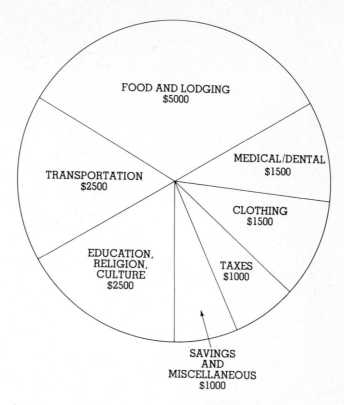

A pie graph: Where a family income of $15,000 goes!

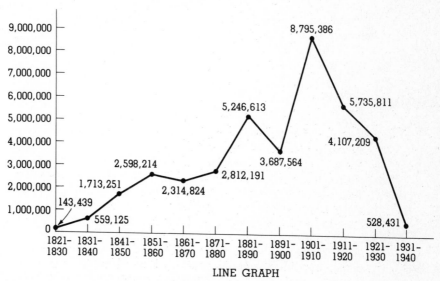

A line graph of immigration to the United States by decade—1821–1940. (Source: U.S. Immigration and Naturalization Service)

and it drew the smoke from a lighted cigarette through some clean cotton. Seeing the "gunk" from one cigarette in the clean cotton shocked even the most devoted smokers in class. Imagination, mechanical ability, and availability are the limiting factors for your use of models, along with, of course, the topic of your speech.

OTHER OBJECTS

Paris! New York! San Francisco! Three cities you may have visited, with enough history and culture for a wealth of speeches. Perhaps you brought back a model of the Eiffel Tower, a theater program, or a toy cable car. These souvenirs might enhance an informative speech about the respective cities. Even a tee shirt from a faraway place might add to your verbal message. Virtually any souvenir might be used for such a situation.

Hobbies and sports equipment provide visual aids, especially for demonstration of techniques or processes. A baseball, football, or basketball is a fairly common object, even for those not interested in athletics or sports. How many people are familiar with mountain-climbing equipment, however, especially if they live in flatlands? How many know the difference between downhill and cross-country skiing equipment? How many nonplayers are familiar with the protective equipment football players use? To show the equipment used in a baseball game would probably be dull for most of your audience; neither would it pose much of a speaking challenge. To talk about the major injuries in a sport such as football, however, gives you the opportunity to compile interesting statistics. In addition, you might show some equipment and demonstrate how it protects the players from injuries. If used well, such aids would enable you to deliver a speech of depth and quality.

Musical instruments are often of value in a speech. In a speech about a violin the audience would profit from seeing the various parts and learning how they are put together. A loud trumpet blast, however, might cause apoplexy in an adjoining classroom, so be discreet. Remember, too, that most classrooms are acoustically atrocious and will not help the sound of even a well-played instrument.

Audiovisual Equipment

Most modern colleges have audiovisual equipment available that you may find helpful in your speaking. Here are some common devices with some of their advantages and disadvantages.

The *overhead projector* is an excellent device for showing lists of facts and figures, using a typewriter or wax pencil instead of posterboard and pen and ink. The overhead uses specially processed film that will take and project grease markings. Unfortunately the processing takes time and special equipment, and the room must be darkened.

The *opaque projector* is simpler to use and requires no special preparation. Books, magazines, photographs, and any other two-dimensional work can be projected. You cannot alter or mark with grease pencil as you can with the overhead, but the flexibility of material compensates for the drawback. It too requires a dark room.

A *slide projector* shows photographic slides of various subjects, and a small slide can be enlarged greatly by projecting it. Slides are available from libraries, various collections, and your own camera. A slide projector also needs a darkened room.

A *motion picture projector* can be used for your own home movies, usually 8 mm or Super 8, or for commercial and educational movies, usually 16 mm. The darkened room and the time needed to show the film may pose some problems.

Videotape recorders are becoming available on more campuses. Immediacy and live action are the primary reasons for using videotape. If you are granted permission, you could show portions of a city council meeting, committee proceedings, or a classroom session by videotaping with "porta-pack equipment." Equipment is expensive, and there is some delay between taping and viewing. Tape does not require the lengthy processing that film does, but it is somewhat trickier to produce. Advances in technique are being made yearly in this field, and prices are constantly dropping.

Many speeches, on-the-spot broadcasts, plays, and other aural events of the past have been captured on *phonograph records*. Records unfortunately become scratchy easily, and it is difficult to find a particular spot on a record. They are light and portable, however, and equipment is readily available and inexpensive. You might do well to transfer your phonograph record sound to audio tape.

Audio tape is light, portable, and with modern cassettes, readily available at small cost. Most of the better tape recorders have a numbering device so you can always find the same place easily and quickly. Virtually any sound can be captured on audio cassettes; the only restriction is the availability of the sound to the person recording.

The *chalkboard* is found in almost every classroom in any school in the United States. Where they are not built in, portable boards usually are available. The chalkboard is readable, erasable, cheap, and convenient, but it can become messy, and writing on the board forces the speaker to face away from the audience. For lengthy or complex ideas the chalkboard has this disadvantage: it takes time to write on it. Then you must erase it or leave the idea in view when you have gone on to other ideas.

What is the best kind of audiovisual equipment? There is no one answer. The purpose and ideas of the speech dictate the kinds of audiovisual aids that suit that speech. Availability, your resourcefulness, and your creativity determine what kinds of aids you use and how you use them. They are almost always desirable as long as they violate no copyright or other laws, are not offensive or embarrassing, and, most important, are pertinent to the topic.

How to Use Visual Aids

One question that often plagues the speaker is whether to pass around a visual aid that is small or that needs to be touched, tasted, or smelled. The advantages of passing the aid around, in addition to the sensory stimulation, are that each person can hold the object and study it at length; everyone can see it equally; and small, important objects become visible. On the other hand, when someone's attention is focused on an object he or she is holding, that person cannot devote attention to the speaker. In addition, the physical act of passing an object from one person to another can be distracting to both speaker and audience. The answer? If you feel that an aid is vital to your presentation and it must be passed around, then do so. If it is not vital, you might do better to pass it up.

Another possible danger of passing a visual aid was demonstrated by a young man who spoke about the most valuable stamp in his collection. He estimated the value at over $2000. Realizing that something that valuable might get "lost" in the crowd, he wisely chose to show the stamp while keeping a firm grip on it. He might have walked among the audience and showed it that way, but that would have consumed a great deal of time, especially with a large audience.

Any visual aid must be large enough to be seen, but small enough to be manageable. The postage stamp was an example of an aid that was too small. Few aids that make it through the classroom door are too large, but shape and contour still may make them hard to manage. If you use posters or other displays, make sure you have tape, tacks, or whatever is necessary to hold them where you want them, without being destructive to property in the room.

One of the most common errors that student speakers commit is displaying the aid to only a segment of the audience, usually the part directly in front of them. The size of the audience is a factor here, but do not forget the shape of the audience. If the audience is widely dispersed, you have to *pan* the aid in order to let everyone see it. Make sure that nothing blocks anyone's view of you and your visual aid. If the audience cannot see it, it will not aid you much.

Try to keep your visual aids out of sight until you are ready for the audience to see them. You do not want your audience wondering what all the figures on the graph represent while you are still introducing the topic. If you use a series of posterboard displays, either put them on an easel with a blank sheet covering them, or place them face down on a table or desk until you are ready for them. If you write on the chalkboard ahead of time, try to cover it with a blank sheet or a screen. If you use smaller objects, keep them in a box or paper bag until you need them, and keep the box in an inconspicuous place. When you have finished with "Exhibit A," put it back in the box, and pull out "Exhibit B" only when you need it.

Try not to compete with yourself when you are using visual aids. Human beings can focus on only one thing at a time. If we are examining your visual aid, we cannot give you our full attention, so do not give vital information at that time. If we are listening to you giving vital information verbally, we cannot devote much attention to your visual aids. A visual stimulus does not need as strong concentration as an aural stimulus, so we might be able to listen while the visual aid reinforces what you say. Nevertheless, when you want undivided attention, get visual aids out of sight when they are not in use.

One final admonition, do not talk to your visual aids. Your graph or photograph will not hear you anyway. We in the audience have ears, however, and we want you to direct your words to us. Too often novice speakers talk to the chalkboard, a chart, or some other object as a way of avoiding direct contact with the audience. It is not only bad audience psychology, but it will not help your nerves. Use a pointer, if available, and talk to your audience as much as you can.

Where to Find Visual Aids

The best way to find visual aids is to use your own resources. Probably you will not talk about photography or cameras unless you own a camera or about macramé unless you practice the craft yourself. Usually speakers choose topics that they are interested in, and because of their interest, they often have aids available.

For statistics or other facts, newspapers and magazines furnish information or photographs and charts that you can copy or project with an opaque projector. Often books have reproducible art work.

Family and friends often can help with visual aids. If you speak about air transportation and your friend makes model airplanes, why not use that resource? A parent's yearbook can furnish interesting material on changing styles in clothes and language.

Use your creativity. Not everyone is artistic, but if a visual aid is artistically well done, that is a plus. The real test of an aid, however, is whether it conveys the information intended. It is far better to have a crude, hand-lettered graph that lets the audience know what they need to know, than nothing at all. A pencil, ruler, ink or poster paint, and blank paper or posterboard are all you really need to produce passable, informative charts and graphs. Remember to make your graphics large enough to read, with broad, thick letters and numbers. Purple or green posterboard may be pretty for some uses, but for visual aids you will want the sharp contrast you can get only from a white background and black or very dark printing. A less professional look also might give a visual aid an individual, personal touch.

Photographs are available from many sources: personal collections, books, magazines, newspapers, and friends' collections. If you need a photograph of a specific object, try the library or a teacher who specializes in a field where such pictures might be commonplace. Doing a speech about Paris? Try the French faculty for posters, maps, and photographs. About police work? See your local or campus police. Most teachers and public officials are cooperative if you are polite and if they know it is for a class project. Use your imagination, and chances are you will find something that will stimulate the audience's imagination.

SUMMARY AND CONCLUSION

It is almost impossible to overemphasize the impact good visual aids can have on an audience. Virtually every speech will benefit from well-planned, relevant appeals to the audience's senses. You should remember that aids can appeal to any of the senses. A good aid will

1. reinforce the verbal message
2. stimulate or renew interest in the subject
3. illustrate factors that are difficult to visualize or imagine

The aid that accomplishes two or even three of these purposes will do the most good.

Aids come in all sizes, shapes, and colors. Some common aids that prove useful in speaking situations are the following:

1. real objects, such as cameras, instruments, gadgets, or souvenirs
2. graphs, in the three basic forms of bar, pie, and line

3. models of engines, buildings, automobiles, and so on
4. live examples, such as pets or children
5. photographs or drawings
6. sound effects

Go ahead and use virtually anything else that appeals to the senses and is appropriate to the speech—the only limitations are the speaker's imagination and resources, and the aid's relevance to the subject.

Many electronic and mechanical devices are available for displaying visual aids. Overhead, opaque, slide, and motion picture projectors can enlarge and display pictures and other objects not ordinarily available. They do require, unfortunately, a darkened room. Videotape recorders, audio tape recorders, and phonographs can add an aural dimension to the speech. The chalkboard is an old friend to the speaker and is found in almost every classroom.

When using visual aids, you should always take into account these suggestions for their use:

1. Make sure that the aid is large enough to see clearly and easily.
2. Make sure that all segments of the audience see it.
3. Keep your aids out of sight until you want the audience to focus on them.
4. Try to keep the audience's primary attention in one place—either you or the visual aid.
5. Avoid talking to the visual aid.
6. Do not circulate a visual aid in the audience unless it is absolutely necessary to your presentation.

If you follow all these suggestions you will find visual aids can be of enormous help in your presentations. The sources for these aids are numerous, but the most important factor is that you use imagination and creativity in finding them. They will be worth the time and energy you spend thinking about them, finding them, creating them, and practicing with them.

EXERCISES

1. What kinds of visual aids would help you give these speeches?
   a. a speech advocating increased emphasis on the use of solar energy
   b. an informative speech about the duties of the Presidency
   c. a speech tracing the history of the guitar
   d. a speech asking the audience to contribute to a specific charitable organization
   e. a speech comparing the energy requirements of compact cars and luxury sedans
2. Assume you are giving a speech on Renaissance art. The only visual aids you can find are in expensive art books in the library. How will you handle the situation? (You will *not* cut the pictures out of the books.)
3. Give three examples of speeches that could utilize some form of sound recording.
4. List some good sources for visual aids for a speech about changing fashions in clothing.

14

delivering your speech

1. *What factors about the physical setting should I take into account before the speech?*
2. *What is a lectern, and how can it help me?*
3. *When does my presentation begin?*
4. *Why should I make eye contact?*
5. *How do I vary my voice?*
6. *What kinds of gestures will work for me?*

You have written the perfect speech. Your research has been exhaustive. Your organization could not be clearer or easier to follow. Your grammar, syntax, and punctuation are surpassed only by your logical, emotional, and personal appeals. Your introduction immediately will capture and maintain the undivided attention of anyone within earshot. Your conclusion will have the audience on their feet cheering and ready to do what your speech has led them to. Only one thing remains to be done! Deliver it!

HEEELLLLPPP!

In this chapter you will find advice for delivering a speech. It gives *guidelines*, not absolutes or rules. Good speakers not only adapt to the situation, but also adapt the situation to themselves.

Some of the hints may seem so obvious that you will be tempted to treat them lightly. Remember that things that seem obvious and simple when you are relaxed may become extremely difficult in a tense, anxiety-provoking situation. And what is more tense and anxiety-provoking than delivering a speech? Chances are you will be frightened when you approach the moment, and the better prepared you are for some of the mechanics, the fewer problems they will pose.

The Physical Setting

Most of you will be delivering your speeches in a classroom. You must take the room itself into consideration when you plan your speech. Size, shape, acoustics, lecterns, and light are some of the physical factors of the room that you must include in your planning.

SIZE AND SHAPE OF THE ROOM

If the room you are in is long and narrow with the speaker at the head of the rectangle, eye contact is easier, a comfortable 60-degree angle of vision includes everyone. Acoustically, however, a long, narrow room forces you to project your voice more in order to be heard farther away. Unless you are on an elevated platform, people in the back rows may have a difficult time seeing you because there are so many heads in front of them. This kind of room arrangement lends itself to formality and serious speeches. Humor becomes more difficult, although not impossible, because of the distance of some of the audience from the speaker.

A room in which the speaker stands at the center of the long side of a rectangle poses other problems. For eye contact, for instance, you may have to turn your head from side to side a great deal more to take in everyone's territory. Your angle of sight may be as much as 180 degrees. Probably vocal projection will not be as difficult because your audience is not so far away, but when you use visual aids, you had better be sure that everyone can see them, which may mean taking much more time to *pan* them from side to side. Because the audience is spread around you, but closer, it becomes more difficult to establish the distance necessary for dealing with serious, highly emotional topics, but there is more intimacy.

A square room incorporates some advantages and disadvantages of these designs. In any of the three designs, however, a vital factor is the size of the audience. A speaker will react negatively to a room that is almost empty; none of us likes to talk to emptiness. The degree of emptiness or fullness depends on the size of both the audience and the room. Twenty-five people in a room that seats eighteen is jam-packed. Most of you will be speaking to classes with from twenty to thirty-five people in them. Ideally there will be room to breathe but also a feeling of unity and closeness. Early in my career, I tried giving a high-school speech class experience in auditorium speaking. Students were faced with the situation of speaking to audiences of twelve or fifteen scattered in an auditorium that seated about four hundred. The speakers found it frustrating and depressing, and the experiment died soon after it was born.

Sitting in a circle or horseshoe has some advantages over rectangular or square arrangements. The speaker and audience obtain a sense of intimacy not available in the other situations. Intimacy leads to informality, so the design does not do well for formal, weighty topics.

Probably your instructor will give you some choice of where to stand. Whether you are given free rein or restricted to one position, consider where you will be in relation to the audience and how large that audience will be. You had better do that considering long before you have to get up and face that audience.

USING A LECTERN

A *lectern* is a stand on which you place notes or other material; a *podium* is a platform on which you stand—*pod* means "foot." Should you keep your notes on a lectern? Your instructor may have some definite ideas about that, and you would be wise to go along with that advice.

The lectern has advantages and disadvantages. The biggest advantage to the lectern is, of course, that it holds notes and papers at a place where you can refer to them easily, where they remain without falling, and where they are invisible to the audience. The physical presence of the lectern, however, establishes a *psychological distance* between the speaker and audience, a mental barrier to intimacy and informality. If you want a formal, distant relationship for the topic you are dealing with, you want a lectern between you and the audience. If you are dealing with an informal topic and want closeness, you place as little between you and your audience as possible.

Too often speakers use the lectern as a leaning post that supports the elbow that props the hand that keeps the head from falling off. Unless you have a condition in which your head may fall off your shoulders, avoid using the lectern that way. The lectern also gives a degree of confidence to insecure speakers who envision the audience rising up en masse and attacking. Do not use the lectern if your primary purpose is keeping "them" away.

Finally, short people have to be especially wary of a lectern. A young lady who was four feet, eight inches tall spoke from behind the lectern in a class of mine. All we in the audience could see were her bangs and an occasional glimpse of eyebrow. Obviously that did not do much for eye contact and hindered her vocal projection, and the humor of the situation overshadowed her attempt to deal with a serious topic. Decide ahead of time whether the lectern will help you, and do not use it for a crutch, either physical or mental.

LIGHTING AND ACOUSTICS

One minor problem that can become major without your realizing it is standing in front of a light source while you address a group. A window with bright light may silhouette you, hindering the audience from seeing the expression on your face. A window also may pose difficulties because of outside traffic or other distractions. Usually such a decision will not be necessary in a classroom, but if you speak in unfamiliar surroundings, it is good to keep window and light placement in mind.

The room's acoustics pose another problem over which you have no control. Sometimes instructors give classes the opportunity to speak in a room just to get used to the sound problems. Outside noises from freeways or airplanes can affect the way you need to project vocally in a class. If the sound outside is so loud that you cannot be heard, wait until it is quiet again, if possible. One rule of thumb for sound is always to speak to the back row of your audience. If you are loud enough for the back row to hear, the rows in front also will be able to hear you.

You're On!

No matter how well prepared you are, there comes that horrible sensation when your instructor finally announces your name. Often students will go through an elaborate series of apologies, explanations, and pleas for sympathy. Don't!

There are reasons for not going through a song and dance that begs for sympathy or special understanding. First is that it probably will not work. More important is that when you change from Student-sitting-in-the-class-and-forming-part-of-audience to Speaker-upon-whom-all-eyes-are-focused, you immediately become the center of attention and start to form an impression in the audience's mind, their impression of you as a *speaker*. If you hem and haw and indicate that you really do not want to speak to them, their reaction most often is, "If he does not want to speak to me, I do not want to listen to him." Before you have even begun, you have alienated your audience, not entirely, but enough that you will have to work just that much harder to get them back. They are going to be faced with the same situation, or perhaps they already have been, and they will not find it easy to forgive your nerves when you—as a group—did not forgive theirs.

Some more enterprising individuals attempt a variation on this theme by talking about how nervous they are, what a miserable job they are going to do, and how unprepared they are. These people think all the time that they are going to do a fantastic job, but that if they diminish our expectations, we will be dazzled by the product. Nope!!! It does not work that way. If you have led an audience to believe one thing and then do something else, beware. Audiences do not like to be tricked. The best course of action—*always*—is to do the best job you can without excuses or apologies. If you cannot do it, accept a "zero" or "F" and retain your dignity. It will probably pay dividends when you finally are prepared for an assignment and give it your best.

From the instant that you are identified as the speaker until you sit down after finishing your speech, you are on; you are the center of attention. Audiences appreciate pride, self-confidence, and poise. We want our speakers to take charge of the situation, enjoy speaking, and give us new and interesting insights into some aspect or problem of life. Get up, speak, sit down, exhibiting all the poise and confidence you can possibly muster. After the imaginary spotlight is off you, you can faint or do some of the less attractive things, figuratively. You will find, in most cases, you are relieved that the situation is over; more important, you will find that the experience was rewarding far beyond your expectations.

Eye Contact

Another vital aspect of speech delivery is *eye contact*. Our culture demands that we look others in the eyes when we are communicating with them. The more intense and serious the communication, the more intense and necessary the eye contact. When someone refuses to look in our eyes, we become suspicious and less receptive to that person's message. We have all heard someone accuse someone else of stretching the truth by saying, "Look me in the eye when you say that." The saying assumes that it is more difficult to lie when direct eye contact takes place.

CONTACT WITH THE TELEVISION EYE

As in so many other aspects of communication, television has had impact on eye contact. When speaking on television, the speaker has only one eye to be concerned with—the television camera. Each of us watching the screen at home sees the speaker looking right at us, and we become confident and at ease "knowing" that the person speaks truth. This single eye can pose a problem for speakers working on television while in front of a live audience. The speaker's instincts and training dictate speaking to the live audience, but the audience in "televisionland" may be hundreds of thousands times as large; a speaker who concentrates on the live audience of, for instance, three hundred is alienating an audience of three million, "avoiding" them by not looking at the television camera.

The live audience speaker, who is our primary concern here, cannot look into several hundred or even fifty sets of eyes simultaneously or even consecutively. Eye contact, therefore, becomes a matter of looking at general directions and places in the audience, actually "contacting" *some* people, while the remainder become secure by identifying as a single audience unit. The speaker is looking at some of us in the audience; we are all part of that audience; therefore, the speaker is looking at all of us. Whether the unit is large, as at a political rally, or small, as in a sales pitch to one family, the principle remains the same.

Just as most of us tend to be right- or left-handed, we also tend to be right- or left-eyed. That is, we tend to favor one side or the other (I tend to favor the left side of an audience as I face them). You may not have had enough experience to notice which side you favor, but you should be on the lookout to avoid ignoring the other half.

DIVIDE YOUR AUDIENCE

You may wish to think of your audience in terms of sections to which you direct your eye focus. A small audience could be divided into four sections; a larger audience into six, nine, or even more. You look at one person in "Section 1" or "North" or however you label it. After a few seconds, or at the completion of an idea, go to another section. Your eyes should stay with a specific person in a specific place long enough to establish rapport; then go to another place at random, but not too close.

You should avoid following the same pattern, or the audience will begin to sense it. Avoid precise, regular eye movement, which makes for a mechanical, dull presentation. A young man in a class of mine tried what we all defined as the "radar-tower" technique. He kept scanning back and forth across the class like a radar tower, about two seconds each way, then back the other way. All of us got so hypnotized by his head movement that we lost sight of his topic, and eventually some people had to suppress smiles and giggles.

Some speakers try to "cheat" by looking *toward* or *past* people, trying to give the impression of looking *at* them. Look at people. Look directly into their eyes, without staring, but with an attitude of wanting to share information.

Some basic suggestions for eye contact:

1. Try to include all parts of the audience.
2. Do not even try to include each individual.
3. In a large group, try not to repeat individuals.
4. Do not fake eye contact.
5. Do not hold on any one person too long.
6. Avoid regularity and rhythmical movement.
7. Whenever you refer to your notes, make sure you look toward a different place when you look back to your audience.

Your Voice

VOCAL CONTACT

The need for vocal contact in a speaking situation seems almost too obvious to mention, but surprisingly many student speakers reduce their effectiveness by ignoring it. Eye contact and vocal contact are related, because when you point your head in one direction to see, you "point" your mouth in the same direction. It is possible to face a manuscript or lectern while looking up and out with the eyes and not moving your head. This mannerism is detrimental to effective communication. It gives an appearance of being "shifty-eyed" and avoiding direct contact. The speaker seems to be talking to the manuscript or lectern. Often the speaker may not be heard. The solution is that eye and vocal contact should work together.

Suppose, however, you are in a large room or auditorium and you have a less than strong voice. You want to move your eyes to include everyone, yet you want to be heard. As long as you are facing your audience and not burying your chin in your chest, the audience will respond favorably to your contact. Therefore, always be sure that the people sitting farthest from you, the back row, can hear you. If you talk to them, you will project your voice sufficiently for everyone to hear. After all, if people fifty feet away can hear you easily, those twenty-five feet away also will hear you.

A speech is an *oral* event, and your audience should be able to hear you without straining or wanting to put on earmuffs. Your note cards have been exposed to the speech a dozen times — if you have been practicing — and so far as medical science can tell us, note cards cannot hear anyway, so talk to the ears that can hear, your audience.

VOCAL VARIETY

In your oral delivery you will want a variety of expression in order to emphasize your key points and avoid monotony. Vary your *rate* of delivery, the speed with which you speak; vary your *volume*, loudness and softness; vary the *intensity* of your voice; and make sure you *pause* to give effective meaning to key words or phrases. When you want the audience to digest difficult material, such as statistics, deep philosophical ideas, or awkwardly phrased quotations, *slow down* and let one bit of information sink in before you bombard them with another. Do not be afraid to be dramatic when it is called for. Remember, the most important aspect of being dramatic is variety or contrast. If, however, you try to be dramatic through the whole speech, you probably will lose the effect you are striving for and may even get an unwanted laugh or two.

Your Body

GESTURES

Many students question whether they should gesture as they speak. Of course! However, the degree to which you gesture and the kinds of gestures you make should be consistent with your personality and the topic of the speech. In the United States generally — and it is a broad generalization — we are not demonstrative in everyday communication. We do not wave our hands about or have great shifts of vocal emphasis, as do some people, such as the French or Italians — again a generalization. If you are normally *phlegmatic* (a good word for word games) and you attempt large, dramatic movements of your arms, hands, and face while delivering a speech, you may look as ridiculous as you feel. Instead you can use a few well-timed, small gestures to add a great deal of emphasis to the speech. Gestures, like rate and volume of speech, are relative to the whole situation and must be taken in context. The gesture that is small and ineffectual for a demonstrative person may be strong and powerful for the phlegmatic speaker, just as slow and fast vary from person to person and depend upon the content of the speech.

Gestures should come from inside the speaker and be inspired by the words and thoughts of the speech. To examine your speech and say, "Oh, this looks like a good spot to point my finger," just does not work for most people. If in the context of delivering the speech, your hand "wants to reach out" to emphasize your point, let it. Planned gestures usually look planned. Allow yourself to be free with your gestures; keep them fresh and spontaneous.

FACE AND POSTURE
Facial expression and bodily attitude are the two most important aspects of your physical emphasis. In most people the eyes are the most expressive parts of the anatomy. Talk with your eyes; let your eyes and face lead the vocal emphasis and show the audience the intensity with which you regard your topic. Oddly enough, the more relaxed you are, the more expressive your face and voice will be.

Bodily attitude is the nonverbal information your body conveys through the way you stand. Are you slouching and leaning on the lectern with your legs crossed while delivering a serious speech telling the audience that they should take an important action? It won't work. Stand erect with a relaxed, confident air, not military erectness; face the audience head on; and keep your feet apart a few inches so you are balanced and comfortable. If you want to move around, why not do so? If these hints seem like simple advice about obvious things, they are — until you are standing in front of a live audience, tense and nervous, with a million things to remember about the speech. If you can think about them ahead of time, they become more natural and easier.

Taking Your Time

One final bit of advice for the presentation: take your time. Sometimes inexperienced speakers start speaking before they are even in front of the audience. Get into your position, get your notes and visual aids ready, look out at your audience for a second or two, and *then* begin your speech. You will be ready to speak and follow your plans, and the audience will be ready to listen and follow your ideas.

You should also take your time during the presentation. Speak slowly enough so the audience catches every word. On the other hand, do not speak so slowly that they think you are trying to stretch the time.

When you are finished, look at your audience, hold the mood for a moment or two, gather up your materials with dignity and poise, and return to your seat calmly; *then* you can collapse, at least inwardly. You will certainly deserve a moment of relaxation after delivering your fine speech.

SUMMARY
AND CONCLUSION

This chapter deals with ways to deliver a speech. It offers advice that people have found successful over the years. Probably it will work for you, and you owe it to yourself to give it a try. Then, if you find it does not work, replace it with your own ideas. Chances are, however, that you will find it helpful as countless other speakers have.

What *physical factors* about the room in which you will present your speech do you need to be concerned with? Be aware of the *size* and *shape* of the room, where you will stand, and how these factors will affect your speech. If at all possible, give yourself a chance to hear the way the room acts acoustically, remembering that *acoustics* will change some from an empty room to one filled with people. Determine whether a *lectern* is available, and decide whether to work with it.

What do you do during the presentation itself? Try to be poised and in control at all times. Your audience wants you to be. Never play on an audience's sympathy for your problems, and never try to fool an audience.

Try to maintain *eye contact* during the speech. It is vitally important. If your audience is large, divide it into imaginary segments. Do not look past or through your audience. Include all parts of the audience, but do not try to include each individual. Some other don'ts: Try not to repeat looking at individuals; do not fake eye contact; do not hold on any one person too long; and avoid regularity and rhythmical eye movements. After looking at your notes, make sure you look toward a different place when you look back to your audience.

For *vocal contact*, if the back row can hear you, so can the others. Try to add a good deal of variety and emphasis by your rate of speech, pitch of voice, volume, and intensity. Remember, gestures add a great deal to a speech, but they must be spontaneous and look unrehearsed. Posture and facial expression are important, but your eyes are the most expressive part of your body.

Perhaps the single most important factor to remember is to *take your time*. You are in charge of the situation, or at least you should appear to be so. If you take your time, it will make you appear more confident, and the appearance will probably make you feel more confident. If you take your time, you will be more likely to remember some of the little things you did in practice, like the proper use of notes, lectern, and audience contact.

There is no substitute for practice. When you think you have mastered your speech, practice it again. The practice sessions may not be fun or stimulating, but they will pay enormous dividends when the moment of truth is finally at hand.

EXERCISES

The time has come, so Do It!!

CHAPTER 15

speaking in groups

1. *How does group speaking differ from public speaking?*
2. *How do groups solve problems?*
3. *What are the purposes of groups?*
4. *Can a committee ever accomplish anything?*
5. *What are the differences between a panel, symposium, and forum?*
6. *What functions does a leader serve in a group?*

A camel is a horse designed by a committee.

Anonymous

Chapter 1 discussed differences between interpersonal communication and public speaking. There are, however, specialized situations involving multiple speakers that retain some of the characteristics of interpersonal communication and some of public speaking.

When we get together in a small group to share ideas, we have group discussion at its most basic level. The group may simply consist of mutually attracted people deciding a social outing, such as which movie to see on Saturday night, or it may be a group composed of experts called together to solve an international crisis. It also can, of course, consist of anything in between these extremes.

This chapter will examine how such groups are formed, how they function, and the role of the individual within the group, especially as it pertains to the principles of public speaking.

The Objectives of Group Discussion

Human beings form discussion groups in order to accomplish certain tasks or objectives. As with many human endeavors, there may be some overlap or duplication in the objectives, but generally they form to serve one or more of three functions: problem solving, the gathering of information, or the dispensing of information.

Problem Solving

The gathering of a group of friends deciding what to do for a social evening represents a simple example of a *problem-solving* group. Three couples may meet in the college cafeteria and decide that they would like to spend an evening together. They will need to establish a date that is mutually acceptable and that poses no conflicts for any of the six; they will need to decide what to do from a series of choices, such as going to the movies, bowling, dancing, attending an athletic event, or having a party. Where they will go will be determined in part by what they do, as may the time in which they do it. If they opt for a party, there are even more decisions to be made, but if they decide to go to the latest horror movie, meeting at 7:30 at the high-school parking lot, the whole decision-making process may take just three or four minutes, after which the group disbands and members go their separate ways until the appointed meeting time.

On the other hand, an automobile manufacturer's board of directors may be faced with a technical problem that could potentially cost lives and billions of dollars. They decide to put their ten top engineers on the problem, giving them instructions to drop everything else, get together to work out the problem, and report back in three months.

Although one group is about as informal as can be and the other equally as formal, both are faced with a task of identifying a problem and resolving it to the satisfaction of the parent organization. The parent organization may simply be the group itself, as in the social situation, or it may be a group with a larger constituency and greater responsibility, such as the board of directors of the automobile company.

STEPS IN PROBLEM SOLVING

In each of the extreme examples used, the group follows a similar pattern in order to arrive at its solution. In the informal social group the process may take just a few minutes and will certainly not be formalized; in the formally organized group with great responsibility beyond just themselves, the structure may be formal, formidable, and lengthy.

Defining the Problem. The first step each group takes will be the process of defining the problem. In the social group the problem is as follows: a group of friends wishes to spend some time together in an enjoyable, mutually satisfying interchange, complicated by six different work and school schedules, as well as other responsibilities. It is unlikely that the group would take the time to articulate and define the problem formally, because they all recognize the problem as their reason for being together.

The engineers, on the other hand, may have a vastly more difficult problem. They must first read the reports that show, for instance, that the proposed model has a tendency to go out of control at medium speeds on moderate curves. Although they begin with the known result of the problem, they still do not have the problem defined. After they know the results of the problem, they must define and pinpoint the problem, requiring, perhaps, months of testing. Is the problem in the steering mechanism? In the suspension system? In the metal itself? Only when they are certain that X causes Y can they define the problem.

For any group, regardless of size, formality, or structure, the process of defining the problem is the first step in solving it.

Examining Possible Solutions. After the problem has been defined, the next step is suggesting possible solutions. With our social group, some of the suggestions may be bowling, movies, a dance, or a party. Each person will probably suggest the solution that he or she prefers. The group will probably go through a "brainstorming" session, in which people throw out possible solutions in order to get as many alternatives as possible.

In the more formal group of engineers, possible solutions may need highly-skilled efforts in design, structure, metallurgy, or other technical areas. Each expert may have to look for some time for possible solutions.

Evaluation. After the possible solutions have been proposed, each must then be evaluated for its merits relative to the problem and its feasibility. A suggestion for our social group to fly to Paris, France, for the evening may sound like great fun, but the logistics of time and money will probably prohibit that solution. Perhaps one member of the group has a broken hand, ruling out bowling; the only dances in town feature bands no one in the group cares for; there may be a variety of reasons for not having a party; consequently, the group eliminates all the choices except for the movie.

The engineering problem may involve months of more testing and laboratory analysis before the group can limit its choices, but each possible solution must be evaluated and examined.

Reaching a Solution. The fourth step is, of course, reaching a decision. After the possible solutions have been evaluated and the ones that are not feasible eliminated, arriving at a solution may be fairly simple, as in the case of the group going to a movie. In the more complex situation facing the engineers, chances are that the choices will not be that clear-cut. One choice may solve the original problem, but develop several others. The engineers may have to propose a solution as a compromise, indicating that there are several possibilities, but that their research and expertise indicates that solution X will be the best, or perhaps the "least worst."

Regardless of the complexity of the situation or the group, the problem-solving/decision-making process follows the same four steps:

1. Define the problem.
2. Suggest possible solutions.
3. Evaluate the possible solutions.
4. Decide.

Information Gathering

Your community's governing body decides to permit the building of some new high-rise apartments specifically for senior citizens. The city council, town board, or whatever it calls itself, holds hearings in which local business people, gerontologists, utility operators, environmentalists, and other concerned citizens can voice their opinions about the new project. The group gathers information from diverse sources in order to help make a more valid judgment on the desirability of the project.

A jury hears testimony in a murder case. Police officers, medical experts, and various other witnesses are called before the judge and jury. Their testimony is monitored and kept within strict boundaries, but the information the jury gathers from these witnesses should be the determining factors in the legal decision.

You may have noted that the information-gathering of these two groups aids them in the decision-making process. In a sense they are dealing with the final two steps of the problem-solving pattern. The town council has determined that there is not enough low-cost housing for its senior citizens (defining the problem) and that the building of the project is a proposed solution for the problem. The people who come before the committee help them to evaluate the specific possible solution and then to decide whether or not to go ahead with the plans. The jury too deals with the evaluation and decision steps; the problem being defined as someone having broken the law by murdering X and the possible solution is that Y is the culprit. Again, the jury must evaluate the proposed solution and make a decision based on that information.

Usually a group that attempts to gather information as its principle function or objective will be a specialized group with highly specific responsibilities. Part of those responsibilities involves evaluating possible solutions and then arriving at decisions that at times may literally involve life and death, as in the case of the jury, but that will almost always bear heavy responsibility.

Information Dispensing

A seemingly unending debate continues to rage in the United States about the issue of abortion where the mother's life is not at stake. Perhaps your college or some other civic group wants to be informed about the subject. They decide to have an open discussion and invite clergy who represent both sides of the issue, medical and legal experts, and perhaps a philosopher or a social worker. Each of these people has a specialized interest in abortion and can offer information based on their area of expertise and experience.

Some colleges offer courses dealing with special topics that require varied background and expertise. Assume that your school offers a course in nineteenth-century American culture. Someone from the English department may discuss literary trends; a professor from the art department will talk about the growth of art in America; a philosopher may add information about that discipline; and a historian may discuss the politics and other historical movements, perhaps tying the entire package together.

Both of these are examples of small groups dispensing information to larger gatherings of people. On a smaller scale, members of your class may have an assignment to discuss before the entire class a topic such as intercultural communication. The group may consist of a black, a Latino, a Jew, a native American, and someone representative of the so-called White, Anglo-Saxon, Protestant (WASP) majority point of view. Probably the group would include both females and males. Each person would be expected to research some aspect of the topic and also offer personal experiences with intercultural communication. The same assignment might also be given to a group that is entirely homogeneous, that is, all of the group have essentially the same racial, ethnic background. They might be expected to do more research into theory and testimony by experts in the field. Either pattern would constitute a group dispensing information to a larger body.

The format for any of these groups can take several forms. These will be discussed later in the chapter.

For Whose Benefit Does the Group Exist?

Groups exist for their own benefit, for the benefit of the larger group that they are speaking to, or for some third outside party or institution.

A group whose primary function is problem solving/decision making really exists for itself. It studies the problem in order to make a valid judgment and perhaps implement a specific course of action. The informal group of friends deciding on its social function obviously exists strictly for its own benefit. A group that is formed by a larger or more responsible body, such as the town council or board of directors of the corporation, exists less for its own good than for the good of the community, of the stockholders, and of the corporation in general. The jury gathers information for itself, but in a larger sense, it benefits society in general when the guilty are sentenced to prison and the innocent are set free. The group in the classroom discussing intercultural communication receives the most good from its own existence, but the classroom audience will, we hope, also benefit from its discussions.

The information-dispensing group of experts should exist for the benefit of its audience. The faculty discussing nineteenth-century culture already possess knowledge and expertise about the subject. They come together to share that information with a group who want to learn about the subject.

Types of Groups

Groups and group discussion range in degrees of formality from the highly informal social group of friends to the rigid formality of bodies such as the United Nations, Congress, or the World Court.

THE COMMITTEE

After the informal social group which requires no comment here, perhaps the most frequently convened group is the committee. Your student body organization undoubtedly has many committees, some which have ongoing responsibilities, called "standing committees," and some which are organized for one specific problem and then disbanded, often called "ad hoc." The organization probably has a board of officers which meets regularly and discusses a wide range of problems. Within the structure, if it is a large school, there may be smaller committees that deal with specific issues, such as a Grade Appeals Committee, a Fee Assessment Committee, or a committee to deal with problems and disputes between and among fraternities, sororities, and other campus organizations. Special committees may need to be convened to deal with an emergency situation, such as raising money for flood victims, or to deal with specific tasks, such as a Homecoming Day Committee.

Too often groups will form committees and sub-committees because no one person is willing to take responsibility for decision making. That should not, of course, be the reason for establishing a committee. Theoretically, we establish committees to deal with problems that can benefit from the attention of more than one person.

Committees usually are constituted to deal with decision making and problem solving, but sometimes they will gather information, and occasionally they will be formed to dispense information.

The structure of a committee and its rules for operation vary depending on the size, formality, and purpose. The larger and more formal a committee is, the more it will have to have specific rules of conduct and organization. The Homecoming Day Committee may meet on a fairly informal basis, with the chair calling the meeting to order and then getting reports from the person or persons in charge of tickets, bands, floats, or other necessary functions. In all probability, everyone on the committee will contribute in a relaxed, informal manner, unless the committee is unusually large. A Congressional fact-finding committee composed of twenty Senators and dozens of witnesses, on the other hand, will need to have strict rules of operation or else chaos will result. The chair will need to exercise a firm hand in seeing that the committee operates smoothly, everyone is heard from, and that it accomplishes its task.

While we sometimes feel that we are being "committeed to death," committees have become an important part of society and a necessary component to democratic decision making.

PANEL

A group of people come together and discuss a topic such as alternate forms of energy. Although they discuss the topic among themselves, they discuss the topic for the benefit of the audience assembled there. The audience does not enter into the discussion, but rather it benefits from the discussion within the group. Such a group is called a *panel*.

A panel will usually have a chair* who performs a few set procedures. The chair will officially open the meeting and then introduce the panel members, stating their qualifications if necessary and appropriate. He or she will then throw the discussion open, preferably having a prepared question or two to get the interchange of ideas flowing. From time to time, the chair will summarize the discussion, change the direction of discussion, help with transitions from one idea to

---

*Traditionally, the leader of a group or committee was called a "chairman" and referred to as "Mr." or "Madam" Chairman. In order to avoid sexist language, the term "chairperson" came into usage, but many consider that an awkward expression. Although many people object to the usage of "chair" because it denotes a piece of furniture, I prefer it to the sexist or awkward terms.

another, and, when necessary, see that everyone on the panel has the opportunity to contribute and that no one or two members of the panel dominate discussion. When the discussion is completed, the chair will summarize the most important points and close the meeting. If there is an *open forum* after the panel discussion, the chair will lead and monitor the questions from the audience.

Members of a panel will generally be prepared by virtue of expertise acquired long before the panel discussion. They do not prepare anything specifically for the discussion, but rely upon previous knowledge and established ideas and attitudes toward the subject at hand. A panel discussion in a classroom situation may involve the members researching a topic in a general way, implying a breadth of knowledge as opposed to depth.

THE DIALOGUE
The *dialogue* is similar to the panel discussion, except that it implies just two persons, rather than a larger panel.

SYMPOSIUM
In a *symposium* each member of the group is an expert, and each member prepares a talk about a specific area of the topic, usually designed for a specific time period. The symposium will have a more defined topic, and each member's talk will cover a set portion of the topic. For instance, a symposium on the problems of drug abuse in the public schools might have participants each presenting a ten- to fifteen-minute presentation on topics such as these:

1. A police officer discussing the legal problems of drug abuse.
2. A physician or pharmacologist discussing the medical and chemical processes involved.
3. A high-school principal discussing the effects of drugs on the people in his or her school.
4. An ex-addict discussing the experiences of a heavy user.

In the symposium, as in the panel, the group discusses for the benefit of the audience, not for their own information.

The leader of the symposium usually does not speak to the topic. Instead the leader will introduce speaker #1, stating the qualifications and experiences the speaker brings and what he or she will talk about. Then the speaker #1 delivers a prepared speech to the audience. The leader will then introduce speaker #2, and so on. Between speakers the chair should offer whatever transitions are necessary, commenting on #1's topic and using it as a transition to #2. Using the example of a symposium about drug abuse, the chair might go from the police officer to the physician like this:

Thank you, Officer Jones. I am sure that everyone found those stories as frightening and horrible as I did. The question that naturally arises is, "Why would young people behave in such a bizarre manner?" Our next speaker, Dr. Betty Smith, will describe the way in which this chemical affects the nervous system and the controlling mechanisms of the brain.

The chair would then go on to state Dr. Smith's qualifications and why we should listen to her.

If there is an open forum after the symposium, which there often is, the chair will conduct that session, seeing that it runs smoothly and that as many audience members as possible get a chance to ask their questions. The leader should also insure that time limits are adhered to and that the audience that comes for a two-hour discussion does not have to sit through four or five hours. At the completion of the symposium or forum, the chair should summarize the pertinent points, thank the participants, and officially close the session.

THE FORUM

As indicated in the descriptions of the panel and the symposium, the *forum* opens up the discussion to questions or comments from the audience. A forum could be held without a panel or symposium preceding it, but it is unlikely. Usually, the chair of the panel or symposium will conduct the forum to insure that as many questions or comments as possible are aired, and that a small faction of the audience does not dominate or monopolize the forum.

Leadership

In any group there are two possible kinds of leaders: first, the leader who has received some sort of official appointment, such as a committee chair being named by the presiding officer of an organization or someone leading a panel or symposium as an assignment; second, the leader who emerges from within the ranks of the group and leads by example and interaction with other members of the group. Often the second type of leader will assume leadership because of strength of personality or other factors. Ideally, in any group *everyone will assume some of the leadership functions.*

FUNCTIONS OF THE LEADER

The group leader will attempt to keep any discussion on the topic and prevent stray, nonproductive issues from overshadowing the group's primary purpose. That is not to say that a group cannot have some tension-relief through an occasional diversion or humorous episode. Actually, such relief is necessary, especially if the group is dealing with matters of substance and meeting for long periods of time.

The leader should also help keep the conversation flowing at all times by being prepared to ask provocative questions. Occasionally a group will bog down and conversation comes to a standstill. The well-informed leader will then ask an open-ended question that should elicit response from virtually every member of the group. A question with a simple or obvious answer will do little to resume the flow of conversation. For example, the question, "Is solar energy too expensive?" may elicit a simple "Yes" answer. The wiser leader will ask an open-ended question such as, "What can we do to reduce the cost of solar?" or "Can we make solar energy economically feasible?"

The leader will also need to insure that everyone in the group has a chance to speak. Often because of enthusiasm for the subject or because of personality factors, some members may attempt to dominate the conversation. Others, for a variety of reasons, will permit themselves to be bullied or dominated and hesitate to contribute. The leader must be prepared to control the situation without insulting anyone or making anyone feel awkward or embarrassed. A simple statement may suffice, such as, "Thank you for those comments, Mr. Eager. Mr. Shy, how do you feel about the situation as we have described it?" Unfortunately, there are times when one person simply will not relinquish the spotlight or when another will not contribute. The leader must try to involve everyone as equally as possible.

From time to time, the leader should summarize and help the group define where it has been and what it has accomplished. This can be especially important when the discussion becomes heated and factions begin to develop. A summary of the agreed-upon points may show that the group has more area of agreement than of contention, in spite of the emotional pitch. The more formal the setting, the more such summary becomes important.

Finally, the leader must strive to suppress his or her own attitude toward the subject at hand. If a symposium or panel is discussing a controversial, sensitive issue, such as abortion or censorship, the leader should maintain a neutral position and avoid his or her own biases. A leader who subtly informs the group and the audience of a favored position not only acts unfairly to some of the participants, but that leader also forces some of the group members to become suspicious and defensive. Even if a member of the group is unprepared or makes statements the leader feels are inappropriate, the leader must maintain an objective neutrality and attempt to keep the discussion flowing.

STYLES OF LEADERSHIP

Generally, leadership styles are separated into three basic types: autocratic, laissez faire, and democratic. These are generalities, however, rather than absolutes, and no leader is always one or the other. Roles may change depending on the composition and circumstances of the group.

The Autocratic Leader. The *autocratic leader* is one who controls the group rigidly, imposing his or her own values, beliefs, and answers on everyone else. As you can imagine, the autocrat stifles discussion and the free flow of ideas by being overbearing and self-centered. Often the autocratic leader treats the group as if it were there to reflect and impose the leader's own solutions to the problem at hand.

The autocratic leader will permit only selected discussion and will insure that the participants who have the opportunity to speak are those whose opinion parallels the leader's. With an autocratic leader the philosophy that engenders group discussion, two (or more) heads are better than one, falls by the wayside. Members of the group feel frustrated and angry that they cannot be heard or that they are, in essence, censored. Free and open discussion suffers and cannot exist under the autocrat.

The Laissez Faire Leader. *Laissez faire leadership* is exactly the opposite of autocratic. The laissez faire leader abandons the sense of responsibility that marks a real leader. Instead he or she allows the group total freedom and brings no sense of direction or purpose to the discussion. The laissez faire leader may simply get the group going, then allow nature to take its course, offering no organization, direction, or sense of purpose. The group will usually deteriorate into a state of anarchy with some members vying for status and recognition while others simply give up and feel frustrated and angry.

The Democratic Leader.   The *democratic leader* avoids the pitfalls that plague the other two styles. The democratic leader will subvert his or her own feelings and desires to the direction the group is taking, exerting sufficient influence to keep the group on the subject and to insure that everyone has an opportunity to be heard. The democratic leader guides and leads the group, allowing each member to retain a sense of personal dignity and worth.

The sensitive leader will shift position on the continuum between no guidance and dictatorship, suiting the style to the participants. If some members of the group attempt to dominate and control, the leader may have to lean toward the autocratic side of the scale in order to control the aggressive faction. Conversely, if a group is composed of secure individuals who stick to reasoned, well-thought-out discussion that gives everyone equal opportunity to participate, the leader can be less obtrusive and allow the group to direct itself.

Often leadership will emerge from within the group itself, and the appointed leader can allow the natural leadership to come forth. The appointed leader, however, retains the ultimate responsibility for the group, and must, therefore, remain ready to step in and redirect discussion, involve reluctant participants, and summarize as necessary.

Maintenance Functions
Within the Group

Within the group itself, members will perform "maintenance functions," usually without consciously attempting to do so. A maintenance function is a behavior that contributes to the overall welfare and cooperative orientation of the group.

SUPPORT

Members of a group should reinforce other members by stating aloud or nonverbally their agreement or understanding of others. If a member of the group who has been reluctant to participate contributes a positive suggestion, it will help that person grow and feel more a part of the group is other members show their approval with comments such as, "Hey, George, that's a good idea," or "Good suggestion, George." It seems so simple, yet sometimes we get so involved with our ideas that we ignore other people's ideas, thereby inhibiting the other person's contributions.

GATEKEEPING

Along similar lines as support is gatekeeping. The gatekeeper encourages others to participate and helps the appointed leader keep the dominant members in check. Without attempting to embarrass or put the other person on a spot, the "gatekeeper" may say something like, "Angela, what do you think about the comment Fred just made?" or "Wait a minute, Fred, let's give Angela a chance to throw her two cents in." The gatekeeper helps each member retain a sense of self-worth and well-being while also helping to involve everyone in the discussion.

TENSION-RELIEF

A group discussion of an important subject can become quite heated and tense as participants become emotionally involved. The ability to laugh at oneself or the humor in the situation can be a great relief for the tension. The humor should not, of course, ridicule or berate anyone in the group, but it may point out some of the human frailties that the group has developed. A group discussing a serious question may find itself sidetracked, and a simple, humorous comment about the situation may get the group back on the track, as well as having the laughter ease the tension. The humor should be gentle, nonaggressive, and in keeping with the situation. Abraham Lincoln was well-known for making a point by saying, "That reminds me of the story about . . . ," and then proceeding to tell an anecdote that made the group laugh, but that also made a point relative to the topic at hand.

The sensitive leader will realize that humor cannot be brought forth on demand and will, therefore, seek other ways of relieving tension: taking a break or changing the focus of the discussion.

Relationship of Group Discussion to Public Speaking

It is obvious that a symposium in which experts present a prepared talk to an audience is much more closely aligned with public speaking than is a social group that comes together in an informal manner. The panelist appearing before an audience of five hundred is much more of a public speaker than is the person in a private, problem-solving group of four or five experts. Most group participants, however, share in varying degrees the skills necessary for the public speaker.

Any person discussing any topic should *be prepared*. A social situation does not demand the rigid, organized preparation that a public appearance does, but why discuss a topic if you know nothing about it?

Public-speaking experience can help a person in a group situation see the basic organizational patterns and how to analyze and organize thoughts. Certainly the leader in a group needs to know how to organize and must be able to do so on the spur of the moment.

Public-speaking techniques such as use of visual aids or statistics will help the discussant get ideas across to the rest of the group.

Finally, in a task-centered group, each person will want to convince the others of the worth and value of his or her ideas. Many of the principles that apply to public speaking also apply to the group situation. The discussant must appeal to the needs of the others, must establish his or her credibility, and must use arguments that are rationally sound and well-thought out. The basic needs of persuasion are the same in any communication situation, public, interpersonal, or group.

SUMMARY AND CONCLUSION

Group communication forms a vital part of our complex of human communication functions. We form groups to solve problems, to gather information, and to dispense information, as well as to provide a social outlet. Solving problems can be much easier if a logical sequence is followed:

1. Define the problem.
2. Propose possible solutions.
3. Evaluate possible solutions.
4. Reach a conclusion.

These group functions can be carried out in committees, panels, dialogues, symposia, or forums.

Leadership in groups varies according to personalities involved and the composition of the group itself. The three most common types of leaders are the autocratic leader who controls the process tightly; the laissez faire leader who lets the group function without central leadership; and the democratic leader who leads subtly and without intruding on the group process. Other members of the group offer support, serve as gatekeepers, and provide tension-relief in their unofficial leadership roles.

EXERCISES

1. You are chairing a symposium/forum about a controversial issue in your community. One of the audience members insists on asking question after question and interspersing his or her own comments and ideas. How would you keep the forum moving and in the proper balance?
2. In a panel/forum one audience member gets the floor to ask a question but instead proceeds to call a panel member vulgar names and to make aggressive, angry comments. How would you handle that situation?
3. List five topics that would be reasonable for a class project and still be interesting to the panel members and to the class.
4. Develop on paper a hypothetical symposium that you would find interesting. Use faculty members or local experts.

APPENDIX A

sample speeches

The speeches that follow are not really speeches; they are instead *manuscripts* or *transcriptions* of speeches. The nonverbal qualities of delivery, voice, timing, and personality cannot be captured on paper, nor can the qualities presented by the speech setting. A speech is much more than its verbal content. As you read them, try to imagine the setting or context, the audience, and the personality of the speakers.

Both major political parties held long, hard-fought primary campaigns in 1980. Democratic incumbent Jimmy Carter narrowly won over a variety of candidates, with the strongest challenge coming from Senator Edward M. "Ted" Kennedy of Massachusetts. For the Republican nomination Ronald Reagan won over an even larger contingent, including former President Gerald Ford, George Bush who became Reagan's running mate and Vice President, and Senator John Anderson who split from the party to run as an independent.

Both speeches were delivered to thousands of party faithful at the respective conventions. To appreciate them fully, try to imagine thousands of screaming, cheering partisans in a festive mood in a huge convention auditorium. Each delegate was certain that his or her party would win the national election in November. The setting is frantic and exciting; the audience is exuberant; and the speakers are admired and loved. Many libraries have audio or video tapes of one or both speeches. Check with your speech department or your library. The speeches come to life much more when you can hear and possibly see the speakers and the context.

Principles of the Democratic Party: Common Hopes for the Future

Senator Edward M. Kennedy, U.S. Senator from Massachusetts

Delivered in New York City, August 12, 1980

Although Senator Kennedy lost the nomination, many felt that he won an emotional victory because of his eloquent address to the convention. Although he immediately sets a tone of reconciliation and party unity, note that at no time does he actually express support for the candidate—only the party. Senator Kennedy echoes a style of oratory made popular by his brother, President John F. Kennedy, in the election of 1960 and during his term in office, 1961–1963. Note the use of repetition for effect: "The pain of defeat is far, far less than the pain of the people I have met. We have learned that it is important to take issues seriously, but never to take ourselves too seriously." Three consecutive paragraphs begin with "Let us pledge that," and five begin, "The same Republicans who are . . ."

Well, things worked out a little different than I thought, but let me tell you, I still love New York. My fellow Democrats and my fellow Americans: I have come here tonight not to argue for a candidacy, but to affirm a cause.

I am asking you to renew the commitment of the Democratic Party to economic justice. I am asking you to renew our commitment to a fair and lasting prosperity that can put America back to work.

This is the cause that brought me into the campaign and that sustained me for nine months, across a hundred thousand miles, in forty different states. We had our losses; but the pain of our defeats is far, far less than the pain of the people I have met. We have learned that it is important to take issues seriously, but never to take ourselves too seriously.

The serious issue before us tonight is the cause for which the Democratic Party has stood in its finest hours—the cause that keeps our party young—and makes it, in the second century of its age, the largest political party in this Republic and the longest lasting political party on this Planet.

Our cause has been, since the days of Thomas Jefferson, the cause of the common man—and the common woman. Our commitment has been, since the days of Andrew Jackson, to all those he called "the humble members of society—the farmers, mechanics, and laborers." On this foundation, we have defined our values, refined our policies, and refreshed our faith.

Now I take the unusual step of carrying the cause and the commitment of my campaign personally to our national convention. I speak out of a deep sense of urgency about the anguish and anxiety I have seen across America. I speak out of a deep belief in the ideals of the Democratic Party, and in the potential of that party and of a President to make a difference. I speak out of a deep trust in our capacity to proceed with boldness and a common vision that will feel and heal the suffering of our time—and the division of our party.

The economic plank of this platform on its face concerns only material things; but is also a moral issue that I raise tonight. It has taken many forms over many years. In this campaign, and in this country that we seek to lead, the challenge in 1980 is to give our voice and our vote for these fundamental Democratic principles:

Let us pledge that we will never misuse unemployment, high interest rates, and human misery as false weapons against inflation.

Let us pledge that unemployment will be the first priority of our economic policy.

Let us pledge that there will be security for all who are now at work. Let us pledge that there will be jobs for all who are out of work—and we will not compromise on the issue of jobs.

These are not simplistic pledges. Simply put, they are the heart of our tradition; they have been the soul of our party across the generations. It is the glory and the greatness of our tradition to speak for those who have no voice, to remember those who are forgotten, to respond to the frustrations and fulfill the aspirations of all Americans seeking a better life in a better land.

We dare not forsake that tradition. We cannot let the great purposes of the Democratic Party become the bygone passages of history. We must not permit the Republicans to seize and run on the slogans of prosperity.

We heard the orators at their convention all trying to talk like Democrats. They proved that even Republican nominees can quote Franklin Roosevelt to their own purpose. The Grand Old Party thinks it has found a great new trick. But forty years ago, an earlier generation of Republicans attempted that same trick. And Franklin Roosevelt himself replied "Most Republican leaders . . . have bitterly fought and blocked the forward surge of average men and women in their pursuit of happiness. Let us not be deluded that overnight those leaders have suddenly become the friends of average men and women. . . . You know, very few of us are that gullible."

And four years later, when the Republicans tried that trick again, Franklin Roosevelt asked: "Can the Old Guard pass itself off as the New Deal? I think not. We have all seen many marvelous stunts in the circus—but no performing elephant could turn a handspring without falling flat on its back."

The 1980 Republican convention was awash with crocodile tears for our economic distress but it is by their long record and not their recent words that you shall know them.

The same Republicans who are talking about the crisis of unemployment have nominated a man who once said—and I quote: "Unemployment insurance is a prepaid vacation plan for freeloaders." And that nominee is no friend of labor.

The same Republicans who are talking about the problems of the inner cities have nominated a man who said—and I quote: "I have included in my morning and evening prayers everyday the prayer that the federal government not bail out New York." And that nominee is no friend of this city and of our great urban centers.

The same Republicans who are talking about security for the elderly have nominated a man who said just four years ago that participation in Social Security "should be made voluntary." And that nominee is no friend of the senior citizen.

The same Republicans who are talking about preserving the environment have nominated a man who last year made the preposterous statement, and I quote: "Eighty percent of air pollution comes from plants and trees." And that nominee is no friend of the environment.

And the same Republicans who are invoking Franklin Roosevelt have nominated a man who said in 1976—and these are his exact words: "Fascism was really the basis of the New Deal." And that nominee, whose name is Ronald Reagan, has no right to quote Franklin Delano Roosevelt.

The great adventure which our opponents offer is a voyage into the past. Progress is our heritage, not theirs. What is right for us as Democrats is also the right way for Democrats to win.

The commitment I seek is not to outworn views, but to old values that will never wear out. Programs may sometimes become obsolete, but the ideal of fairness always endures. Circumstances may change, but the work of compassion must continue. It is surely correct that we cannot solve problems by throwing money at them; but it is also correct that we dare not throw our national problems onto a scrap heap of inattention and indifference. The poor may be out of political fashion, but they are not without human needs. The middle-class may be angry, but they have not lost the dream that all Americans can advance together.

The demand of our people in 1980 is not for smaller government or bigger government, but for better government. Some say that government is always bad, and that spending for basic social programs is the root of our economic evils. But we reply: The present inflation and recession cost our economy $200 billion a year. We reply: Inflation and unemployment are the biggest spenders of all.

The task of leadership in 1980 is not to parade scapegoats or to seek refuge in reaction but to match our power to the possibilities of progress.

While others talked of free enterprise, it was the Democratic Party that acted — and we ended excessive regulation in the airline and trucking industry. We restored competition to the marketplace. And I take some satisfaction that this deregulation was legislation that I sponsored and passed in the Congress of the United States.

As Democrats, we recognize that each generation of Americans has a rendezvous with a different reality. The answers of one generation become the questions of the next generation. But there is a guiding star in the American firmament. It is as old as the revolutionary belief that all people are created equal — and as clear as the contemporary condition of Liberty City and the South Bronx. Again and again, Democratic leaders have followed that star — and they have given new meaning to the old values of liberty and justice for all.

We are the party of the New Freedom, the New Deal, and the New Frontier. We have always been the party of hope. So this year, let us offer new hope — new hope to an America uncertain about the present, but unsurpassed in its potential for the future.

To all those who are idle in the cities and industries of America, let us provide new hope for the dignity of useful work. Democrats have always believed that a basic civil right of all Americans is the right to earn their own way. The party of the people must always be the party of full employment.

To all those who doubt the future of our economy, let us provide new hope for the reindustrialization of America. Let our vision reach beyond the next election or the next year to a new generation of prosperity. If we could rebuild Germany and Japan after World War II, then surely we can reindustrialize our own nation and revive our inner cities in the 1980s.

To all those who work hard for a living wage, let us provide new hope that the price of their employment shall not be an unsafe workplace and death at an earlier age.

To all those who inhabit our land, from California to New York Island, from the Redwood Forest to the Gulfstream waters, let us provide new hope that prosperity shall not be purchased by poisoning the air, the rivers and the natural resources that are the greatest gift of this continent. We must insist that our children and grandchildren shall inherit a land which they can truly call America the beautiful.

To all those who see the worth of their work and their savings taken by inflation, let us offer new hope for a stable economy. We must meet the pressures of the present by invoking the full power of government to master increasing prices. In candor, we must say that the federal budget can be balanced only by policies that bring us to a balanced prosperity of full employment and price restraint.

And to all those overburdened by an unfair tax structure, let us provide new hope for real tax reform. Instead of shutting down classrooms, let us shut off tax shelters.

Instead of cutting out school lunches, let us cut off tax subsidies for expensive business lunches that are nothing more than food stamps for the rich.

The tax cut of our Republican opponents takes the name of tax reform in vain. It is a wonderfully Republican idea that would redistribute income in the wrong direction. It is good news for any of you with incomes over $200,000 a year. For the few of you, it offers a pot of gold worth $14,000. But the Republican tax cut is bad news for middle income families. For the many of you, they plan a pittance of $200 a year. And that is not what the Democratic Party means when we say tax reform.

The vast majority of Americans cannot afford this panacea from a Republican nominee who has denounced the progressive income tax as the invention of Karl Marx. I am afraid he has confused Karl Marx with Theodore Roosevelt, the obscure Republican President who sought and fought for a tax system based on ability to pay. Theodore Roosevelt was not Karl Marx — and the Republican tax scheme is not tax reform.

Finally, we cannot have a fair prosperity in isolation from a fair society.

So I will continue to stand for national health insurance. We must not surrender to the relentless medical inflation that can bankrupt almost anyone — and that may soon break the budgets of government at every level.

Let us insist on real controls over what doctors and hospitals can charge. Let us resolve that the state of a family's health shall never depend on the size of a family's wealth.

The President, the Vice President, and the Members of Congress have a medical plan that meets their needs in full. Whenever Senators and Representatives catch a little cold, the Capitol physician will see them immediately, treat them promptly, and fill a prescription on the spot. We do not get a bill even if we ask for it. And when do you think was the last time a Member of Congress asked for a bill from the federal government?

I say again, as I have said before: if health insurance is good enough for the President, the Vice President, and the Congress of the United States, then it is good enough for all of you and for every family in America.

There were some who said we should be silent about our differences on issues during this convention. But the heritage of the Democratic Party has been a history of democracy. We fight hard because we care deeply about our principles and purposes. We did not flee this struggle. And we welcome this contrast with the empty and expedient spectacle last month in Detroit where no nomination was contested, no question was debated and no one dared to raise any doubt or dissent.

Democrats can be proud that we chose a different course — and a different platform.

We can be proud that our party stands for investment in safe energy instead of a nuclear future that may threaten the future itself. We must not permit the neighborhoods of America to be permanently shadowed by the fear of another Three Mile Island.

We can be proud that our party stands for a fair housing law to unlock the doors of discrimination once and for all. The American house will be divided against itself so long as there is prejudice against any American family buying or renting a home.

And we can be proud that our party stands plainly, publicly, and persistently for the ratification of the Equal Rights Amendment. Women hold their rightful place at our convention: and women must have their rightful place in the Constitution of the United States. On this issue, we will not yield, we will not equivocate, we will not rationalize, explain, or excuse. We will stand for E.R.A. and for the recognition at long last that our nation had not only founding fathers, but founding mothers as well.

A fair prosperity and a just society are within our vision and our grasp. We do not have every answer. There are questions not yet asked, waiting for us in the recesses of the future.

But of this much we can be certain, because it is the lesson of all our history:

Together a President and the people can make a difference. I have found that faith still alive wherever I have traveled across the land. So let us reject the counsel of retreat and the call to reaction. Let us go forward in the knowledge that history only helps those who help themselves.

There will be setbacks and sacrifices in the years ahead. But I am convinced that we as a people are ready to give something back to our country in return for all it has given us. Let this be our commitment: Whatever sacrifices must be made will be shared — and shared fairly. And let this be our confidence: At the end of our journey and always before us shines that ideal of liberty and justice for all.

In closing, let me say a few words to all those I have met and all those who have supported me at this convention and across the country.

There were hard hours on our journey. Often we sailed against the wind, but always we kept our rudder true. There were so many of you who stayed the course and shared our hope. You gave your help; but even more, you gave your hearts. Because of you, this has been a happy campaign. You welcomed Joan and me and our family into your homes and neighborhoods, your churches, your campuses, and your union halls. When I think back on all the miles and all the months and all the memories, I think of you. I recall the poet's words, and I say: "What golden friends I had."

Among you, my golden friends across this land, I have listened and learned.

I have listened to Kenny Dubois, a glassblower in Charleston, West Virginia, who has ten children to support, but has lost his job after 35 years, just three years short of qualifying for his pension.

I have listened to the Trachta family, who farm in Iowa and who wonder whether they can pass the good life and the good earth on to their children.

I have listened to a grandmother in East Oakland, who no longer has a phone to call her grandchildren, because she gave it up to pay the rent on her small apartment.

I have listened to young workers out of work, to students without the tuition for college, and to families without the chance to own a home. I have seen the closed factories and the stalled assembly lines of Anderson, Indiana and South Gate, California. I have seen too many — far too many — idle men and women desperate to work. I have seen too many — far too many — working families desperate to protect the value of their wages from the ravages of inflation.

Yet I have also sensed a yearning for new hope among the people in every state where I have been. I felt it in their handshakes; I saw it in their faces. I shall never forget the mothers who carried children to our rallies. I shall always remember the elderly who have lived in an America of high purpose and who believe it can all happen again.

Tonight, in their name, I have come here to speak for them. For their sake, I ask you to stand with them. On their behalf, I ask you to restate and reaffirm the timeless truth of our party.

I congratulate President Carter on his victory here. I am confident that the Democratic Party will reunite on the basis of Democratic principles — and that together we will march toward a Democratic victory in 1980.

And someday, long after this convention, long after the signs come down, and the crowds stop cheering, and the bands stop playing, may it be said of our campaign that we kept the faith. May it be said of our party in 1980 that we found our faith again.

May it be said of us, both in dark passages and in bright days, in the words of Tennyson that my brothers quoted and loved — and that have special meaning for me now:

I am a part of all that I have met . . .
Tho much is taken, much abides . . .
That which we are, we are —
One equal temper of heroic hearts . . . strong in will
To strive, to seek, to find, and not to yield.

For me, a few hours ago, this campaign came to an end. For all those whose cares have been our concern, the work goes on, the cause endures, the hope still lives, and the dream shall never die.

Acceptance Address

Ronald Reagan, Former Governor of California

Delivered in Detroit, Michigan, July 17, 1980

Because of the thunderous applause and long ovation, President, then candidate, Reagan's first sentences are a plea for silence and order so that he can go on, citing the waste of prime television and radio time. Note that he immediately pokes fun at his theatrical background in order to help assuage the fears of those who felt his acting career hurt his serious image. Because he knows that he has won the nomination and will be the party's candidate, Reagan is able to state the party platform and his own views quite specifically and then go on to attack both the Democratic Party and the incumbent, President Jimmy Carter. President Reagan offers a series of campaign promises and deals heavily with international issues, an area where many feared he was too inexperienced. Reagan's style is less oratorical than Kennedy's and is more intimate, personal, and warm, enabling him to conclude his speech with a personal request.

Thank you very much. We're using up prime time. Thank you very much. You're singing our song. Well, the first thrill tonight was to find myself for the first time in a long time in a movie on prime time.

But this, as you can imagine, is the second big thrill.

Mr. Chairman, Mr. Vice President-to-be, this convention, my fellow citizens of this great nation:

With a deep awareness of the responsibility conferred by your trust, I accept your nomination for the Presidency of the United States. I do so with deep gratitude. And I think also I might interject on behalf of all of us our thanks to Detroit and the people of Michigan and to this city for the warm hospitality we've enjoyed.

And I thank you for your wholehearted response to my recommendation in regard to George Bush as the candidate for Vice President.

I'm very proud of our party tonight. This convention has shown to all America a party united, with positive programs for solving the nation's problems; a party ready to build a new consensus with all those across the land who share a community of values embodied in these words: family, work, neighborhood, peace and freedom.

Now I know we've had a quarrel or two but only as to the method of attaining a goal. There was no argument here about the goal. As President, I will establish a liaison with the 50 Governors to encourage them to eliminate, wherever it exists, discrimination against women. I will monitor Federal laws to insure their implementation and to add statutes if they are needed.

More than anything else, I want my candidacy to unite our country; to renew the American spirit and sense of purpose. I want to carry our message to every American regardless of party affiliation, who is a member of this community of shared values.

Never before in our history have Americans been called upon to face three grave threats to our very existence, any one of which could destroy us. We face a disintegrating economy, a weakened defense and an energy policy based on the sharing of scarcity.

The major issue of this campaign is the direct political, personal, and moral responsibility of Democratic Party leadership—in the White House and in the Congress—for this unprecedented calamity which has befallen us. They told us they've done the most that humanly could be done. They say that the United States has had its day in the sun, that our nation has passed its zenith. They expect you to tell your children that the American people no longer have the will to cope with their problems; that the future will be one of sacrifice and few opportunities.

My fellow citizens, I utterly reject that view. The American people, the most generous on earth, who created the highest standard of living, are not going to accept the notion that we can only make a better world for others by moving backward ourselves. And those who believe we can have no business leading this nation.

I will not stand by and watch this great country destroy itself under mediocre leadership that drifts from one crisis to the next, eroding our national will and purpose. We have come together here because the American people deserve better from those to whom they entrust our nation's highest offices, and we stand united in our resolve to do something about it.

We need a rebirth of the American tradition of leadership at every level of government and in private life as well. The United States of America is unique in world history because it has a genius for leaders—many leaders—on many levels.

But back in 1976, Mr. Carter said, "Trust me." And a lot of people did. And now, many of those people are out of work. Many have seen their savings eaten away by inflation. Many others on fixed incomes, especially the elderly, have watched helplessly as the cruel tax of inflation wasted away their purchasing power. And, today, a great many who trusted Mr. Carter wonder if we can survive the Carter policies of national defense.

"Trust me" government asks that we concentrate our hopes and dreams on one man; that we trust him to do what's best for us. But my view of government places trust not in one person or one party, but in those values that transcend persons and parties. The trust is where it belongs—in the people. The responsibility to live up to that trust is where it belongs, in their elected leaders. That kind of relationship, between the people and their elected leaders, is a special kind of compact.

Three hundred and sixty years ago, in 1620, a group of families dared to cross a mighty ocean to build a future for themselves in a new world. When they arrived at Plymouth, Massachusetts, they formed what they called a "compact," an agreement among themselves to build a community and abide by its laws.

This single act—the voluntary binding together of free people to live under the law—set the pattern for what was to come.

A century and a half later, the descendants of those people pledged their lives, their fortunes and their sacred honor to found this nation. Some forfeited their fortunes and their lives; none sacrificed honor.

Four score and seven years later, Abraham Lincoln called upon the people of all America to renew their dedication and their commitment to a government of, for and by the people.

Isn't it once again time to renew our compact of freedom; to pledge to each other all that is best in our lives; all that gives meaning to them—for the sake of this, our beloved and blessed land?

Together, let us make this a new beginning. Let us make a commitment to care for the needy; to teach our children the virtues handed down to us by our families; to have the courage to defend those values and virtues and the willingness to sacrifice for them.

Let us pledge to restore, in our time, the American spirit of voluntary service, of cooperation, of private and community initiative; a spirit that flows like a deep and mighty river through the history of our nation.

As your nominee, I pledge to you to restore to the Federal Government the capacity to do the people's work without dominating their lives. I pledge to you a Government that will not only work well but wisely, its ability to act tempered by prudence, and its willingness to do good balanced by the knowledge that government is never more dangerous than when our desire to have it help us blinds us to its great power to harm us.

You know, the first Republican President once said, "While the people retain their virtue and their vigilance, no Administration by any extreme of wickedness or folly can seriously injure the Government in the short space of four years."

If Mr. Lincoln could see what's happened in these last three and a half years, he might hedge a little on that statement. But with the virtues that are our legacy as a free people and with the vigilance that sustains liberty, we still have time to use our renewed compact to overcome the injuries that have been done to America these past three and a half years.

First, we must overcome something the present Administration has cooked up: a new and altogether indigestible economic stew, one part inflation, one part high unemployment, one part recession, one part runaway taxes, one part deficit spending seasoned with an energy crisis. It's an economic stew that has turned the national stomach.

Ours are not problems of abstract economic theory. These are problems of flesh and blood; problems that cause pain and destroy the moral fiber of real people who should not suffer the further indignity of being told by the Government that it is all somehow their fault. We do not have inflation because—as Mr. Carter says—we've lived too well.

The head of a Government which has utterly refused to live within its means and which has, in the last few days, told us that this coming year's deficit will be $60 billion, dares to point the finger of blame at business and labor, both of which have been engaged in a losing struggle just trying to stay even.

High taxes, we are told, are somehow good for us, as if, when government spends our money it isn't inflationary, but when we spend it, it is.

Those who preside over the worst energy shortage in our history tell us to use less, so that we will run out of oil, gasoline, and natural gas a little more slowly. Well, now, conservation is desirable, of course, but we must not waste energy. But conservation is not the sole answer to our energy needs.

America must get to work producing more energy. The Republican program for solving economic problems is based on growth and productivity.

Large amounts of oil and natural gas lay beneath our land and off our shores, untouched because the present Administration seems to believe the American people would rather see more regulation, more taxes and more controls than more energy.

Coal offers a great potential. So does nuclear energy produced under rigorous safety standards. It could supply electricity for thousands of industries and millions of jobs and homes. It must not be thwarted by a tiny minority opposed to economic growth which often finds friendly ears in regulatory agencies for its obstructionist campaigns.

Now make no mistake. We will not permit the safety of our people or our environmental heritage to be jeopardized, but we are going to reaffirm that the economic prosperity of our people is a fundamental part of our environment.

Our problems are both acute and chronic, yet all we hear from those in positions of leadership are the same tired proposals for more Government tinkering, more meddling and more control—all of which led us to this sorry state in the first place.

Can anyone look at the record of this Administration and say, "Well done"? Can anyone compare the state of our economy when the Carter Administration took office with where we are today and say, "Keep up the good work"? Can anyone look at our reduced standing in the world today and say, "Let's have four more years of this"?

I believe the American people are going to answer these questions, as you've answered them, in the first week of November and their answer will be, "No—we've had enough." And then it will be up to us—beginning next January 20—to offer an Administration and Congressional leadership of competence and more than a little courage.

We must have the clarity of vision to see the difference between what is essential and what is merely desirable; and then the courage to bring our Government back under control.

It is essential that we maintain both the forward momentum of economic growth and the strength of the safety net between those in our society who need help. We also believe it is essential that the integrity of all aspects of Social Security be preserved.

Beyond these essentials. I believe it is clear our Federal Government is overgrown and overweight. Indeed, it is time our Government should go on a diet. Therefore, my first act as chief executive will be to impose an immediate and thorough freeze on Federal hiring. Then, we are going to enlist the very best minds from business, labor and whatever quarter to conduct a detailed review of every department, bureau and agency that lives by Federal appropriation.

And we are also going to enlist the help and ideas of many dedicated and hardworking Government employees at all levels who want a more efficient Government just as much as the rest of us do. I know that many of them are demoralized by the confusion and waste they confront in their work as a result of failed and failing policies.

Our instructions to the groups we enlist will be simple and direct. We will remind them that Government programs exist at the sufferance of the American taxpayer and are paid for with money earned by working men and women and programs that represent a waste of their money — a theft from their pocketbooks — must have that waste eliminated or that program must go. It must go by Executive Order where possible, by Congressional action where necessary.

Everything that can be run more effectively by state and local government we shall turn over to state and local government, along with the funding sources to pay for it. We are going to put an end to the money merry-go-round where our money becomes Washington's money, to be spent by states and cities exactly the way the Federal bureaucrats tell us it has to be spent.

I will not accept the excuse that the Federal Government has grown so big and powerful that it is beyond the control of any President, any administration or Congress. We are going to put an end to the notion that the American taxpayer exists to fund the Federal Government. The Federal Government exists to serve the American people and to be accountable to the American people. On January 20, we are going to reestablish that truth.

Also on that date we are going to initiate action to get substantial relief for our taxpaying citizens and action to put people back to work. None of this will be based on any new form of monetary tinkering or fiscal sleight-of-hand. We will simply apply to government the common sense that we all use in our daily lives.

Work and family are at the center of our lives, the foundation of our dignity as a free people. When we deprive people of what they have earned, or take away their jobs, we destroy their dignity and undermine their families. We can't support families unless there are jobs; and we can't have jobs unless the people have both money to invest and the faith to invest it.

These are concepts that stem from an economic system that for more than 200 years has helped us master a continent, create a previously undreamed-of-prosperity for our people and has fed millions of others around the globe and that system will continue to serve us in the future if our Government will stop ignoring the basic values on which it was built and stop betraying the trust and good will of the American workers who keep it going.

The American people are carrying the heaviest peacetime tax burden in our nation's history — and it will grow even heavier, under present law, next January. We are taxing ourselves into economic exhaustion and stagnation crushing our ability and incentive to save, invest and produce.

This must stop. We must halt this fiscal self-destruction and restore sanity to our economic system.

I've long advocated a 30 percent reduction in income tax rates over a period of three years. This phased tax reduction would begin with a 10 percent "down payment" tax cut in 1981, which the Republicans in Congress and I have already proposed.

A phased reduction of tax rates would go a long way toward easing the heavy burden on the American people. But we shouldn't stop there.

Within the context of economic conditions and appropriate budget priorities during each fiscal year of my Presidency, I would strive to go further. This would include improvement in business depreciation taxes so we can stimulate investment in order to get plants and equipment replaced, put more Americans back to work and put our nation back on the road to being competitive in world commerce.We will also work to reduce the cost of government as a percentage of our gross national product.

The first task of national leadership is to set realistic and honest priorities in our policies and our budget, and I pledge that my Administration will do that.

When I talk of tax cuts, I am reminded that every major tax cut in this century has strengthened the economy, generated renewed productivity and ended up yielding new revenues for the Government by creating new investment, new jobs and more commerce among our people.

The present Administration has been forced by us Republicans to play follow-the-leader with regard to a tax cut. But in this election year we must take with the proverbial "grain of salt" any tax cut proposed by those who have already given us the greatest tax increase in our nation's history.

When those in leadership give us tax increases and tell us we must also do with less, have they thought about those who've always had less — especially the minorities? This is like telling them that just as they step on the first rung of the ladder of opportunity, the ladder is being pulled out from under them. That may be the Democratic leadership's message to the minorities, but it won't be our message. Ours, ours will be: We have to move ahead, but we're not going to leave anyone behind.

Thanks to the economic policies of the Democratic Party, millions of Americans find themselves out of work. Millions more have never even had a fair chance to learn new skills, hold a decent job or secure for themselves and their families a share in the prosperity of this nation.

It's time to put America back to work, to make our cities and towns resound with the confident voices of men and women of all races, nationalities and faiths bringing home to their families a paycheck they can cash for honest money.

For those without skills, we'll find a way to help them get new skills.

For those without job opportunities we'll stimulate new opportunities, particularly in the inner cities where they live.

For those who've abandoned hope, we'll restore hope and we'll welcome them into a great national crusade to make America great again.

When we move from domestic affairs, and cast our eyes abroad, we see an equally sorry chapter in the record of the present Administration:

—A Soviet combat brigade trains in Cuba, just 90 miles from our shores.

—A Soviet army of invasion occupies Afghanistan, further threatening our vital interests in the Middle East.

—America's defense strength is at its lowest ebb in a generation, while the Soviet Union is vastly outspending us in both strategic and conventional arms.

—Our European allies, looking nervously at the growing menace from the East, turn to us for leadership and fail to find it.

—And incredibly, more than 50, as you've been told from this platform so eloquently already, more than 50 of our fellow Americans have been held captive for over eight years—eight months—by a dictatorial foreign power that holds us up to ridicule before the world.

Adversaries large and small test our will and seek to confound our resolve, but we are given weakness when we need strength; vacillation when the times demand firmness.

The Carter Administration lives in the world of make-believe. Every day, drawing up a response to that day's problems, troubles, regardless of what happened yesterday and what'll happen tomorrow.

But you and I live in a real world, where disasters are overtaking our nation without any real response from Washington.

This is make-believe, self-deceit and, above all, transparent hypocrisy.

For example, Mr. Carter says he supports the volunteer Army, but he lets military pay and benefits slip so low that many of our enlisted personnel are actually eligible for food stamps. Re-enlistment rates drop and, just recently, after he fought all week against a proposed pay increase for our men and women in the military, he then helicoptered out to our carrier the U.S.S. Nimitz, which was returning from long months of duty in the Indian Ocean, and told the crew of that ship that he advocated better pay for them and their comrades. Where does he really stand, now that he's back on shore?

Well, I'll tell you where I stand. I do not favor a peacetime draft or registration, but I do favor pay and benefit levels that will attract and keep highly motivated men and women in our volunteer forces and back them up with an active reserve trained and ready for instant call in case of emergency.

You know, there may be a sailor at the helm of the ship of state, but the ship has no rudder. Critical decisions are made at times almost in comic fashion, but who can laugh?

Who was not embarrassed when the Administration handed a major propaganda victory in the United Nations to the enemies of Israel, our staunch Middle East ally for three decades, and then claimed that the American vote was a "mistake," the result of a "failure of communication" between the President, his Secretary of State and his U.N. Ambassador?

Who does not feel a growing sense of unease as our allies, facing repeated instances of an amateurish and confused Administration, reluctantly conclude that America is unwilling or unable to fulfill its obligations as leader of the free world?

Who does not feel rising alarm when the question in any discussion of foreign policy is no longer, "Should we do something?" but "Do we have the capacity to do anything?"

The Administration which has brought us to this state is seeking your endorsement for four more years of weakness, indecision, mediocrity and incompetence. No. No. No American should vote until he or she has asked: Is the United States stronger and more respected now than it was three-and-a-half years ago? Is the world safer, a safer place in which to live?

It is the responsibility of the President of the United States, in working for peace, to insure that the safety of our people cannot successfully be threatened by a hostile foreign power. As President, fulfilling that responsibility will be my No. 1 priority.

We're not a warlike people. Quite the opposite. We always seek to live in peace. We resort to force infrequently and with great reluctance — and only after we've determined that it is absolutely necessary. We are awed — and rightly so — by the forces of destruction at loose in the world in this nuclear era.

But neither can we be naíve or foolish. Four times in my lifetime America has gone to war, bleeding the lives of its young men into the sands of island beachheads, the fields of Europe and the jungles and rice paddies of Asia. We know only too well that war comes not when the forces of freedom are strong; it is when they are weak that tyrants are tempted.

We simply cannot learn these lessons the hard way again without risking our destruction.

Of all the objectives we seek, first and foremost is the establishment of lasting world peace. We must always stand ready to negotiate in good faith, ready to pursue any reasonable avenue that holds forth the promise of lessening tensions and furthering the prospects of peace. But let our friends and those who may wish us ill take note: the United States has an obligation to its citizens and to the people of the world never to let those who would destroy freedom dictate the future course of life on this planet. I would regard my election as proof that we have renewed our resolve to preserve world peace and freedom. That this nation will once again be strong enough to do that.

Now this evening marks the last step, save one, of a campaign that has taken Nancy and me from one end of this great nation to the other, over many months and thousands and thousands of miles. There are those who question the way we choose a President, who say that our process imposes difficult and exhausting burdens on those who seek the office. I have not found it so.

It is impossible to capture in words the splendor of this vast continent which God has granted as our portion of His creation. There are no words to express the extraordinary strength and character of this breed of people we call Americans.

Everywhere we've met thousands of Democrats, Independents and Republicans from all economic conditions, walks of life bound together in that community of shared values of family, work, neighborhood, peace and freedom. They are concerned, yes, they're not frightened. They're disturbed, but not dismayed. They are the kind of men and women Tom Paine had in mind when he wrote, during the darkest days of the American Revolution, "We have it in our power to begin the world over again."

Nearly 150 years after Tom Paine wrote those words, an American President told the generation of the Great Depression that it had a "rendezvous with destiny." I believe this generation of Americans today also has a rendezvous with destiny.

Tonight, let us dedicate ourselves to renewing the American compact. I ask you not simply to "trust me," but to trust your values — our values — and to hold me responsible for living up to them. I ask you to trust that American spirit which knows no ethnic, religious, social, political, regional or economic boundaries; the spirit that burned with zeal in the hearts of millions of immigrants from every corner of the earth who came here in search of freedom.

Some say that spirit no longer exists. But I've seen it—I've felt it—all across the land, in the big cities, the small towns and in rural America. It's still there, ready to blaze into life if you and I are willing to do what has to be done; we have to do the practical things the, down-to-earth things, such as creating policies that will stimulate our economy, increase productivity and put America back to work.

The time is now to limit Federal spending; to insist on a stable monetary reform and to free ourselves from imported oil.

The time is now to resolve that the basis of a firm and principled foreign policy is one that takes the world as it is and seeks to change it by leadership and example; not by harangue, harassment or wishful thinking.

The time is now to say that we shall seek new friendships and expand others and improve others, but we shall not do so by breaking our word or casting aside old friends and allies.

And the time is now to redeem promises once made to the American people by another candidate, in another time and another place. He said:

"For three long years I have been going up and down that country preaching that government—Federal, state and local—costs too much. I shall not stop that preaching. As an immediate program of action, we must abolish useless offices. We must eliminate unnecessary functions of government.

"We must consolidate subdivisions of government and like the private citizen, give up luxuries which we can no longer afford." And then he said:

"I propose to you my friends, and through you, that government of all kinds, big and little, be made solvent and that the example be set by the President of the United States and his Cabinet."

That was Franklin Delano Roosevelt's words as he accepted the Democratic nomination for President in 1932.

The time is now, my fellow Americans, to recapture our destiny, to take it into our own hands. And to do this it will take many of us, working together. I ask you tonight, all over this land, to volunteer your help in this cause so that we can carry our message throughout the land.

Isn't it time that we, the people, carry out these unkept promises? That we pledge to each other and to all America on this July day 48 years later, that now we intend to do just that.

I have thought of something that's not a part of my speech and worried over whether I should do it. Can we doubt that only a Divine Providence placed this land, this island of freedom, here as a refuge for all those people in the world who yearn to breathe free? Jews and Christians enduring persecution behind the Iron Curtain; the boat people of Southeast Asia, Cuba and of Haiti; the victims of drought and famine in Africa, the freedom fighters of Afghanistan, and our own countrymen held in savage captivity.

I'll confess that I've been a little afraid to suggest what I'm going to suggest. I'm more afraid not to. Can we begin our crusade joined together in a moment of silent prayer.

God bless America.

Thank you.

APPENDIX B

Speech Evaluation

Name of Speaker _____

Title _____ Date _____

I. ORGANIZATION

    A. Attention or Introduction

    B. Summary/Conclusion

    C. Preparation

    D. Composition

II. DELIVERY

    A. Audience/eye contact
       or adaptation

    B. Voice and Articulation

    C. Language/Style

    D. Body Use and Poise

III. CONTENT

    A. Support/Evidence

    B. Visual Aids

    C. Subject Selection

    D. Thesis or Central Point

IV. OVERALL EFFECTIVENESS

COMMENTS

taken from Edwin Cohen's
Speaking the Speech, 2nd Edition
Holt, Rinehart and Winston, Chicago, 1982

Speech Evaluation

Name _____ Date _____

Title _____

I. CONTENT   1   2   3   4   5
   Good logical support? Evidence? Emotional
   appeals? Were visual aids used effectively? Good
   subject selection? A well-stated thesis?

II. ORGANIZATION   1   2   3   4   5
    A good attention-getting introduction? Sum-
    mary/Conclusion? Well prepared? Good compo-
    sition?

III. DELIVERY   1   2   3   4   5
     Good audience contact? Eye contact? Use of
     voice? Articulation? Language? Body gestures?
     Poise?

IV. OVERALL EFFECTIVENESS   1   2   3   4   5

COMMENTS

Speech Evaluation

GENERAL CRITERIA

I. DELIVERY
   A. Was there good rapport and contact with the audience?
   B. Was the speaker's voice loud enough? Strong enough?
   C. Was the speaker's articulation clear and easily understood?
   D. Was the language of the speech clear, precise, and in keeping with the topic?
   E. Was the speaker in control of the situation and seemingly at ease?

II. CONTENT
   A. Did the speaker present adequate evidence and support for the ideas of the speech?
   B. Were visual aids used when necessary? Effectively?
   C. Was the subject selection good for this speaker?
   D. Was a thesis or central idea stated clearly and adequately?

III. ORGANIZATION
   A. Was the speech well organized?
   B. Was there a good attention-getting introduction?
   C. Was there a good summary and conclusion?
   D. Did the speaker seem well prepared?
   E. Was the speech easy to follow?

index